*A Place in History*

STANFORD STUDIES IN JEWISH HISTORY AND CULTURE

EDITED BY *Aron Rodrigue and Steven J. Zipperstein*

# A Place in History

*Modernism, Tel Aviv, and the Creation
of Jewish Urban Space*

Barbara E. Mann

STANFORD UNIVERSITY PRESS

STANFORD, CALIFORNIA

2006

Stanford University Press
Stanford, California

Printed in the United States of America on acid-free, archival-
quality paper

Library of Congress Cataloging-in-Publication Data
Mann, Barbara E.
   A place in history : modernism, Tel Aviv, and the creation of
Jewish urban space / Barbara E. Mann.
      p. cm.
   Includes bibliographical references and index.
   ISBN 0-8047-5018-1 (cloth : alk. paper) — ISBN 0-8047-5019-X
(pbk. : alk. paper)
   1. Sociology, Urban—Israel—Tel Aviv.   2. Tel Aviv (Israel)—
History.   I. Title.
HT147.I7M36   2006
307.76′095694′8—dc22

2005022960

Original Printing 2006

Last figure below indicates year of this printing:

15   14   13   12   11   10   09   08   07   06

Typeset by G & S Typesetters in 10.5 on 14 ITC Galliard

Published with the assistance of the Koret Foundation and the
Lucius N. Littauer Foundation.

*This book is dedicated in loving memory to my father, Carl, who frequented Tel Aviv in the early 1950s, and to his granddaughter, Maya Rose, who made her first trip there with her mother and her "Bubbie," Bertha, in 2003.*

# Contents

# Acknowledgments

Remembering and writing about Tel Aviv has occupied me for over a decade, and it is impossible to acknowledge everyone who has aided and abetted me along the way. However, in the spirit of urban exploration, I am grateful to conference and seminar audiences in the following cities: Beer Sheva, Berkeley, Boston, Denver, London, New York, Palo Alto, Philadelphia, Princeton, St. Louis, Tel Aviv, and Washington, D.C.

A year-long Fulbright-Hayes Faculty Research Abroad Grant in 1999–2000 provided an opportunity for this book's core research. Generous support from the University Committee on Research in the Humanities and Social Sciences at Princeton University enabled ongoing research and writing. A Bicentennial Preceptorship from Princeton provided the means and the time to complete the manuscript, one month before my daughter's birth.

I am indebted to Nili Varzarevsky, Tsiona Raz, and the staff of the Tel Aviv–Jaffa Municipal Archives, Reuven Koffler of the Central Zionist Archives, Yoav Dagon of the Nachum Gutman Museum, and Batia Carmiel of the Historical Museum of Tel Aviv–Jaffa. Their professional expertise as well as their passion for all things Tel Aviv have contributed immensely to my appreciation of the city. I also thank Vivienne Silver of the Silver Print Gallery, Ein Hod, Miri Ben-Moshe of the Israel Phoenix Insurance Collection, Yaffa Goldfinger of the Tel Aviv Museum of Art, and the staffs of the Rubin Museum and the Lavon Institute for Labor Studies for their help with the illustrations.

For their feedback and support during the writing of this book, I would like to acknowledge Karen Alkalay-Gut, Tamar Berger,

Deborah Bernstein, Gisela Dachs, Ronit Eisenbach, Sidra Ezrahi, Michael Gluzman, Michal Govrin, Deborah Hertz, Miki Kratsman, Sandra Moog, Guy Olami, Ilana Pardes, Eli Robinson, Gil Ronen, Esther Schor, Nancy Sinkoff, Vered Vitnitzky-Seroussi, Charlie Yawitz, and Yael Zerubvel. Abigail Jacobson afforded indispensable research assistance in the final stages. Steven Zipperstein encouraged my work early on in the pages of *Jewish Social Studies* and later in the editorial process. Norris Pope and Judith Hibbard, my editors at Stanford University Press, made seeing this book to press an experience any author would envy. An anonymous reader provided comments which helped focus my arguments. I am grateful to Chana Kronfeld, who has nurtured my intellectual growth since she was my Ph.D. advisor at the University of California, Berkeley; I also thank her for her careful reading of this new project. Any errors or omissions are my own.

Rachel Feit, Eilon Schwartz, Emily Silverman, and Amy Singer have all provided years of unparalleled hospitality, conversation, and friendship in Tel Aviv. I cannot imagine the city without them.

# Preface

How long has it been since the Jews have built a city? Somewhere between two thousand and three thousand years. And during that period the task of building and administering a city has become, to speak mildly, more complicated.

—Ludwig Lewisohn, "Letter from Abroad: A City Unlike New York," 1925

Over the years, a recurring demand has been that the land "must be made to speak." But in the end someone must speak for it.

—Brian Ladd, *The Ghosts of Berlin*

All cities are unique and each city is unique in a different way. Tel Aviv's uniqueness stems from the complex set of historical factors that occasioned its founding and development—from a utopian garden city suburb in 1909 to a sprawling, cosmopolitan metropolis. This book examines how the creation of Tel Aviv has both shaped and reflected collective identity. Initially viewed as an exemplary "Jewish" space, Tel Aviv was later seen as the paradigmatic Israeli city, a site that turned its back on diasporic Jewish life to embody Zionism's secular ethos of self-determined productivity. However, although a utopian vision of Jewish urban space led to the creation of a vibrant metropolis, any claims to the "Jewishness" of this space were destabilized and eventually subverted by both the vision's own inner contradictions and the material conditions of twentieth-century Palestine.

The establishment of Tel Aviv in 1909 was part of a fundamental revolution in modern Jewish culture regarding notions of space and place. Broadly speaking, many forms of cultural and political expression in European Jewish life sought to critique the normative notion of Jews as "rootless" and a "people of time."[1] These forms of expression included the movement for national, territorial autonomy (political Zionism), a call to settle the land and train as physical laborers (workers' movements), and new aesthetic forms (literary and artistic modernism). The establishment of Tel Aviv as "the first Hebrew city" was the most complex and sustained example of this desire to instantiate the Jews as a "people of space," to give them a place in history. As Michel Foucault has reminded us, whereas our present era is "the epoch of space," the nineteenth century was obsessed with history.[2] Tel Aviv is very much a product of the cusp of these two eras, proof that an obsession with one is inextricably intertwined with a preoccupation with the other. This necessary relation between space and history provides the organizing principle of this book; each chapter is organized around a specific site or abstract notion of space integral to Tel Aviv's urban identity. However, identity, especially in its collective form, is necessarily a by-product of time, "subject to the play of history."[3] Therefore, although not a historical study per se, this book moves in roughly chronological fashion, from Tel Aviv's "pre-history" in European Jewish life and thought, through the city's formative early decades, and into the first years of statehood. The concluding chapter revolves around the temporal axis of the years immediately following the Rabin assassination in 1995, an event that dramatically changed the city's relation to history.

Tel Aviv is a city founded primarily by immigrants and refugees. Coming from a variety of ethnic and class backgrounds, they arrived with vastly disparate material possessions. More importantly, though, immigrants who voluntarily settled in a new land out of an ideological belief in Jewish political autonomy, and refugees who fled an oppressive regime, had radically different attitudes toward the meaning of Tel Aviv as their new home. One of the ways these disparities were ostensibly dissolved was through the conception of Tel Aviv as a "Jewish" city. What exactly this meant, and how ideas of Jewishness shaped Tel

Aviv's emerging urban fabric, cannot, of course, be entirely understood in isolation from the ethnic and social context of the Mediterranean landscape within which Tel Aviv developed. Though identity is not static, but a process observed over time, it is also necessarily a product of interaction with difference. Attitudes toward "the other"—whether concerning internal Jewish differences of gender, religiosity, ethnicity or social/economic status, or vis-à-vis the local Arab population—therefore played an important role in the city's self-perception, and the urban space that evolved in concert with this image. While recognizing the merit of historiographical work that situates analysis of Israel within the wider nexus of the modern Middle East, this book primarily is an examination of the "internal Jewish factors which have shaped Israeli collective consciousness and national-cultural identity during the past 100 years—in all their pluralism, ambivalence and contradictions."[4] This kind of analysis of Israeli culture and history does not myopically isolate Jewish life from the full diversity of its historical settings; rather, distinguishing the internal "contrasting narratives"[5] that comprise Tel Aviv's early self-image is a necessary step toward understanding how the city fits into its Mediterranean surroundings. Moreover, examining Tel Aviv's self-proclaimed status as a modernist city par excellence sheds light on the more general nexus of nation-building, modernism, and urban identity.

The city's modernist birthright is grounded in the historical timing of its establishment, both in fact and in fancy. As the following chapters will demonstrate, Tel Aviv's actual existence on the ground paralleled its aesthetic invention. Both "Tel Aviv constructed" and "Tel Aviv imagined" were shaped during the decades when international modernism flourished, as both a powerful architectural vision and a cluster of aesthetic movements. An urban center created wholly from scratch, the city embodied the ideals and contradictions of the paradigmatic modernist architects such as Le Corbusier. Literary modernism's valorization of exile and newness found its most problematic treatment in the representation of Jewish urban space in Tel Aviv. On the one hand, Tel Aviv's public sphere reflected the ostensibly revolutionary aspirations of its citizenry. On the other hand, public and private space inevitably bore traces of its founders' diasporic origins. Although the promise of newness implied a future-oriented enterprise with no past to remember, this new home also came to be seen as a form of exile for many of its citizens. These inner tensions between public and private, history and the present, home and exile, manifested themselves repeatedly in literary and artistic depictions of the city. This study draws on representations of Tel Aviv and reads the city itself as a text in order to demonstrate how its relatively shallow roots—its ostensible lack of memory—has shaped both imagined versions of the city and its physical plane. Memory is Tel Aviv's constitutive principle as well as its nemesis.

A brief examination of the recent history of two buildings in Tel Aviv sheds light on the significance of modernism and memory in this study. The first building is a high-rise apartment smack in the city center, named for the building to which it stands adjacent—Beyt Hana (Chana House). Dating from the city's "golden years" of Bauhaus-inspired construction, the structure was originally an agricultural school for women, named after its founder, Chana Chizik. The site thus neatly fuses two of the city's founding myths—the pristine qualities of its pastoral beginnings and the International Style. An enormous billboard advertising the newly constructed luxury apartments tries to trade on the site's historical cachet, using the slogan *lagur betel aviv shel pa'am, lichyot betel aviv shel hayom* (Dwell in Tel Aviv of once upon a time, live in Tel Aviv of today). The phrase contains two different verbs for "live," the first a limited, even temporary, condition (akin to "reside"), the second a more generalized and expansive notion. The advertisement seamlessly links Tel Aviv's idealistic, idyllic, and simpler past with the material comforts of the present, promising the best of both. For current Tel Avivians, however, the site is also inextricably linked with a terrorist incident that killed three women there in the 1990s, when Chana House's ground floor contained a café called Apropos. A small memorial structure with details of the attack can be found across the street in the middle of the boulevard.

Several miles north and slightly east of Chana House, another building has recently come under public scrutiny. Located within the Tel Aviv University complex in the suburb of Ramat Aviv, it is the university's Marcelle Gordon Faculty Club, known colloquially as Habayit ha-yarok, the Green House. The original structure dates back to the late nineteenth century and was part of the Arab village of Sheikh Munis, a site "abandoned" in 1948. Jewish immigrants lived for a time in the village, as was the case in many such sites during the state's early years. The building was eventually purchased by the university and restored in 1991 according to plans chosen by architectural competition. The Green House's highly ornamental style in fact bears little resemblance to the original structure. The building has been landmarked by the Israeli group Zochrot (Remembers [fem. pl.]), an organization dedicated to raising awareness of Palestinian life in Israel prior to 1948. Among its activities is the placing of signs, in Arabic and Hebrew, marking demolished Palestinian structures. An official plaque placed by the university at the entrance names the Italian architect responsible for the renovation, but contains no mention of Sheikh Munis or the building's history.[6]

Despite their different functions and histories, both Chana House and the Green House typify Tel Aviv's official, and unofficial, memorial practices, and illustrate the difficult pasts faced by the city. In good modernist fashion, both buildings recycle the appeal of the old with the solid facts of the new. Yet this process has begun to unravel, even implode; the erasure of the past has been undone by the pressures of the present, forces that are themselves unpredictable and selective. Chana House aspires to ground its top-of-the-line amenities in the ostensibly austere, pioneering lifestyle of Tel Aviv's early citizenry. This combination of sophistication and simplicity is inevitably marred by the Israeli-Palestinian political conflict as it has erupted in Tel Aviv's streets. The Green House has been renovated in a style intended to convey a sense of authentic "Oriental" nativeness. However, the rooted indigenousness of Sheikh Munis's displaced inhabitants inevitably comes back to haunt, a "return of the repressed" on the urban grid. This book investigates the historical dilemmas posed by structures such as Chana House and the Green House, dilemmas that possess an ongoing and immutable relevance within the city's historical and contemporary landscapes.

The field of urban studies has burgeoned in recent years in terms of both geography and theoretical approach. Studies of urban cultures had traditionally focused on the European "big three"—London, Berlin, and Paris. American studies widened the arena slightly, with efforts devoted mostly to New York. More recently, cities such as Los Angeles, Brasilia, and Hong Kong have attracted debate and discussion, with their potent mix of motivated planning, financial and cultural capital, and enormous physical expansion. The field is now as large as the globe is wide, and has acquired a less utopian, more postmodern edge, as well as its own section in many bookstores, with titles reflecting a diverse range of urban cultures on every continent.[7] This book introduces Tel Aviv to this ongoing and ever-expanding study of cities, citizens, and city life.

Though this study engages Tel Aviv's history, it is less concerned with the past per se than with its cultural and aesthetic construction. Each chapter seeks to create a "thick description" of a particular site or set of sites in the city. By locating artifacts, traces, and representations of the past, and placing them both in their respective historical contexts and in dialogue with one another, it tries to approximate some idea of the city's "sense of self." This potentially slippery term suggests a problematic erasure of human agency; what creates a city's identity if not the citizens, artists, and bureaucrats who inhabit, represent, and regulate it? Yet the cumulative effect of these multiple imprints and impressions—the often inchoate whole that is any city—is best described by a model that admits its necessarily limited, subjective scope. This synchronic approach does not aspire to a panoramic or comprehensive history of agents and sources, but instead offers specific spatial and temporal slices of the city, chosen for their seemingly paradigmatic quality, as well as their instability and their tendency to trouble or question their very exemplariness and indeed the possibility of any single coherent rendition of the city. I am ultimately less interested in historical agents and sources than in the palpable effects of history—or its absence—on the contemporary plane of the city.

Walking through the city does not necessarily and always entail a history lesson for each and every pedestrian, nor is Tel Aviv's history somehow an immanent presence in its streets. Ultimately, as Brian Ladd notes above regarding Berlin, someone must speak for the land. Just as the politics of space is largely related to position and perspective, so my own location as an author necessarily guides my approach. This book was initially conceived when I lived in Tel Aviv during the late 1980s and early 1990s, a time during which the Palestinian question became a matter of everyday public discourse. This historic period was punctuated by two important events—the beginnings of the first Intifada in 1987 and the election of Yitzhak Rabin as prime minister in 1992. To the limited extent that this book explores the heretofore buried presence of Arab life in and around Tel Aviv, it owes this impulse to the atmosphere of turmoil and possibility during those years. Finally, this book is part of a general trend in Israeli scholarship that undertakes to critique certain normative notions of Israeli history and identity—in this case, the story of the establishment of Tel Aviv.

Any description of Tel Aviv that I offer, then, in the following pages grows out of two concurrent dialogues: this dialogue between me and the place, and a second dialogue between the place and the terms of its description. My primary source material consists of literary and journalistic accounts of the city. Tel Aviv's growth as a Jewish urban center is inseparable from the creation of a vernacular Hebrew literature, both in logistical and ideological terms. The city provides the backdrop for innumerable works of fiction and poetry, and served as the material center of Hebrew literary life from the early part of the twentieth century. One of the crucial tasks faced by early Hebrew writing in Palestine was the depiction of space, often before it existed in physical, concrete form, a situation that created a unique set of problems and challenges. Though many writers saw their work as expressly contributing to the creation of a new secular Jewish culture, it was often the case that literature served as a site of critique and opposition. In this study, therefore, literature operates as a kind of longitudinal space spanning the length of the book, within which Hebrew writing's heavily intertextual tradition thrives.

Tel Aviv's evolving centrality to modern Jewish life coincided with another important element of the spatial revolution in Jewish culture, that is the burgeoning of fine arts and photography by Jewish practitioners. What began in the early 1920s as a trickle with the photographic work of Avraham Soskin and the painting of the Tel Aviv school, became in the late thirties a torrent of visual records, particularly after the immigration of many German photographers, who brought with them an awareness of the "New Objectivity." Tel Aviv was understood as the site where normative notions regarding Jewish antipathy to image making would come to an end. This enthusiasm for visuality also typified Hebrew modernist writing about the city, work that expressly exploited the word's figurative potential. Thus ideas about the significance of imagery generally, and visual images in particular, are integral to the book's core argument regarding the transformation of Jewish culture. This material includes different photographic genres (street scenes, studio portraits, and historical landscapes), paintings, postcards, guidebooks, and images of public art and architecture. Indeed, the inseparability of identity and representation is most evident within these examples of material culture that seek to portray the dynamism of an evolving society.

Chapter 1 outlines Jewish culture's particular and ambivalent relation toward space, and contextualizes materials concerning modern Jewish life within the general frame of urban studies. It surveys attitudes toward Jewish urban experience and Zionist visions of urban space, including Theodor Herzl's utopian novel *Altneuland* (1902), in light of theoretical models regarding the production of space and urban experience and its representation. This general discussion lays the groundwork for the following two chapters, which are "case studies" of specific sites integral to the city's early history. Tel Aviv is virtually unique among cities in that its first cemetery preceded the establishment of the city itself. Chapter 2 examines the Old Cemetery's place in the city's collective memory. Though generally ignored in general civic consciousness, the cemetery, an example of what Anthony Vidler calls the "architectural uncanny," represents an important link with the diasporic landscapes from which Tel Aviv's founders hailed.[8] Chapter 3 turns to the central thoroughfare of Rothschild Boulevard, one of Tel Aviv's first public spaces. The boulevard's evolving depiction in literature and photography may be understood as an indication of the city's attempts to create a sense of rootedness and history for its citizens.

Chapters 4 and 5 turn away from these more site-specific encounters with the city to examine broader, more abstract notions of urban space and their evolution. Early visions of the city called for an intertwined relation between public and private space, where customs traditionally associated with the private sphere became idealized in the public realm as a new urban collective identity. This vision is both manifest in the city's International Style architecture and serves as the focus of early writing about its spatial character. Chapter 4 discusses these ideas about public and private space in Tel Aviv through the dualistic image of the balcony. Chapter 5 moves out of the city and presents a more "macro" level view of Tel Aviv vis-à-vis its immediate environs. Even while still a small neighborhood, Tel Aviv imagined itself as the center of modern Jewish life in Palestine, a center with distinct, though shifting, boundaries. This chapter demonstrates how Tel Aviv's imagined geographical borders—including the surrounding settlements, the Arab city of Jaffa, and the Mediterranean—have signified aspects of the city's evolving social, cultural, and political identity. Together these two chapters describe how abstract notions of space, ideas that in fact undergird the establishment of any city, were informed by ideas of a specifically Jewish, Hebrew urban space. Ostensibly intrinsic characteristics of these spaces were themselves construed in relation to Jewish urban experience in the Diaspora, normative notions of modern urban planning, and the reality of the local Middle Eastern landscape.

Chapter 6 returns the book's focus to a specific site, Rabin Square— the public plaza where Yitzhak Rabin was assassinated in 1995. The square, a site saturated with memory, is essentially the antipode to the Old Cemetery, an all-but-forgotten site that is the subject of Chapter 2. Chapter 6 demonstrates how, with the memorial practices in the years following Rabin's death, Tel Aviv has entered into a radically new relationship to history. It concludes with a discussion of the relatively unknown site of Summayl, an Arab village adjacent to the square, whose inhabitants fled in 1947. Adopting Michel de Certeau's suggestion that urban space is produced by footsteps, as people walk among the city's revealed and hidden structures, the chapter reads Rabin Square and Summayl together as exemplifying Tel Aviv's problematic and ongoing negotiation with its past.[9]

*A Place in History*

> Why is the Holy-One-Blessed-Be-He named in such a way that he is
> called *Makom* [place]? Because He is the place of the world.
>
> —Genesis Rabah 58:8

> When space feels thoroughly familiar to us, it has become place.
>
> —Yi-Fu Tuan, *Space and Place*

## Space, Place, and *Makom*

In the last decade or so space has become an increasingly important
term in critical analysis. Like the concept of "the text" for poststruc-
turalism, "space" is now a catch-all category within a growing number
of interdisciplinary projects that may be loosely grouped under the
rubric of cultural studies. Much of this intellectual work takes its inspiration from the writings of Henri Lefebvre, whose *The Production of
Space* provided a seminal set of conceptual tools with which to discuss
the social experience of the city. What Michel Foucault did for knowledge, Lefebvre has done for space: space, in this view, is a discourse; it
is neither given nor transcendent, but "produced." However, even
Lefebvre himself seems a bit wary of this notion: "To speak of 'producing space' sounds bizarre, so great is the sway still held that empty
space is prior to whatever ends up filling it. Questions immediately
arise here: what spaces? and what does it mean to speak of producing
space?"[1] However, Lefebvre resists the impulse to divide space from its
usage, and insists that "an already produced space can be decoded, can
be read" in order to uncover the forces involved in its creation.[2] Indeed, "every society . . . produces a space, its own space."[3] The process
is both mutual and dialectical: society produces spaces, and these very
spaces produce the society. In a sense, we may find here a relation like
that between identity and representation; just as identity does not exist a priori to language, but is always produced and understood
through language, space is never a given or static entity, but always the
product of its usage.

I

Although Lefebvre's work relates mainly to space in the modern period, he also writes about what he calls "absolute space," a kind of leftover space, often located in nature, that is inevitably associated with myth, religious worship, and ancient rites and ceremonies. Absolute space was "a product of the bonds of consanguinity [affiliation?], soil and language." Modern architecture and urban planning often capitalized on the cache of these ancient forms in their attempts to create viable and appealing social environments: "Not that absolute space disappeared in the process; rather it survived as the bedrock of historical space and the basis of representational spaces (religious, magical and political symbolisms)."[4] For the purposes of this study, this "absolute space"—to the degree that it exists—may be understood as Eretzyisrael (Land of Israel), primarily in its ancient, biblical incarnation, characterized by Jewish political autonomy and a largely agrarian lifestyle.[5]

For analytical purposes, Lefebvre divides space into three zones or modes of definition: spatial practices (*la pratique spatiale*), representations of space (*les représentations de l'espace*), and spaces of representations (*les espaces de représentation*).[6] The first category consists of the economic base, and is the domain of the social sciences. Analysis of this zone includes descriptions of networks—how goods and people circulate and services are rendered; this is "space as empirically observed." This study is primarily concerned with Lefebvre's final two categories of spatial analysis: "representations of space," which includes architecture and anything else having to do with the city's physical plan, and "spaces of representation," a category encompassing the realm of the imagination, that is, all art.[7] However, as even devout followers of Lefebvre note, "these kinds of spaces are not exclusive zones, but only analytic categories. [They] therefore necessarily incorporate each other in their concrete historical-geographical combinations."[8] In the case of Tel Aviv, as we will see, these last two categories are especially intertwined: the city was imagined in various forms years before its establishment. Even during the relatively modest stages of its initial construction as a suburb of Jaffa, it was conceived as a grandiose center of Jewish cultural renewal. Therefore, each chapter's "thick description" of space includes sources that predate the city's physical existence.

By now it should be clear that space is always an ideologically loaded concept. Yet, the idea of space as an abstract, even neutral, entity persists and can even be methodologically valuable, especially when contrasted to the notion of place. In his study *Space and Place: The Perspective of Experience*, Yi-Fu Tuan parses the difference between the two categories in the following way:

> "Space" is more abstract than "place." What begins as undifferentiated space becomes place as we get to know it better and endow it with value. . . . The ideas of "space" and "place" require each other for definition. From the security and stability of place we are aware of the openness, freedom, and threat of space, and vice versa. Furthermore, if we think of space as that which allows movement, then place is pause; each pause in movement makes it possible for location to be transformed into place.[9]

Tuan's phenomenological description focuses on the biologically grounded aspects of the human experience of space. This notion of space as a universal preexisting condition, to which the characteristics of place are "added," has historically been the normative view in Western culture—the great "sway" referred to by Lefebvre regarding empty space. Whether viewed through an anthropological or semiotic lens, this prevailing understanding of the relation between space and place construes the former as an inert, primal form to which "layers" are added. This deposit—in the form of signs, culture, custom, and built form—can then be dissected and explored for the motivating forces of its particularizing qualities. But what is the nature of this preexisting space? Does space really precede place, and if so how is it perceived or measured? Or is all space always already place, given that the very act of perception implies a subject, a position, a "horizon," "constituted by cultural and social structures that sediment themselves into the deepest level of perception"?[10]

Tuan's notion that "when space feels thoroughly familiar to us, it has become place" is nonetheless useful when complicated by simply noting that he describes a process—not a magic trick—that includes a beginning, a middle, and an end, and during which familiarity is taught and acquired.[11] This process of becoming familiar (or native) involves a certain selectivity, and implies agents as well as objects of instruction, both of which are somewhat effaced in Tuan's formulation. Except in religious or transcendental views, this process is neither predetermined nor teleologically driven. Though often unacknowledged until complete (that is, a "success"), this process may nonetheless be retrospectively identified, described, and unpacked. Furthermore, there often remains an abiding strangeness that inheres beneath the feverishly built-up surface that we call place.

Lefebvre and Tuan may seem like odd bedfellows. However, regarding their depiction of human experience, both Marxism and phenomenology embrace a deterministic view, even though their motivating factors may differ. Both Lefebvre and Tuan view space as fabricated, as inevitably a product of *something*, whether that "something" is ideology, historical forces, social functions, or the simple fact of human skin. Both essentially argue that space is not a *tabla rasa*, a blank slate existing a priori to human experience, onto which the characteristics of place are imposed. In this sense, both approaches would militate against the conception of space as a blank slate typifying early Zionist thought, which saw the Land of Israel as "a land without a people for a people without a land." Both approaches also treat space as the product of social experience, whether that sociability is constituted by a family, a city, or a nation. The conceptual frames of both Lefebvre and Tuan can help us to understand how Tel Aviv sought to become—and was gradually perceived as—a Jewish urban space.

The special connotations of place in Jewish tradition further complicate this relation between space and place in urban form. Within classical Jewish sources, the Hebrew word for place—*makom*—is often considered a synonym for God.[12] In the Hebrew bible, when the word "makom" is used in association with God's appearance, it usually refers to a concrete place as in, for example, the sacrifice of Isaac on Mt. Moriah, referred to as "the place that God had told him of" (Genesis 22). Makom in this usage generally signifies the intimacy or closeness between God and humanity, as opposed to the term *shamayim* (heavens), which may signify God's distance or remove.[13] The biblical God is associated with tactile components of the physical landscape: a cloud, a bush, or a mountain. However, the later works of the sages (*sifrut chazal*), written largely in exile after the destruction of the temple in Jerusalem, developed a more abstract interchange between God and place. It is there, in rabbinic commentary on the Book of Genesis, that we find an explanation for their synonymous association: "Why is the Holy-One-Blessed-Be-He named in such a way that he is called *Makom* [place]? Because He is the place of the world."[14] No longer understood in relation to specific locales of the biblical landscape, makom is more than just associated with the sacred; it is a metaphor for conceiving of a godhead who has no visible form, for a people who perceive themselves to be in exile.

Clearly the notion of God as a transcendent, all-encompassing space—"He is the place of the world"—is seriously compromised if space is always socially produced à la Lefebvre. How can God—the ultimate space—ever be known or described, let alone created by human design? God's transcendence is potentially undone by the notion of space as a social production. Yet Zionism—a movement of national redemption and rehabilitation—stems directly, though not without difficulty, from this paradoxical meeting of transcendence with social experience. Zionism's largely secular thrust exploited Judaism's transcendental, historical connection to the "Land of Israel," while bypassing the divine presence at its root. This ancient attachment, however, existed mainly on the level of the word—the "homeland of the text."[15] The power of the biblical bond notwithstanding, part of Zionism's task in "imagining" a national tradition was creating a place to house that tradition and to locate its collective, ritual sites.[16] Thus, the creation of a new Jewish nation-state may have depended on the land's putative qualities as an ancient Jewish homeland; however, in the modern context, the space had to be (re)produced. Tel Aviv was perhaps the central site of this explicitly modern endeavor.

In a certain sense, the imagining and construction of Tel Aviv was an attempt to secularize space, to make what had been the biblical Land of Israel—dreamt and written about for thousands of years, and in which God's presence abided—into an actual place—a place with the attributes of home. This gap or tension—between the biblical story about the Place and the place itself, and between space as transcendent and space as socially produced—undergirded the creation of modern

Hebrew culture in Palestine, including the production of urban space. Loyalty to the place itself, as opposed to its historical or narrative dimension—a duality that Zali Gurevitch has called "the double site of Israel"—is also a rejection of the theological dimension of "Place . . . , the law of a divinity that transcends the earthly realm of place."[17] Aesthetic representation of Tel Avis is thus at once a profanity and a reconfiguration of what sacred space could be.

## Jews, the City, and Representation

Tel Aviv's founders were largely Eastern European, and the successive waves of immigrants who initially molded its urban sphere and gave rise to literature and painting devoted to the city also hailed largely from Eastern and Central Europe. We can therefore reasonably expect that the city's nascent qualities as an urban space, and the imaginative work it inspired, bore some relation to the prior urban experiences of its inhabitants, and to the European city's long imaginative tradition. Historically, the rise of the city has given birth to certain literary forms—in the modern era, most notably the novel: "As literature gave imaginative reality to the city, urban changes in turn helped transform the literary text."[18] These literary forms were tied to various conceptions of history underlying the city, even in its premodern stages. For example, ancient myths took their cue from Athens and Rome, both of which were supported by a cyclical view of history in which Dionysian and Appollonian forces drove the city's mastery over time and space. Later, Augustine developed an essentially linear view of history progressing inevitably toward the City of God. Ideas about the city and its imaginative representation also developed in conjunction with different conceptions of human nature. Thus an appreciation of the city as divinely inspired led to an allegorical reading of God's signs in urban, social settings. Later, deterministic understandings of human nature—exemplified by the work of Spencer and Darwin—led to the treatment of the city as a living organism, whose inner workings resemble the natural processes of rejuvenation and decay. The literary naturalism of Balzac and Zola allowed for a more individual, symbolic interpretation of the city, which eventually paved the way for the wholly internalized, subjective view of the city that was modernism. The development of modernist forms in London and in Paris has itself been linked to Marxist notions concerning the relation between industrial production and the human psyche.[19]

The following chapters will indicate how specific aspects of European urban thought directly impacted both the imagined and constructed Tel Aviv—in Lefebvre's terms, both the "representations of space" and the "spaces of representation." Here we briefly survey Jewish urban experience in Europe, focusing on those aspects that bear most directly on the establishment of Tel Aviv. Urban historians agree that the formative era for what we now recognize as the modern city occurred during the passage from a feudal to a commercial society, and the concomitant transformation of the city from a spiritual to a mercantile center. During a period in which the Church officially condemned commercial profit, Jews were unavoidably, intimately, connected to this process. The concern here is not the actual social or economic conditions of Jewish communities in Europe, which varied widely from region to region.[20] Nor is it in determining whether urbanization was ultimately "good" or "bad" for Jews, or in uncovering some essential relation between urbanization and acculturation. Rather, the focus is how urban discourse has "figured" the Jew, how writing about the city has involved writing about Jews, and how these ideas about Jews and cities informed certain basic tenets of modernism. All of this eventually permeated writing about Tel Aviv, a modernist city conceived and perceived in somewhat anomalous terms as a "Jewish" city.

There is certainly a long history of anti-Semitic polemics linking Jews with a critique of modernity and the money economy, especially concerning the rise of urbanism and cosmopolitanism.[21] One can appreciate these connections without slipping into the easy formula linking the terms "Jewish" and "urban" with some sort of "degeneracy," by going beyond the abstract terms of the argument and paying attention to the specific social institutions and agents that actually produced, and were victims of, anti-Semitism. In fact, the rise of modern anti-Semitism is directly related to the development of modern civic society. As Hillel Kieval notes: "Anti-Semitic orderings of reality, in which Jewish and non-Jewish moral spheres and physical realms are carefully demarcated, have constituted one of the crucial ways in which urban societies in the past have created a sense of civic identity."[22] In the late Middle Ages, Jews were seen as a potential threat to Christian communities, resulting in frequent expulsions of Jews connected to charges of ritual murder, this at a time when Jews were often not even allowed to live within city walls. Jews were seen as a deleterious element of the evolving urban fabric that could not be tolerated by civil society. Christian piety was explicitly connected to ridding urban society of Jews, a kind of "urban cleansing."[23] Anti-Jewish edicts and expulsions of Jews should be seen against the general background of unease and anxiety regarding the breakdown of feudal society and the expansion of towns and commercial centers.

The urban space most frequently associated with premodern European Jewish communities is the ghetto. For example, in his study of the relation between the body and urban form, *Flesh and Stone: The Body and the City in Western Civilization*, Richard Sennett devotes a chapter to the Jews as a community. Its focus is Venice, home of Europe's first ghetto, established in 1516 as an institutionally and physically separate site, reachable only by water, that was firmly closed to traffic each night. Despite the fact that Venetian Jews were an integral part of the city's economic and financial infrastructure, according to Sennett, they simply did not exist as individuals in the public sphere. Thus Jews were seen in aggregate, their distinctive dress representing a different lifestyle, even a challenge to normative Christian society. At the same time, the very substance of their Jewishness—prayer, rituals, food, holiday observances, communal institutions, and the like—was unseen, part of the private sphere.[24]

Sennett's analysis of Venetian Jewry, for all its ostensibly au courant discussion of sexuality, actually mobilizes a long history of discourse regarding the ghetto. Robert Bonfils has presented a systematic and cogent critique of modern scholarship about the ghetto, on the part of Jewish historians as well as more "disinterested" scholars such as Sennett.[25] Bonfils argues that it is incorrect to view the ghetto exclusively as a tool of compulsory segregation and exclusion, with both negative implications as well as romantic associations. He notes that scholarship has largely articulated the idea of the ghetto as a place of confinement through metaphors of somatic experience and the body, a rhetoric deriving in part from Renaissance theorists such as da Vinci who conceived of architectural perfection in terms of the human body. Social, racial, or religious difference in the city's physical plane was routinely figured in terms of unpleasant bodily experience, including infection and illness. However, examining Italian ghettos established in their specific historical context produces a radically different assessment. The Venetian ghetto was created shortly after Jews first entered the city, following a war and social unrest. The prevailing "myth of Venice" present in contemporaneous public discussion about the ghetto held that a perfect Christian society was possible only without the presence of Jews. Logically, therefore, the Jews should have been expelled. Instead, they were allowed to stay in the city, albeit in a circumscribed space. The ghetto, instead of excluding them, actually incorporated Jews into Venice's urban landscape for the first time. The ghetto, in this view, may therefore be seen not as an instrument of *exclusion*, but in fact as one of *inclusion*, an intermediary step toward greater tolerance and fuller integration of Jews into European urban society. Negative stereotypes of the ghetto, however, persisted and eventually became part and parcel of modern ideas about Jewishness and urbanity, including Zionist polemics regarding the need for Jewish renewal and rebirth. Max Nordau, for example, in his essay calling for a new "Jewry of Muscle," blames "the narrow Jewish street" and "the dimness of sunless houses" for the physical and spiritual degeneration of European Jewry.[26] It would not be overstating things to say that, in a nutshell, Tel Aviv was conceived as an urban space that would negate the unsavory aspects of ghetto life while turning its ostensibly invisible realm of Jewish practice into the very substance of the public sphere (see Chapter 4).

In modern times, the Jew became a cipher for diverse, often contradictory ideas about urban society and city life. In her introduction to *The Jew in the Text*, Tamar Garb presents a psychoanalytic model of gentile-Jewish relations, reading society as a consciousness that invents stories to explain itself to itself. In this sense, Jews were understood as both "origin" and "rupture" vis-à-vis Christian society.[27] This relation produced a strong need to police the boundary between Christianity and Judaism, and inscribed the Jews in texts as both indispensable and villainous. Jews in Europe were a part of the new world but also a visible reminder of the old, restricted both externally by legal codes, as well as internally by Jewish dietary laws and the prohibition on intermarriage. They were both "a part of" and "apart from" Christian society, a visibly distinct communal identity.[28] While in premodern times this difference had been expressed in religious terms, it later developed a scientific, racial rationale, most notoriously articulated by Richard Wagner in "Jewry in Music" (1850). In Wagner's influential polemic, Jews had no authentic attachment to the soil, and their participation in German national life (especially its cultural dimension) was therefore a degenerate threat to the creation of a genuine German culture. Jews were perceived as rootless and cosmopolitan, a group that highlighted modernity's inner contradictions regarding its own promise of universal rights and citizenship. Zionism accepted the essential truth of this critique, and sought to remedy Jewish life in Europe through the establishment of a national homeland wherein Jews would achieve the normative status of other modernizing national groups.

One city of the European Jewish Diaspora bears special mention in relation to Tel Aviv, both for its physical locale and urban sensibility as well as for its place—or lack thereof—in Jewish historiographical writing about cities: Odessa. The Black Sea city's image as the cultural center of the Haskalah began to develop in the 1860s, with the establishment of Jewish presses in Hebrew, Yiddish, and Russian.[29] Odessa was the home of numerous writers and ideologues such as Ahad Ha'am, Mendele Mokher Sforim, Chaim Nahman Bialik, Saul Tchernichovski, S. Ben-Tsion, Meir Dizengoff, and Alter Druyanov, all of whom later took up residence in Tel Aviv and/or had streets there named after them. Druyanov became Tel Aviv's first historian. The poet Bialik, perhaps Tel Aviv's most famous Odessan transplant, and the lynchpin of the connection between the two cities, lived in Odessa for twenty years (1900–1920), longer than in any other place. The idea of a secular Jewish culture drawing explicitly upon traditional Hebrew sources permeated much of Bialik's public work in Odessa (and later in Tel

Aviv), including his publishing enterprise and his work as a teacher at the "Reformed School" (*cheder metukan*), whose goal was to give children "both a national and a universal education."[30] In fact, of the Odessa Hebrew writers associated with Bialik and his creative enterprises who eventually moved to Palestine, all but one (Yosef Klausner) settled in Tel Aviv.

Early cultural life in Tel Aviv, especially in the interwar period, may be understood within the context of Ahad Ha'am's cultural Zionism, as nurtured in the particular environs of Odessa. Odessa possessed a distinctly cosmopolitan character, and foreigners constituted the overwhelming majority of the population. Visitors noted its distinctly European character and Jews were especially drawn to its relative economic and social tolerance: "Jewish immigrants looked upon Odessa, with its wide streets and limestone buildings, as a world apart from the ancient settlements to which they were accustomed, and Odessa came to represent to Jews elsewhere, particularly in Lithuania, the option of a fresh start, offering a change of climate, economic possibilities, and perimeters of acceptable religious behavior."[31] In contrast to prevailing notions of Jewish parasitism, Odessa, with its large class of successful Jewish merchants, was singled out as evidence of the Jews' ability to contribute productively to the economic life of the city, once allowed unhampered access to its commercial institutions.[32] The city's geography seemed to reinforce the sense of "freedom and purposefulness" of its inhabitants. The sea, an especially exotic attraction, was often the first large body of water seen by Jews who settled there; one new resident's account noted the contrast between Odessa's relative cleanliness and the "stench of generations in my town."[33] (Later descriptions of Tel Aviv would contrast the vitality of the city's seashore with the "stink" and "backwardness" of the European shtetl. See the discussion in Chapter 5.) Odessa's Jewish community also possessed an erratic liberality concerning public religious observance: regular synagogue attendance was accompanied by smoking on the Sabbath, on which day 90 percent of Jewish shops remained open.[34] These elements of Odessa's social life and public sphere, and its distinction as an urban center for Jews—the city's European character, the notion of Jewish productivity, an evocation of the sea, the importance of public hygiene, and religious tolerance—all also feature prominently in early depictions of Tel Aviv's uniqueness as a city, both prescriptively and descriptively. That is, both early Tel Aviv imagined, and Tel Aviv in fact, came to resemble the Odessa that was a home for so many of its founders.[35]

However, in addition to these more tangible, quantifiable ingredients of city life, Odessa and Tel Aviv share a deeper, more essential quandary as centers of Jewish culture. In his introduction to *The Jews of Odessa*, Steven Zipperstein wonders about the lack of historiographical writing on Odessa, especially as compared to other European centers of Jewish life. He concludes that these urban histories were generally either intellectual accounts of rabbinic life and traditional piety, or records of anti-Semitism and Jewish martyrdom: "Odessa, the site of neither intensive traditional learning nor singular mistreatment at the hands of authorities or local townspeople, did not lend itself to such investigation." Furthermore, those very characteristics that captured the essence of the city did not seem to lend themselves to the telling of history: "the fast pace of life in the new Black Sea port . . . and the alleged preoccupation of its residents, Jewish and non-Jewish alike, with moneymaking and the pleasures of the moment made it a place where the past was considered irrelevant or was overshadowed by the demands of the present." Zipperstein also cites the impressions of Simon Dubnow, who called Odessa "the least historical of cities," and Shmaryahu Levin, who compared the city unfavorably with Vilna and Kiev, where "the dust of generations lay . . . like an invisible shadow," as examples of the prevailing prejudices regarding Odessa in Jewish historiography.[36]

These critiques—and they are damning, at least in the sense that they devalued the city as a legitimate object of study—resonate with later estimations of Tel Aviv, particularly as compared to Jerusalem. Indeed, many of these claims regarding Odessa found their way into both negative and positive characterizations of Tel Aviv: a rejection of rabbinic culture and traditional scholarship, and the creation of a new, secular replacement; the "freedom from history" and a hyper-attention to the present; a focus on utility as opposed to ideology; the effects of a highly competitive, mercantile economy on cultural transformation; and other features commonly associated with port cities—especially a relatively liberal lifestyle and a cosmopolitan mix of cultures. Chapter 4 examines how these traits eventually became linked in Tel Aviv to the creation of a distinctly Jewish public space. Ironically, and this was perhaps Tel Aviv's crowning achievement, the city turned its ostensible lack of history into a virtue, making the very idea of newness the core of its urban identity. The city's novelty became its primary challenge— creating a sense of history, as well as a sense of place.

One of the clearest imaginative statements of the importance of urban renewal to Jewish renewal can be found in the plethora of Zionist utopian novels published in the late nineteenth and early twentieth centuries. Written in German, Hebrew, and even English, works such as *Ein Zukunftsbild* (A Picture of the Future; 1885), by the Hungarian merchant Edmund Eisler, and *Looking Ahead* (1899), by the American rabbi Henry Pereira Mendes, conceived of an autonomous Jewish life in Palestine, in a society composed of a variety of urban forms and rural settlements.[37] Although the novels generally contained a majestic depiction of a rebuilt Jerusalem with some version of a restored temple, the focus here is on examples of what was imagined as a wholly new and modern Jewish urban society, usually in the form of commercially successful port cities. One of the earliest, *A Voyage to the Land of Israel in 2040* (1892) by Elhanan Leyb Levinski, a tale of a honeymoon in the Land of Judea, exemplifies Ahad Ha'am's cultural Zionist vision of a thriving Jewish community in Palestine that would serve as a national, cultural center for Jews all over the world.[38] Not surprisingly, given their concern for society's physical form, utopian novels dealt extensively with the importance of aesthetics, both as a prerequisite to internal reform and typically, also externally, as evidence submitted to non-Jews regarding the vibrancy of autonomous Jewish life. In Levinski's *Voyage*, the city of Ashdod is a tour de force of beauty, commerce, engineering, and intellectual achievement:

> The city is very large, some of the streets are longer than eight miles long. Electricity provides light for all the streets and homes, and night is as light as day; the electric train runs throughout the city from end

to end. All the buildings are amazingly beautiful; some are built from white marble. According to the latest statistics, the city's population is over one million. The large and praiseworthy port competes with the trade of Marseilles and Hamburg. Trade from the East in general, and the Land of Israel in particular, is especially great, because the Jews, in light of their location at the crossroads of Asia and Africa, and given their knowledge of the Syrian language and customs of its traders, imported merchandise of the East to Syria, all of it by way of Ashdod.[39]

Jews in Levinski's account were seen as cultural ambassadors as well as natural tradesmen. Interestingly, the text also recapitulates the normative Jewish aversion to aesthetic production and describes its impact on the city's physical plane: "There are no pictures or stone statues, you won't see them in any of the Hebrew cities, because the Jews do not realize their heroes in pictures or stone or clay, which are ultimately mute forms."[40] The most remarkable characteristic of Levinski's utopia is so self-evident one almost misses it; it is especially worth noting here for its similarity to later descriptions of Tel Aviv as a "100 percent Jewish city" (see Chapter 4).

At first glance, Jaffa is no different from . . . other seaside towns. It distinguishes itself in that our feet are standing on Hebrew earth: the spoken language is Hebrew, the courts are Hebrew courts, and the customs are a bit different than in other countries. Total freedom in the city; no one will ask you who you are, what your business is, and from where and to where you are going. You won't be asked for traveling papers, you'll see no judges or police, nor swords or lances, no symbols of rank or uniforms.[41]

Levinski's choice of Hebrew as the language of choice for both institutional and more mundane affairs marks *Voyage* as a product of the Eastern European Haskalah, with its strong emphasis on Hebrew language and classical sources. According to Rachel Elboim-Dror, "the culture described in [Levinski's] utopian Jewish state is therefore the culture of the Jewish shtetl of the Diaspora, reformed and renovated from a physical as well as a spiritual point of view. It is the transformation of the Jewish shtetl in the direction of the enlightened West."[42]

Levinski's urban utopia differs markedly from what is perhaps the best-known of Zionist utopias, Theodor Herzl's *Altneuland* (1902). Herzl's Haifa, encountered in the year 1923, is a near-perfect replica of Viennese high society, complete with cafés, resort spas, opera glasses, and gloves, and reflects a desire to build a Jewish society that is both economically and socially liberal, a haven of cooperative free enterprise and religious tolerance. There seems to be no definitive vernacular, and citizens communicate effortlessly in their imported European mother tongue, most probably German. (Herzl's ignorance of Jewish tradition and the Hebrew language was lambasted by Ahad Ha'am in a review of the novel.[43]) *Altneuland* also contains a healthy dose of futuristic effects, including a sky tram and telephonic newspaper. Herzl's "New Society" is a commonwealth with no judicial functions, and only the symbolic trappings of a central, controlling executive. In short, instead of a modern nation-state, the Jews have created a bourgeois, non-militarized "new center of civilization": "Only we Jews could have done it. . . . It could only have come through us, through our destiny. Our moral sufferings were as much a necessary element as our commercial experience and our cosmopolitanism."[44] Beyond its glorification of architectural and scientific accomplishments, this view of the "New Society" as an inevitable product of the meeting between cosmopolitanism, with its promise of universal rights and transnational freedoms, and Zionism's nationalist particularism, is perhaps *Altneuland*'s most utopian element.[45] Indeed, this incongruity between Tel Aviv's status as a city like any other and its self-proclaimed uniqueness as a Jewish city will prove to be the abiding tension propelling the formation of the city's cultural identity. For all their differences, both Levinski's *Voyage* and Herzl's *Altneuland* share a view of the city as the place where culture is contested and negotiated. Both novels also sidestep or entirely ignore the Arab question. *Altneuland* discounted the influence of native culture and landscape, and assumed the modernizing presence of European Jews would be welcomed by the local population, who would only benefit from the technological and social advances introduced. Levinski does not even mention the local inhabitants, but instead notes the "barren" state of the land itself: "For what was the land before the Jews arrived? It was worthless. Uncultivated fields, mounds of stones, a wasteland."[46]

Finally, neither Levinski's *Voyage* or Herzl's *Altneuland* considered the difficulty of establishing a new urban center so far from the familiar cultural sources of home. They assumed the happy superiority of a new Jewish center in Palestine and an unconflicted relation between this center and the Diaspora. In fact, early writing about Tel Aviv focused explicitly on this distance, and on the troublesome task of (re)creating an authentic sense of place.

## Memory, Exile, and Modernism

European Hebrew writers arriving in Palestine during the early years of the twentieth century encountered a land that seemed at once strange and familiar. Carrying with them memories of their native landscape, these writers were also strongly influenced by biblical images of the Land of Israel. David Frischmann's memoir of his 1913 visit to Palestine parses the experience in this way: "The land that I just came from is the land of geography, and this land that I am walking in right now is the land of history."[47] These two different kinds of memory existed side by side and equally powerfully in the imagination of one of Hebrew fiction's prototypical immigrant-pioneers, S. Y. Agnon's Yitzhak Kummer:

> Yitzhak remembered all the cities and villages and mountains and rivers that he had passed through on his way to Eretzyisrael, and all the mountains and rivers and cities and villages that he saw during his journey and didn't pay attention to because his eyes and heart were in Eretzyisrael, came and stood before him, and each place was more lovely than the next.[48]
>
> When Yitzhak was a child, he learned that Joseph was a shepherd and Moses was a shepherd and King David was a shepherd. Now he stood in the place where the shepherds of Israel had stood, and sheep and goats were grazing, only an Arab shepherded them.[49]

Yitzhak's physical relation to the landscape is mediated by both the memory of specific geographic elements of his past—mountains, rivers, cities, and villages—and the image of biblical figures whose own livelihood connected them to the land in a way that Yitzhak himself only dreams of. Despite his best intentions, with his peripatetic wandering between Jaffa, Jerusalem, and the *moshavot* in between, Yitzhak lives the same kind of essentially rootless existence that, according to Zionism, characterized Jewish experience in the Diaspora. Yitzhak's apprehension of the landscape is similarly "vicarious," a term used by landscape historian Robert B. Riley to describe a situation in which "the real observed landscape leads to an internally experienced landscape that is far richer and more personal than the 'real' landscape."[50] Synthesizing an experience of both the "visible" and the "visual"—the tangible details of ocular perception as well as their "cognitive ordering . . . into meaning"[51]—the vicarious landscape is an expression of one's attitude toward a particular place and often involves a personal narrative of attachment or alienation. The writing and manipulation of the vicarious landscape of Eretzyisrael has been a crucial component of modern Hebrew literary production. Memories of "the land of geography"—whether of the Ukrainian countryside or the boulevards of Paris—seeped into the writing of European immigrants about Palestine, either explicitly by way of comparison, or implicitly through shared imagery and atmosphere.

Writing about Tel Aviv was particularly inflected with the memories of diasporic metropolises because of the perception of the city as new and somewhat of a "blank slate." In Frischmann's narrative, Tel Aviv rises out of the "depths of the sands . . . like a wondrous island in the sea. . . . Lovely, orderly streets capture the eye and the heart. Each house a jewel in and of itself, every dwelling a pearl, every domicile a kind of toy. And all this people did in only two years!"[52] However, even as a modest garden suburb of Jaffa, Tel Aviv conceived of itself as a metropolis, not a province, and as a cultural and political center. This self-conception is clear in the 1905 prospectus of the founders of Achusat Bayit (Tel Aviv's first neighborhood): "Just as the city of New York marks the main gateway to America, so we must improve our city so that in the course of time it will be an Eretzyisraeli New York."[53]

From its inception, the idea of Tel Aviv as well as the city itself was the product of diverse cultural, ethnic, and ideological influences. On the one hand, the city was conceived by its founders, and perceived by its early visitors, as an expressly "European" endeavor, a "speck of Europe in the middle of Asia" (א בּלעק אײראָפּע אין מיטן אַזיע).[54] On the other hand, it was clearly a Mediterranean city on the sea, with the example of Jaffa close by.[55] Tel Aviv was also imagined, for better or for worse, in opposition to Jerusalem with its historical solidity and spiritual authority.[56] Writing that praised the city, as well as writing that maligned it, accepted the essential dichotomies distinguishing Tel Aviv —"the first Hebrew city"—from Jerusalem, distinctions at the center of larger debates over the cultural and political identity of the Jews as a national community.

Tel Aviv was widely taken up as a poetic subject early on, and the city became a focal point of larger ideological conflicts concerning Jewish life in Palestine. Chief among these conflicts was the question of what kind of lifestyle was most conducive to Jewish renewal. Gordonian agrarianism stressed the importance of a return to nature, manual labor, and collective living. Tel Aviv, with its growing, largely petit-bourgeois population, represented the antithesis of these tenets.[57] Urban life was also strongly connected to Jewish life in the Diaspora, and negative elements attributed to Tel Aviv were seen as a continuation or replication of the adverse conditions of Jewish life in the Diaspora.[58] Thus, attacking and defending Tel Aviv in poetry was often a measure of ideological identification. For example, Uri Zvi Greenberg's changing attitudes toward the city in his work can be traced against political and social upheaval and his own evolving political affiliations, particularly after 1929.[59]

The harshness of the local climate for its European-born inhabitants also figured strongly in poetry about the city as a decisive force in its development. Poems from the 1920s and 1930s that are considered among the foundational works of Tel Aviv's poetic tradition— Avraham Shlonsky's early poems and Nathan Alterman's *Kokhavim bachuts* (Stars Outside)—treat the city as a mytho-poetic site of conflict between culture and the natural elements.[60] Shlonsky's work repeatedly stages confrontations between the city's new buildings and the surrounding sands and threatening winds, as in the following lines from *Amal* (Labor):

I bend over the sand.
From the pressure of cement the dunes groan:
why did you come here, man, to the deserts
to bridle us?!

Suddenly a sirocco wind whipped,
and like an unhaltered herd of camels
winds attacked the city being built.[61]

Alterman's work describes the sensual details of city life—its markets, streets, and public spaces—and the various characters who inhabit them. Without actually mentioning Tel Aviv by name, poems such as "Street Day," "Market Day," "The Birth of the Street," and "Boulevard in Rain"[62] capture the city's vitality, the specifics of light and seasonal change, and especially its dynamic youth, in contrast to the old "gray cities" of Europe.[63] Despite its small size, Alterman's Tel Aviv is "not provincial in the accepted sense" but is, in fact, "a dual center for the land and especially for the people."[64] At the same time, Alterman confesses to missing certain aspects of European city life, particularly at the break of day:

I feel at this moment that the city clock is missing here. I remember those clocks jutting forth like the eye of a Cyclops from the turrets of city halls and from the gates of old city walls in Europe. Rusty, hoarse with age, they hide within their musty interiors tales of hidden conversations between dainty, frivolous princesses and courageous knights, wrapped in black rotundas. They ceaselessly mill, like old, tired Samsons, wheat of the bitter and sweet years of the city and its inhabitants, and at this moment, after the rooster's cry, within the grip of death and forgetfulness, seventy times stronger and deeper, they begin to chime from somewhere on high . . . and all the clocks in town answer in jumbled murmur, multi-toned mumbling of prayer, to the leader of the congregation (*shliach tsibur*)—the public clock before them. . . . Like memory, like regret, blind caresses of comfort, the bells of time descend upon the built city, kneeling beneath the burden of its days and nights.

But these don't exist at all in Tel Aviv. Instead there is a single donkey that always begins to bray at someone [also: "to miss or long

for someone"] at the same early morning hour. His tragic voice resembles the playing of a crazed cello, all of whose strings are undone
and wailing together. . . . He himself doesn't seem to know the importance of his position; he doesn't imagine that those with eyes as
open as his at a late hour listen only to his voice, and answer his braying with mute longing, like those clocks that join in song with the
first clock.[65]

The city clocks of European cities, embedded in the solid architecture of old city walls, measure the passage of time itself, symbolizing
Europe's deep historical roots and the culture that had developed
along with it, including Greek myths, fairy tales, and even aspects of
the Bible. Their chimes ring particularly loudly in contrast to Tel Aviv's
single rooster's cry at dawn. Yet the European city and its citizens
also suffer from the memory of their "bitter and sweet years . . . kneel
[ing] beneath the burden of its days and nights." There is something
potentially liberating in the lone braying of the donkey in Alterman's
Tel Aviv neighborhood, even as it calls upon and unites all the individual longings and memories of its citizens. In describing this donkey,
Alterman plays on the word *ga'aguim*, meaning "longing" but deriving from *ga'a*, meaning "bleat" or "bray." Though in colloquial Hebrew, *chamor* (donkey) has negative connotations, the term also
evokes the figure of the messiah and thus notions of redemption. Like
the image of the goat in Reuven's paintings (see Chapter 4), the native
donkey is also a privileged, yet ironic conduit of nostalgia and diasporic
memory.

Thus, the location of memory in Tel Aviv is complex and paradoxical. On the one hand, the city's newness, its lack of memory, is held up
as a virtue. On the other hand, the city potentially suffers from a kind
of excess of memory, due to the collective "homesickness" of its citizens. Certainly, given the largely immigrant nature of Jewish society in
Palestine, it is not surprising that early writing about Tel Aviv often
incorporated memories of the diasporic landscape. However, how
would later writing about the city cope with the literary landscape thus
fashioned for Tel Aviv? For *Israeli* writing, as the following chapters
demonstrate, memories of the city in its early decades are inevitably
linked to a stubborn bedrock of diasporic memories, almost as if in

compensation for the city's own shortage of history. Modernist literature generally has "[overlaid] the modern city with the city of antiq-
uity," that is, with ideas drawn from historical conceptions of urban
space and citizenship.[66] Certain strands of modernist poetry embraced
the modern metropolis's fragmented qualities, its tendency to be experienced as an inchoate mass of invention and ruin. Modernist forms
of subjectivity deftly utilized this perspective to describe the city as
composed of different and often contradictory layers of historical experience, and the poet as a free-floating, alienated observer, whose exemplary state is that of imagined or actual exile.

Indeed, perhaps only modernism could have accommodated Tel Aviv's
paradox-riddled self-image, at the heart of which is a vision of the city
as both the location of homecoming and a radically utopian social
space—both "The Place" and "no place." This meeting of a foundational, redemptive notion of return with the modernist drive to "make
it new," thus makes Tel Aviv an unusual framework in which to examine notions of exile and cultural production. Generally speaking, the
notion of writing and exile in the modern period indicates a physical
condition in which a writer, either voluntarily by way of expatriation,
or involuntarily as a result of political, social, or punitive force, relo-
cates to a new country and continues to write in that new location, either in his or her mother tongue or, in some cases, in the language of
the newly adopted homeland. One need only mention the examples of
Joseph Conrad, Gertrude Stein, Isaac Bashevis Singer, Joseph Brodsky,
Salman Rushdie, and Mahmud Darwish to get a sense of how varied
the literary experience of exile has been in the twentieth century.
Literary creation in Tel Aviv found strength both in a nostalgic longing for the Diaspora's physical contours and in a valorization of exile's psychological disposition. Indeed, modern Hebrew writing might
be a kind of template for what Svetlana Boym has called "ironic nostalgia," that is, an "accept[ance] . . . of the paradoxes of exile and
displacement."[67]

Poets working in Tel Aviv during its culturally formative period—
the 1920s to the 1940s—were largely modernist in practice; literary
modernism privileged both the location of exile and the position of the

alienated poet-citizen within the city. Moreover, Hebrew poetry, as a genre, bears a special relation to the situation and trope of exile; the very conditions for poetry, for song, are inextricably linked within the Hebrew literary imagination to Exile. In the famous section from Psalms beginning "By the rivers of Babylon, we lay down and wept," what starts as a declaration about the impossibility of poetry—"how shall we sing the Lord's song on foreign soil?"—culminates in one of the most resonant and memorable series of images in the history of the lyric: "If I forget thee, O Jerusalem, may my right hand loose its cunning; if I do not remember thee, let my tongue cleave to the roof of my mouth" (Psalms 137:1–6). Memory, a necessary by-product of exile, leads to the creation of song.[68]

This tension between the native son or daughter, returned to the ancient homeland, and the alienated flâneur possessing anonymity and critical distance, was a formative element of Tel Aviv's urban imagination. A 1927 series of poems entitled "In Tel Aviv," by Shlonsky, a major figure of the *moderna*, or first generation of Hebrew modernism in Palestine, exemplifies this tension.

"In Tel Aviv" (excerpts)
(a)
Street lamps before evening falls
Ah—who lit you, yellowed eyes?
For what did you bring, empty auto, untimely,
a strange guest to the wine house?

Hackerbrau pictures on the walls,
overturned glasses on the bar.
And in a neglected nook a clock drowses,
and a Jew asleep at the counter.

I, a Jew, came for no reason,
I, a Jew, returning home,
an empty car shifts another moment,
and silence returns to what it was.

And a snoring shofar roars,
a scratch in the skin of silence.

And only streetlights still throw
Yellow rings to the earth.

. . .

(d)
A peddler yawns, bent over his stand.
A gang of porters on the street corner.
An auto sprays mud. Camel caravan. Babies.
An Arab with a monkey.

The tower clock a Cyclops.
"A—RETZ" screams a Yemenite.[69]
Abandoned stalls at the crossroad:
*Gazoz* [soda]!

Day after day, idleness, idleness.
Tired be I, and always hungry. . . .

. . .

(e)
Last walk in the city-after-midnight,
stillness reckons [subtracts] his steps from slumber.
Weary face of houses stretched out beneath,
eyes shut.

What if I wander the streets, the wind behind me,
wagging his tail?
And what if I go home, and my room like a coffin
waiting for its dead: he will come . . . he will come . . . [70]

The series opens with the familiar details of what is perhaps the most
privileged setting in modernist poetry, the beloved *Dämmerung* of
a Mitteleuropa metropolis: the lighting of street lamps, a lone auto-
mobile with a mysterious traveler, the neighborhood winehouse with
atmospheric decorations, and a hint of benign neglect of both glass-
ware and regulars. The poem wavers between an existential state of
loneliness and despair—"Last walk in the city-after-midnight, / stillness reckons [subtracts] his steps from slumber. / Weary face of houses
stretched out beneath, eyes shut"—and a routinely disaffected sense
of both public and private space: "What if I wander the streets, the

wind behind me, / wagging his tail? / And what if I go home, and
my room like a coffin / waiting for its dead: he will come . . . he will
come . . ."

At the same time the poem demonstrates loving attention to the
newfound sensual details of daily life in the city: the snoring shofar—a
ritual object both humanized and desacralized by its position on the
street, asleep—the yawning peddler, the cries of the Hebrew-newspa-
per seller and soda fountain–boy, and the almost pointillist delineation: "Camel caravan. Babies. / An Arab with a monkey." The eye
stumbles to absorb the full range of stimuli, to order and arrange the
plethora of details within stanzas that, while not tightly metered, maintain some allegiance to regular rhyme. The clash of alienation and attachment—between displacement for the sake of one's poetic temperament, and migration in the name of some transcendental cause—is
best captured in the couplet: "I, a Jew, came for no reason / I, a Jew,
returning home."

The notion of home is complicated in early Tel Aviv by two different modalities—the modality of newness and the modality of strangeness. The place that is understood as an ancient homeland must somehow be "made new"—"the first Hebrew city"—and is also, inevitably,
foreign. What kind of site could possibly accommodate this difficult
knot of contradictory desires and impulses? Foucault's "heterotopia,"
a space that functions as a mirror or "counter-site" to a utopia, serves
as an instructive model. Heterotopic spaces are places

> formed in the very founding of a society—which are something like
> counter-sites, a kind of effectively enacted utopia in which the real
> sites, all the other real sites that can be found within the culture, are
> simultaneously represented, contested, and inverted. Places of this
> kind are outside of all places, even though it may be possible to indi-
> cate their location in reality.[71]

The Old Cemetery on Trumpeldor Street is Tel Aviv's foundational
heterotopia—in both its physical locale and its discursive representation over the last one hundred years. Given its status as a site that predates the city itself, the cemetery is an excellent place to begin considering Tel Aviv's history. At the same time, however, its implicit

connection to historical Jewish cemeteries of the Diaspora complicates the very notion of definitive beginnings and authentic origins. An exploration of the Old Cemetery and its history will demonstrate just how firmly Tel Aviv's modernity and newness were anchored in its diasporic past.

## Two

The Zionist Uncanny: Reading the Old
Cemetery on Trumpeldor

It is easier to drain the Emek [Valley] of its swamps than our soul of
its rotten accumulation of centuries. It is easier even to remember
Zion than to let our right leg forget its cunning at the foxtrot.
　　　　　—Marvin Lowenthal, "This Hebrew Renaissance" (1925)

If I forget thee O *golah* . . .
　　　　　—*The Book of Tel Aviv Street Names* (1944)

The city is constructed by its gaps.
　　　　　—Stephen Barber, *Fragments of the European City* (1995)

## Snapshot

A photograph of Ahad Ha'am's funeral in 1927, in Tel Aviv's Old Cemetery (Figure 2.1).[1] Amidst a group of people surrounding the fresh grave,
the poet Ch. N. Bialik eulogizes the ideological mentor of a generation
of Eastern European Jewish intellectuals. Most of group look at the
grave or each other. Some are in uniform, police or officials of some sort;
a white-bearded Alexander Siskind, dark glasses reflecting back into the
camera, stands just behind Bialik's left shoulder. Bialik is at the center of
the photograph; he looks into the camera with an expression of fatigue
and sadness—an Eastern European Jew, wearing a heavy coat over a
nondescript suit, with a modest cap on his head, standing by a freshly
dug grave in the dunes of the Trumpeldor Cemetery. More panoramic
photographs of the ceremony show that the grave is located in the cemetery's newer section, surrounded largely by sand, a few other graves, and
some spare, newly planted shrubbery (Figure 2.2). The dark suits of the
crowd, their European dress, contrast sharply against the bareness of the
place, the emptiness of the dunes, the dirt, the stone wall of the cemetery looming in the background, the large, triangular stone of a mass
grave strongly visible on the horizon. What is most affecting, however,
about this particular photograph is the result of a belated, surreptitious

*Fig. 2.1* Ch. N. Bialik eulogizing Ahad Ha'am, 1927. Soskin Archive, Historical Museum of Tel Aviv–Jaffa.

knowledge: Bialik stands in almost precisely the spot where he will be buried seven years later. His fatigue seems more than simply grief for his friend and mentor; it seems almost a kind of surrender, an admission, but of what precisely? Is he simply tired of standing in the center of yet another photograph?

It is the nature of photography that the viewer often possesses some knowledge of the world outside the frame that those within the photograph lack. This is especially the case with photographs of historic events, where the retrospective knowledge of hindsight produces belated, unconscious judgments regarding the photograph's subjects, who themselves appear oblivious to future events. This photograph, however, disturbs this knowledge, and the viewer's sense of power, in that Bialik's fatigued expression seems almost a premonition of his death. The photograph of Bialik standing awkwardly upon his own "final resting place" profoundly unsettles the notion of death as "at peace." It also complicates the association contained within the Hebrew terms for graveyard

*Fig. 2.2* Panorama of cemetery during Ahad Ha'am's funeral, 1927. Soskin Archive, Historical Museum of Tel Aviv–Jaffa.

—a "house of graves" (*beyt-kvarot*) or an "eternal home" (*beyt-olam*)— between the cemetery and home. The photograph links these two oscillating and unresolved relations—death as *not* rest/cemetery as *not* home. Its early Tel Aviv historical setting—and the centrally defining roles played by Bialik and Ahad Ha'am in the creation of modern Hebrew culture—implicitly raise the contradiction of creating something that is at once radically new, and a home.

In this, the Trumpeldor Cemetery is emblematic of Tel Aviv's own repeated and paradoxical attempts to be a "home" for modern Hebrew culture. An exploration of the Trumpeldor Cemetery will serve as an exemplary entry into Tel Aviv's troubled relation to history, and to the idea of home. This chapter examines the cemetery—its physical plan and tombstones, its relation to the surrounding city, and its representation in public consciousness—in order to illustrate how Tel Aviv has expressed and symbolized the paradoxes inherent in European Jewish settlement in the Middle East. Reading the cemetery as a text will illuminate what was lost in the migration of diasporic Jewish culture, and what was displaced and effaced in the process. As Chapter 1 suggests, the origins of Tel Aviv and the Old Cemetery may be found in the European Diaspora and in the memory of grand architecture and public spaces.

## Portraits of Home

At the end of Gershon Shofman's "Between a Rock and a Hard Place," a story of physical and moral destitution set in a small corner of Vienna during World War I, we read of the Hebrew writer Shlomo Pik's return to Palestine. Having arrived in Vienna to "inhale Europeaness," Pik finds himself weakened and wandering, as if there were "no soil beneath his feet." He returns to the apparent solidity of the "Land-of-Israel" soil, nearly suffocated by the omnipresent atmosphere of "Europeaness," leaving behind his portrait, painted by Mundo, a young Jewish émigré mistakenly arrested for espionage while painting landscapes outside the city. Mundo, whose name signifies the "world-liness" of Europe, has spent the war in relative ease, imprisoned in a psychiatric ward where he occupied himself painting portraits of the doctors. For Pik, a thinly disguised version of Shlomo Rabinowitz, "there's no soil beneath his feet here, but his portrait stands ready; for this there is room even in Europe." As Mundo himself concludes: "Given that the portrait has already been made, he no longer desired the original."[2]

Shofman's story raises the specter of the Wandering Jew, an image that Zionism was meant to erase, returning the Jews to their ancestral homeland. Absence in Vienna/Europe was meant to attain presence—"soil beneath his feet"—in Tel Aviv/Palestine, with all its attendant political, economic, and cultural accessories. This valorization of terri-toriality, even a qualified or ironic version, flew in the face of the pre-dominant modernist aesthetic of alienation and exile.[3] Yet if Zionism was also a form of modernism, then Tel Aviv was one of its more inter-esting and problematic texts, an ultimate exercise in "making it new." In fact, Tel Aviv was a kind of "laboratory for urban design,"[4] subject to the competing ideological desires of the successive waves of immigrants who built its infrastructure. However, this future-oriented drive toward newness was continually thwarted by the rhetoric of place and homeland, of a *return* to a privileged space, the "Land of Israel." This return envisaged a new Hebrew culture deriving from ancient Jewish life in the region, based on biblical depictions and archaeological excavations of synagogue ruins. Thus, the desire to be new was inevitably undercut by a desire to appear old. Tel Aviv was a modernist invention, not only or even primarily in its urban planning and architectural style—both of which are discussed in Chapter 4—but in terms of its own paradoxical self-conception: a city both new and authentic, wrought by a break with the immediate, exilic past, yet rooted and connected to an ancient, more venerable tradition. This paradox provided much of the creative tension within early Hebrew literature in Palestine, which worked to depict local Jewish life as both natural and redemptive, in contrast to the Diaspora's unhealthy rootlessness. For this formulation to work, the fundamental "unhomeliness" of European Jews in Palestine had to be overcome, or at least downplayed.

What was repressed by Zionism's negation of exile surfaced within modern Hebrew culture as *das Unheimlich*, "the uncanny," a phenomenon related to Shofman's ghostly portrait of the Jewish "haunting" of Europe. In Sigmund Freud's terms, repression marks the uncanny, "that class of terrifying which leads us back to something long known to us, . . . something familiar and old-established in the mind and which has become alienated from it only in the process of repression."[5] Ironically, the uncanny is most itself, recognized as most "unhomely," when it is most "at home." Freud's conclusions derive in part from a secondary meaning of *heimlich*, that is, "hidden" or "buried." His use of examples from an 1860 dictionary suggest home's more ominous side, something walled in and secretive: "I have roots that are most *heimlich*, I am grown in the deep earth" (198). His further references from the Brothers Grimm are consonant with this darker sense: "From the idea of 'homelike,' 'belonging to the house,' the further idea is developed of something withdrawn from the eyes of strangers, something concealed, secret" (200). This catalog leads to the conclusion that "*heimlich* is a word the meaning of which develops towards an ambivalence, until it finally coincides with its opposite, '*unheimlich*'" (201). Emerging historically in a period of enormous migration and global homesickness, the uncanny was a way of describing a home that no longer felt like one; it was, in a sense, a foregone by-product of the drive toward home.

A major part of Freud's essay "The Uncanny" is devoted to a discussion of literary works, for it is within the realm of the imagination that the uncanny achieves its greatest disturbances: "An uncanny effect is often easily produced when the distinction between imagination and reality is effaced, as when something that we have hitherto regarded as imaginary appears before us in reality, or when a symbol takes over the full functions of the thing it symbolizes" (221). This last symbolic operation constitutes the power of Shofman's portrait, the mesmerizing effect that images of Jews held in Eastern Europe.[6] This uncanniness had permeated European Hebrew culture, which had been produced in a language without a territory. Some element of this European "unhomeliness" was also transplanted in Palestine, and was, in a sense, "true": despite the rhetoric of homecoming, and despite its linguistic origins in the East, Hebrew culture in Palestine was fundamentally foreign. This twinned relation of home and the uncanny lurks in an early Tel Aviv vignette, Devora Baron's "At the End of Summer," which features a Tel Aviv population circa 1920, panic-stricken by the spread of disease: "In our crowded neighborhoods, gentlemen, in this climate at the end of summer, disease is liable to take a serious form. The form, in every detail, of a plague."[7] Baron's brief sketch repeatedly creates, then shatters, a sense of calm. Just as a "closed car" carries off the latest victim, "incurable consumptives" appear, a reminder that the respite is only temporary. As the story builds toward a "feeling of relief" and an end to the epidemic, a wagon appears "at the end of the street with someone stepping slowly at its side, holding the reins in his hands":

> A sick man being taken to the hospital, or a corpse? . . .
> At the sight of the sheet-wrapped body, swaying with the jolts of the approaching cart, every face wilts. Only now do many realize that the night has already fallen and the last glimmers have gone out on the

surface of the sea. The windows are lit up the entire length of the local hospital. Half-people in bandages can be glimpsed through the iron bars; the mattresses hanging over the balcony railings are exposed to the electric light in all their suspect stains. . . .

The funeral is enormous.

With the low-sided *Eretzyisraeli* bier in their hands, the beadles are immediately swallowed up in the mob, and to anyone watching from the rooftops, the procession might look almost festive with its myriad, quietly burning candles; not a single cry or groan or sound of human speech is heard. At the crossroads, where the road ends, the mourners turn right, slide down the slope with a momentary flickering of their candles, and instantly disappear into the darkness of the dunes. And in the empty neighborhood a long silence falls, the silence of relief. Shutters are soundlessly opened.[8]

The neighborhood of the living and the resting place of the dead are two distinct and separate spheres, yet they exist side by side, in close, even intimate, proximity. The crowd accompanies the dead into a kind of underworld—the "crossroads," resonant of death and the world beyond, where the road ends and the darkness of the dunes engulfs the flickering candles—while back in town comes a feeling of relief as life starts up again. Yet there is something deathlike about the "empty neighborhood," with its "half-people in bandages," its long silence and soundless shutters, while the cemetery, known euphemistically as "an eternal resting place," is somewhat humanized, filled, temporarily, with life.[9] "At the End of Summer" thus evokes the chilling proximity of daily life to the site of death, for Freud, the supreme locus of the uncanny: "Many people experience the feeling in the highest degree in relation to death and dead bodies, to the return of the dead, and to spirits and ghosts" (218). The story's pre-State setting—a detailed evocation of a sweltering 1920s Tel Aviv—is rare for Baron, much of her work being set in the Eastern European shtetl. It is, however, not surprising that Baron's often darkly grotesque sensibility would settle upon a funeral as the thematic climax of a tale set in what was conceived as a supremely life-giving project—the founding of the first Hebrew city, spearhead of a new Hebrew national culture in Palestine.[10] Her story suggests the contours of the psychological landscape of death in

Tel Aviv during this period; it represents the death of a single individual as a collective experience, a reminder of the community's own tenuous condition.[11]

The fictional depiction of the geographic relation between the cemetery and the town bears a strong resemblance to the actual location of Tel Aviv's cemetery in the 1920s. The cemetery was founded during the 1902 cholera epidemic in Jaffa. Ottoman officials forbade the burial of the dead within the city walls, particularly given the proximity of the Jewish cemetery in Adjami to the center of town. Jewish community leaders requested an alternative, and Shimon Rokach was granted permission to purchase twelve dunam of land in the name of the Committee of the United Communities of Ashkenazi and Sephardi Groups, in what was then called the Lands of North Jaffa. According to a story, the area consisted largely of shifting sand and was thus difficult to cultivate.[12] Legend also has it that holy books were buried in a special grave and two "black weddings" were held at the site in an effort to halt the epidemic. (It was believed that these community-sponsored ceremonies, in which orphans were married off, would lead God to look favorably upon the charity of the community, and have mercy, thus easing the epidemic.[13]) It was only five years later that the first plan to build a modern Jewish neighborhood outside of Jaffa was announced. In essence, then, Tel Aviv began with its dead. In the words of a historian, "the city followed its graves."[14] The cemetery received the designation "old" as early as the late 1920s, in the wake of plans to build a new site. According to literary historian Dov Sadan, "the term *old* [gave] it a special flavor, so that thinking of it, one would link it with truly old cemeteries in famous communities in the Diaspora. Just as this term indicated the glory of old age, and lent them respect and affection, so it was with [the Trumpeldor Cemetery]."[15] The Old Cemetery (*beyt ha-kvarot ha-yashan*) is today situated at Tel Aviv's geographic center, a walled-in pastoral patch, occupying prime real estate in a desirable location. The uncanny experience it represents—the city's distance from a disaporic "home"—also remains at the heart of the Israeli culture that has grown around it. Specifically, the Old Cemetery is an example of what Anthony Vidler has called an "architectural uncanny," a site symbolizing or enclosing some fundamental "unhomeliness."[16] Vidler's literalized interpretation regrounds the psychoanalytic term in its spatial origins—a profound physical disorientation that nonetheless feels vaguely familiar.

Jewish tradition insists on an intimate connection between the very idea of burial in "the Land of Israel" and homecoming—a motif stretching from the biblical story of the Cave of the Patriarchs to the contemporary desire of Jews living abroad to be buried in Israel. Ironically, the Trumpeldor Cemetery inverts this relation between burial and homecoming; an awareness of this reversal seemed to flicker within the expression on Bialik's face, as he eulogized Ahad Ha'am in the dunes. The cemetery's exposed location, and the fact that its existence predated the city itself, rendered it a constant reminder of not being at home, and of an instability at odds with the longevity of the diasporic Jewish cemeteries with which it was implicitly compared.

The Trumpeldor Cemetery therefore has a unique relation to modern Hebrew culture's historical attempts to be "at home" in Palestine, being the resting place of key figures in early Hebrew culture, including Max Nordau, Ch. N. Bialik, Ahad Ha'am, and Meir Dizengoff. It is, in other words, a virtual mapping of modern Hebrew culture. The site of the cemetery, as well as its fragmentary, textual history, may be read as exemplary of Tel Aviv's own understanding of itself, as well as tensions between secular and religious civic institutions, conflicts that still permeate Israel's cultural and political spheres. For example, decisions regarding the cemetery's establishment were made in conjunction with several separate institutions: the Burial Society (*chevre kadisha*), under the auspices of the Chief Rabbinate; the *kehliya* (representatives of the Jewish community); and the Tel Aviv–Jaffa Municipality.[17] Their official correspondence deliberated a variety of issues, from funding to repair the surrounding wall and build a new entrance, to the designation of a special section for the burial of children. Concern for the upkeep and maintenance of the cemetery was already evident in 1932, with the establishment of a citizen's group dedicated to its preservation—the Association for the Improvement of the Old Cemetery—and discussion of the cemetery as a national pantheon began as early as 1935.[18] The protocols from a meeting of the association reveal an interest in the site as a valuable cultural commodity for the new city, even as the precise contours of this culture were still being shaped. In connection with suggested repairs and alterations in the cemetery, one participant notes: "I do not miss Christian or Moslem cemeteries. We should simply make the existing cemetery appropriate for Tel Aviv. . . . In the Old Cemetery, trees cannot be planted because of the edict that forbids allowing the roots to take the spirit out of the dead. . . . The cemetery should be left as it is so that generations to come will know that this was how the Old Cemetery in Tel Aviv was."[19]

Thus the example of the Old Cemetery offers insight into the way Tel Aviv tried to define itself as a new, secular, Hebrew city, the ostensible bedrock of contemporary Israeli culture. The Old Cemetery is a foundational site in Tel Aviv's history in terms of both time and space: temporally, because its establishment predated that of the city itself, and spatially, due to its central relation to the city's subsequent physical expansion around it. In an essay on semiotics and urbanism, Roland Barthes observes that "as a general rule, the studies made of the urban core of different cities have shown that . . . the center of the city . . . does not constitute the culminating point of any particular activity, but a kind of empty 'heart' of the community's image of the center . . . , a somehow empty place which is necessary to the organization of the rest of the city."[20] Tel Aviv's Old Cemetery is the "somehow empty place" around which Tel Aviv organized itself, however subconsciously. In addition to its textual representation, however, the cemetery also deserves scrutiny as a potential "site of memory" in comparison with similar European cemeteries and in light of the central place of mourning in Israeli society.

## The Old Cemetery, Mourning, and Sites of Memory

The death of the writer Yosef Haim Brenner in the Jaffa riots of May 1921 was among the most traumatic events in the history of Jewish settlement in Palestine (Figure 2.3).[21] According to an account in the Hebrew daily *Ha-aretz*:

> All the residents of Tel Aviv gathered by the Herzliya Gymnasium. They removed the corpses from the school, and laid them in a row.

Comrade Dizengoff eulogized the dead. Afterward *El Male
Rachamim* was said, and the entire people cried bitterly. Pioneers
took the bodies one by one to the cemetery. Hebrew writers, among
them the aging Alexander Ziskind Rabinovitz, carried Brenner's body.
A defensive chain surrounded the huge crowd. At the cemetery there
was also a huge crowd, and one of the workers said a few words.
A moment of mourning was announced, and the entire crowd sat on
the ground for a few minutes. At dark, the crowd came back from
the cemetery in grieving silence.[22]

In *Ha-poel Ha-tsair*, Yitzhak Tabenkin wrote: "The victims were
buried together in a mass grave because they fell together (*ba-tsavta*).
Brenner's body is also buried there, but there are no separate graves."[23]
This mass grave—in Hebrew, *kever achim*, literally, a "grave of brothers"—is today located near the entrance of the cemetery (Figure 2.4).
Each name is engraved on its own slab, except for that of Yosef Ben
Moshe Lowyard, who, according to the inscription, "was killed together with Brenner and his comrades, and whose body has disappeared." The plaque reflects the importance of the recovery of personal
remains; an attachment to the land during a lifetime is reconstituted after death by "returning" the body to the earth.

*Fig. 2.3* Funeral of Y. H. Brenner, 1921. Historical Museum of Tel Aviv–Jaffa.

*Fig. 2.4* Mass grave for victims of 1921 disturbances, including Y. H. Brenner.
Photo by author.

A version of the story of the Old Cemetery on Trumpeldor Street
consists of precisely the kind of narrative I have just offered regarding
Brenner: an oscillation between a description of its physical aspects—
location, layout, and tombstone inscriptions—and its "metaphysical"
aspects—its own history, as well as the many individual histories it cir-
cumscribes. Obviously it is impossible to include a description of every
person buried in the cemetery.[24] I choose to comment at length on
Brenner, a major historical figure in his own right who died a violent
and dramatic death, and not, for example, on Sarah Baratz, who apparently loved the sea, or on the many graveside photographs preserving the faces of children (Figures 2.5, 2.6). This egalitarian comming-
ling of the cultural elite with the population as a whole is consonant
with the city's early utopian vision, and is characteristically noted in descriptions of the cemetery.[25]

Another dimension should be added to this dual narrative; that is,
an understanding of the Old Cemetery as a "site of memory," in Pierre

*Fig. 2.5* Grave of Sarah Baratz. Photo by author.

Nora's terms a place where "memory crystallizes and secretes itself."[26] Although we may quibble with Nora's now ubiquitous and potentially idealized view of a once "authentic" memory trampled by the debilitating force of history and monumentalized into "sites of memory," his essential distinctions remain provocative and valuable. Memory's power as a stable, coherent concept that seems to preserve aspects of the past is in fact enhanced by its apposite construction, that is, the passage of time and the concept of history. That this is true for the Old Cemetery becomes particularly clear when one considers its location— the center of Tel Aviv's hectic, ever-metamorphosing downtown. Yet suggesting that a graveyard functions as a "site of memory" seems a bit axiomatic, what with its abundant and transparent mix of spatial parameters and textual cues. If the Old Cemetery was perceived in this way, then it would naturally function as a kind of outdoor museum, a mnemonic space through which the visitor moved and activated images linked to a collective memory.[27] A famous example of an urban cemetery functioning in such a fashion is Paris's Père Lachaise, memorialized in Balzac's novels. This mini-neighborhood of the dead, sprawling over a hill to the east of the city center, even has its own Metro stop.[28] Numerous volumes extol the history of the site, the record of which ex-

*Fig. 2.6* Child's grave. Photo by author.

tends back to the year 418.[29] Père Lachaise's authority is thus constituted both discursively, in canonical literary works and historical studies, as well as geographically, on the urban grid. A similar authority is
indicated in somewhat different fashion for the old Jewish cemetery in
Prague. There, physical depth functions as a marker of time: more than
twelve thousand graves are contained in a relatively small area in the
city's old Jewish quarter, buried in layers dating back to the fifteenth
century.[30] The cemetery's chaotic, jumbled interior is oddly soothing,
quiet and shaded over with centuries of greenery, reflecting the vibrant
longevity of the Prague Jewish community. Today the cemetery's proximity to other organized Jewish landmarks in the city, especially its immediate physical contiguity to a museum devoted to children's drawings from the Terezin concentration camp, sets it squarely within the
context of the shoah and the destruction of Jewish life in Eastern
Europe.

Neither the example of Père Lachaise nor that of the old Jewish
cemetery in Prague make for the best of comparisons with Tel Aviv's
Old Cemetery. However, bracketing questions of historical longevity,
the degree of authority accruing to the European cemeteries is hardly
the same for Tel Aviv's Old Cemetery, which contains no less significant
a gathering of local heroes. The Old Cemetery receives scant, almost
cursory, mention in most standard written accounts of the city, including local histories and guides in Hebrew, as well as tourist guidebooks in English. My own informal survey of pedestrians in the
streets surrounding the cemetery, conducted over a number of years,
revealed that most people did not know where it was or who was
buried there. I myself come to the cemetery, and to Tel Aviv as a whole,
as a relative outsider, having lived in the neighborhood for four years
from 1988 to 1992. In my frequent visits to the city since, I have returned to the cemetery, observing the minimal changes in landscaping
and the occasional new grave. In contrast to the surrounding rapidly es-
calating skyline, it sometimes seems that the Old Cemetery on
Trumpeldor is the only spot in Tel Aviv that remains static and relatively untouched. This is not to argue against change and in favor of a
kind of fossilized, nostalgic view of the city's origins; neither is it to de-

fend nor attack plans for the city's development as a cultural and economic center, or the preservation of its older neighborhoods. However, from its inception, Tel Aviv's sense of itself as a city has been characterized precisely by these two sensibilities—nostalgia and outsiderness. Literary and artistic expression in the city has even capitalized on the creative tension between the two: nostalgia for the founding vision of Tel Aviv as an intimate "garden city" by the sea—an express rejection of the crowded Jewish quarters of the Diaspora's urban centers—mingled with ambivalent memories of the cultural and social achievements of these metropolises; a feeling of outsiderness in a place where for much of the city's history most of its inhabitants were born elsewhere.

Not only is the cemetery itself virtually ignored, once inside, it is not an easy place to find one's way around. Though landscaping in the main areas is maintained, there is no map at the cemetery's entrance or brochure detailing the "who's who" or providing an official history.[31] The visitor is left to wander freely among the graves, following the path where there is one, treading carefully between the stones where there is not. The lack of a didactic context is at noticeable odds with the overtly historicized and landmarked nature of so much of the Israeli landscape; this is perhaps because many of the writers and famous personages buried there are already overly inscribed elsewhere in the national collective memory—in educational curricula, and in the numerous streets and buildings named after them.

Perhaps one can hardly expect the cemetery to become a kind of leisure park or touristic site like American urban cemeteries, given the centrality of mourning in Israeli society. Yet other Israeli cemeteries attract both touristic and local attention, Mount Herzl being the most salient example.[32] Even a less familiar, "off-the-beaten-track" site such as the cemetery at Kibbutz Kinneret, where the poet Rachel Bluwstein is buried, is nonetheless relatively well tended and well marked. The poet's gravesite is physically situated and arranged so as to construct a specific kind of graveside experience. The visitor is invited to sit on a bench at the poet's grave, overlooking a large palm tree on the shore of the Sea of Galilee, a prominent feature in Rachel's poems. Beside the grave, a copy of the poet's collected works—published in more than twenty editions, a talisman of Ashkenazi–Labor-movement culture—is chained within a protective safe-box. The body of the poet and the body of her poetry are both interred within the land; the graveside visit is thus constituted as kind of a recovery: the pilgrim sits at the grave, reads a poem, and looks up to find the actual landscape represented in the poem. The experience is somewhat contradictory: a kind of static "lyric time" frames the landscape, as if nothing has changed since the composition of Rachel's Kinneret poems in the 1920s; at the same time, one cannot ignore the surrounding agricultural infrastructure, a mainstay of the Zionist narrative of "redeeming" the land.

The cemetery's potential, political volatility in Israel's "culture of mourning" is also the subject of two recent popular novels.[33] In Meir Shalev's *Blue Mountain*, a Jewish farmer exacts revenge on his neighbors by turning his portion of their collectively worked land into a commercial enterprise, an "eternal resting place for pioneers." For a significant fee, wealthy Jewish donors from abroad—former communists, socialists, and utopian dreamers who left Palestine for the "fleshpots" of America—could be (re)united with the soil of Israel, this time for good: "Two hundred and seventy-four old men and women, a mandolin, and one aging mule are buried in my cemetery. Pioneers, fulfillers, and traitorous capitalists."[34] The cemetery in Shalev's novel is the setting for a cross-generational drama: an often comic drama of loyalties and betrayals unfolds upon the graves, and is inscribed in the landscape through the placement of burial plots. Thus the drive to reclaim or redeem the land is mocked by the return of the physical remains of those who had ultimately rejected the pioneering ethos. The omnipresent past hovers like the mosquitoes that threaten to invade the settlement. In Batia Gur's *A Stone for a Stone*, the accidental death of her son during military training provokes a mother to challenge the entire military and judicial establishment regarding the prohibition on individualized gravemarkers. During the unveiling of the standard sixty-by-forty centimeter cement stone, upon which was inscribed the sentence "fell in the line of duty," she bursts out: " 'Murderers. They murdered him and now they tell me "fell in the line of duty." ' . . .

Everyone was afraid. She had broken all the rules. Grieving mothers who were native Israelis, especially Ashkenazi in origin, behave with restraint and respect at their sons' funerals."[35] Both Shalev's and Gur's novels treat the cemetery as a locus of social and political conflict. The relative lack of public or literary discourse about the cemetery on Trumpeldor Street is therefore striking precisely because of the centrality of mourning in Israeli culture; this lack is emblematic of Tel Aviv's difficult relation to its past.[36] For example, since the closure of the Municipal Museum, the city has no museum devoted exclusively to its own history, effectively erasing from the space of the city any institutionalized symbolic representation of its past. (The former Municipal Museum on Bialik Street near the cemetery has been closed for a number of years and there are no definitive plans to renovate it.) Even the official material handed out by the tourist information desk at City Hall devotes only a single page to important sites in Tel Aviv's history, focusing mainly on current nightlife, shopping, and beachfront activities. In recent years, however, with the ninetieth anniversary of its founding, the city has indicated that it is beginning to recognize the degree to which its past must be productively integrated into its present. In conjunction with the anniversary, for example, numerous exhibits were mounted and a spate of glossy volumes on the city's distinctive architecture were published. Even more recently, Tel Aviv's early years have been the subject of major photography retrospectives, in Tel Aviv and at the Israel Museum in Jerusalem.[37] Preservation and quality of life in the city continue to be vigorously debated, and in July of 2003, UNESCO (the United Nations Educational, Scientific and Cultural Organization) designated Tel Aviv as a World Heritage Site, in recognition of the city's distinctive International Style architecture.

Still, the enigma of the cemetery remains untapped. On the one hand, we might say that the Old Cemetery thus functions as a "site of memory" only *in potentia*, as a kind of structuring absence, whose boundaries may define and enclose an important part of Israeli history, but whose actual presence and significance have yet to be addressed.[38] On the other hand, the cemetery has in a sense leaped over, or skipped, the more obvious, explicit processes and signs of commemoration and memorialization, arriving directly at the extreme, ultimate function of a site of memory, that is, *forgetting*. What precisely is at stake in this forgetting, and what happens when we allow the cemetery's own fragmentary textual history to remember? Memory speaks in unpredictable and uncontrollable ways. In giving voice to the Old Cemetery's textual history—the few essays and poems written about it, and its tombstone inscriptions—I seek to understand what is unmanageable about the site, and the experiences buried and forgotten within.

## The Text of the Cemetery

A review of early documents relating to the cemetery, and an examination of its tombstone inscriptions, augment its potential as a site of memory. For example, a short article from 1922 views the Old Cemetery as deserving of preservation and upkeep. In conjunction with another piece, about tree-planting in the city, Y. Segel, Tel Aviv's municipal gardener, urges protecting the graves from the surrounding sands with tamarisk trees. In this way, the "remnants of the past" that characterize the graves' iconic motifs, making it worthy of the title *beyt kvarot yehudi atik* (ancient Jewish cemetery) may be preserved. Segel also happens to be related to one of the local tombstone artisans. He warns against the imposition of "modish" cement gravestones, "those enormous, clamorous stones, decorated with all kinds of irrelevant ornaments, like pictures, photographs of the dead beneath a glass frame on the gravestone, and all other sorts of customs lacking in taste or tradition, which spoil the cemetery's quiet, innocent appearance, lovely in its simplicity."[39] Segel wishes to maintain the cemetery in a manner reflecting the values of the community it serves: simplicity, hygiene, respect for the past, and a connection to Jewish tradition.[40] Though photographs were a relatively new addition, tombstone portraits of the dead were not, and such portraits can be found on graves in older Jewish cemeteries as well.[41] The puritanism regarding visual expression may seem surprising given Tel Aviv's secular aspirations. However, this anti-ornamental view is in keeping with Tel Aviv's minimalist, modernist cultural sensibility, which has found expression in urban planning and architecture as well as in literature.

Segel's article expresses no explicit concern for the Old Cemetery as a site that could bolster Tel Aviv's meager historical foundations. However, aesthetic distinctions concerning modern and ancient tombstone styles are at the heart of the first study to champion the Old Cemetery as a historical site, a 1939 volume that remains the only comprehensive study of the cemetery—*Sefer beyt ha-kvarot ha-yashan* (The Book of the Old Cemetery). This rare volume contains a biographical listing of everyone buried in the cemetery (3,758 names at the time of printing), complete with tombstone inscriptions, a statistical breakdown according to gender, age, and year of death, and photographs of some of the more elaborate tombstones. The idea for the book is credited to the writer Alexander Siskind, who had, by that time, seen many of his friends buried in the Old Cemetery. In the extensive introduction, editors Zvi Kroll and Zadok Leinman distinguish between the various groupings of graves in the cemetery—the famous and the anonymous, newer mass graves and the older, less orderly sections, children and cholera victims—distinctions that remain helpful in navigating one's way around the cemetery.

Kroll and Leinman particularly emphasize the stylistic differences among the various "generations" of graves. The placement of the cemetery's earliest graves—of those who died during the cholera epidemic in Jaffa—is disorderly and unsymmetrical. Their tombstones, typical of Jewish cemeteries of the East, are laid flush with the earth, often covered by marble engraved with biblical verses or devotional acrostics. Despite their haphazard arrangement, and their structural "primitiveness," these stones, according to the editors, demonstrate a "stylistic unity" that is authentically rooted in a specifically Jewish version of the local. Their appreciation of the stones' native qualities parallels views expressed by early Hebrew painters in Palestine, who looked to ancient synagogue mosaics as a model for a new, authentically Hebrew art, in opposition to what they perceived as a diasporic, Jewish sensibility. The cemetery's newer tombstones, those constructed since 1922, stand upright, in the style of European cemeteries. "Modernization," according to Kroll and Leinman, has "overcome" these graves; the text upon their stones is "repetitive" and "empty of content" (x). The editors also comment on the brevity of the newest inscriptions, often consisting of just a name and years: "Of course this is the taste of the new generation, at the bottom of which is a desire to be free of the repetitiveness of the accepted formula" (xii).[42]

These distinctions between the earlier and later graves point to the ideological investment of the editors' judgment, an evaluation rooted in their conception of iconic and textual authenticity. They view the modernity of the later graves as empty and meaningless, and connected specifically to the Diaspora. Ironically, however, the editors measure their own efforts against the example of European Jewish cemeteries; the main line of inquiry followed by scholars of those cemeteries concerned the broken, aging gravestones, and their chief methodological challenge lay in a traditional Jewish realm—textual interpretation, that is, "deciphering" the writing upon the stones, thereby establishing the nature of the Jewish community in which the interred once lived and died. Those studies sought to demonstrate a coherent continuity throughout the generations of Jewish dead. However, the editors of *The Book of the Old Cemetery* declare:

> Research alone is neither fitting nor sufficient in regard to the Old Cemetery in Tel Aviv, whether because of the brief span of its existence—though called the "old" cemetery, it is only thirty-eight years old—or due to the impoverished content of the gravestones. The place lacks the antiquities of the distant, unknown past and even the passage between periods is not palpable (xvi).

The idea that no majestic, historical process may be decoded in the Old Cemetery—"even the passage from period to period is not palpable"— was perceived as a complementary mark of Tel Aviv's newness.[43] The relative shallowness of Tel Aviv's roots is its attraction: there is a touch of defensive pride in the editors' insistence on the need for a method unlike that used to study Jewish cemeteries in the Diaspora, and in their proclamation of the "impoverished" state of their own cemetery.

Instead of the grand genealogy of European graveyards, the Old Cemetery's noteworthy are figures from the present, "the builders of the city of Tel Aviv. . . . The impression of their deeds and activities . . . are still greatly felt in the atmosphere of our time—as if they were still with us, living and working. . . . The history of their lives and actions is the gravestone of a living generation that we knew, and to whom the connection is still unsevered" (xvi). History, the record of events over time, is described as an ossified artifact—a gravestone—that can be tangibly observed in space. The feeling that the dead are "still with us" deflects attention from actual gravemarkers: the fresh memory of their deeds obviates the need for extensive tombstone inscription. This paucity of textual inscription in the cemetery as a whole, its stylistic minimalism, distinguishes it from disaporic Jewish cemeteries. For example, a volume on Vilna's cemetery views textuality as the ultimate memorial: "For memorial in a book is more valuable than that engraved in stone, which will one day be spoiled, while that which is written in a book will last forever."[44]

An example more nearly contemporaneous to the Trumpeldor Cemetery may be found in the Workman's Circle Cemetery in New York. Many of the tombstones in this pantheon of modern Yiddish authors bear elaborate, explanatory epitaphs.[45] In the Trumpeldor Cemetery, however, tombstone inscription is inversely proportional to fame: the most extreme example of this is Aharon Melnikov's austere red marble stone marking Ahad Ha'am's grave; the gravestone indicates neither his real name, nor dates of birth and death. The Jewish cemetery whose sensibility bears the closest resemblance to the Trumpeldor Cemetery's secular pantheon is Warsaw's Okopowa Cemetery, where the modernist writers Y. L. Peretz and U. N. Gnessin are buried. Ironically enough, in 1928, a new immigrant claiming to have worked at the Jewish cemetery in Warsaw offered his services to the Tel Aviv Municipality. Recognizing the importance of maintaining "the only cemetery in the first Hebrew city," he notes that it is currently

> a shame and embarrassment to looking at: there are no paths, visitors
> have to walk over the tombstones, with no trees or plants while this
> place begins to be more and more holy for us. This place of remem-
> brance of our people who have died connects the cemetery with most
> of the residents of our city. . . . Therefore, the time has come for the
> city to find a solution to this question, and I . . . having some experi-

ence in this realm, having worked for years in the Jewish cemetery in Warsaw, known for the beauty of its arrangement, offer my help to the honorable management of the city in solving this dilemma. I would take upon myself partial care of the cemetery, laying paths between the graves, planting trees, and generally making it a place worthy of the name "cemetery."[46]

The fact that the Okopowa Cemetery is also the subject of a book published in 1936, reinforces the similarity between the two sites and their mutual aspirations: both cemeteries encompass religious and secular impulses regarding history and memorialization.[47] The stylistic variety of their tombstones demonstrates the degree to which passage between the religious and the secular was neither smooth nor unequivocal. Both studies emphasize the inventive, individual expression of the newer stones' modernist style, and envision the cemeteries as important repositories of history and cultural change. Despite the radical differences between Jewish life in Warsaw and in Tel Aviv, the cemeteries still share their demarcation of that brief historical window in which a vision of a particular kind of secular, Jewish life was possible.

Despite *The Book of the Old Cemetery*'s modernist preference for "the stone itself," the Trumpeldor Cemetery is characterized by a jumble of styles. With the exception of certain cross-cultural motifs—the candelabra, the charity box, Sabbath candles, a pair of hands raised in blessing—Jewish funerary iconography seems to be more a function of local, ethnic, or national context, than any set of *halachic* dicta.[48] However, visiting the cemetery today, one cannot help but notice an enormous stone that does not fit any of the editors' categories, and seems to violate the uneasy aesthetic coexistence achieved among the disparate gravestone styles. What the stone commemorates, and its radical difference from the cemetery's other stones, marks the degree to which the Trumpeldor Cemetery could *only* have been built in Tel Aviv.

Towering above its eastern section, it is the cemetery's most textual stone: a large rectangular monument built in memory of people who died far from Tel Aviv and whose ashes were brought to Israel—the Jewish community of the Polish town of Zdunska Wola (Figure 2.7).[49] Erected in 1950 by a group of survivors, the reflective black marble slab

*Fig. 2.7* To the right, the Zdunska Wola monument: a piece of Jerusalem in Tel Aviv. Photo by author.

with raised gold lettering is surrounded by a low wall of white marble, upon which are engraved the names and familial connections of the victims, entire families with ten and twelve children. Buried in this spot are ashes brought from the crematoria in Chelmno to Israel by Zelig Frankel, a native of the town. The stone's main text is a series of rhymed couplets describing the virtue of the victims, the brutality of their death, and their commemoration by survivors. The stone's monumental presence disrupts the cemetery's horizon, which otherwise stretches out at a fairly even height and in an almost uniformly pale gray and sandstone palette. This physical disparity highlights the incongruity of the stone's text—its dense lyricism as well as the people and events commemorated—in this particular setting.

Generally speaking, shoah memorials in Israel may be understood in relation to the national narrative of *shoah u-g'vura* (Holocaust and heroism), which emphasized the redemptive building of the Jewish state in the wake of the destruction of European Jewry. Jerusalem provides the most instructive example of how "Holocaust and heroism" are linked together in an urban space, where the Holocaust Museum (Yad Vashem) is located immediately next to Mount Herzl, an enormous military cemetery containing the graves of Israeli prime ministers, including, most recently, that of Yitzhak Rabin. Together with religious sites such as the Western Wall and the Old City, these civic-sacred sites—Yad Vashem and Mount Herzl—reinforce Jerusalem's special status in Jewish and Israeli history. Indeed, Yad Vashem and Mount Herzl often host national ceremonies, and are visited jointly, and in didactic sequence, on touristic itineraries.

The meaning of shoah memorials is generated largely by the landscape within which they are situated.[50] Israeli shoah memorials often represent the discontinuousness of the shoah vis-à-vis the Israeli landscape, what might be called, after Momik, the child narrator of David Grossman's See Under: Love, its essential "Over Thereness." This "else-whereness" of the shoah is a constitutive force in the form and shape of its Israeli commemoration. Thus Israeli shoah memorials generally, and Yad Vashem in particular, "build Europe within Israel."[51] However, whereas in Jerusalem the shoah is commemorated through these state institutions, its presence is more palpable as a matter of daily experience in Tel Aviv, where a higher percentage of the residents are survivors. In a sense, the monumental nature of the Zdunska Wola memorial "builds Jerusalem in Tel Aviv." Its inclusion in the Trumpeldor Cemetery troubles the degree to which this kind of memorialization of the shoah is a "natural" element of the Israeli landscape.[52] At the same time, it points to the difficulty of assimilating the trauma of the shoah to the triumphal narrative of "the first Hebrew city."

The Zdunska Wola memorial, and the events it represents, may also be understood in relation to another important distinguishing feature of the Trumpeldor Cemetery vis-à-vis Israeli cemeteries generally. The Trumpeldor Cemetery contains few of the conventional markers of heroism and national sacrifice often associated with death and mourning in Israel.[53] The presence of both shoah and g'vura is thus quite muted in the Trumpeldor Cemetery, an exceptional quality indicative of the different ways Tel Aviv and Jerusalem mark and memorialize history.

Though *The Book of the Old Cemetery* was published years before the Zdunska Wola memorial was built, the memorial was anticipated by its editors. Kroll and Leinman refer to events unfolding in Europe as the context for a morbid logic: just as Jewish life in Palestine is meant to commemorate, or even substitute for Jewish life in Europe, so this spot marking Jewish death honors the European Jewish dead (xix). While they envision the cemetery as a future landmark that will serve as a stable, bounded "site of memory," the *Book* itself will also serve as a bulwark against forgetting, "come the day that no one will remember [Tel Aviv's] youth, her founding and the process of her growth."[54] In the closing paragraphs of their introduction, the editors plead with the public to maintain the Old Cemetery, and prevent it from falling into disrepair. In a remarkably self-aware moment, they imagine the future preservation of the Trumpeldor Cemetery as precisely the type of cultural landmark Tel Aviv needed.[55] No longer necessary as a functioning cemetery—a new site having been built in 1932 in Nachalat Yitzhak—the Old Cemetery, Tel Aviv's most "precious archives" (xiii), should, however, be maintained in some fashion, because it represents the only authentic historical claim to roots that Tel Aviv can make, slim as it may be. Perhaps they imagined a role for it akin to that of the old Jewish cemetery in Prague, whose "characteristic, unique and wholly inimitable atmosphere . . . often nourished by the dramatic destinies of deceased inhabitants of the ghetto, soon found a place for itself in numerous myths, legends, literary works and paintings."[56] In this scenario, the Trumpeldor Cemetery functions as an inert presence, a site that can be referred to in coherent, stable fashion, and inserted wholecloth into a variety of cultural discourses. Indeed, to the relatively minimal extent that the cemetery figures in subsequent discourse about Tel Aviv, the same set of legendary circumstances and anecdotes appear in almost standardized formulation. The cemetery has become a kind of limited trope, offering a conveniently monumentalized version of the city's founding. Modern Hebrew poets have challenged this story of the cemetery; their ironic treatment of the cemetery as a site of memory uncovers and gives voice to the memories so radically effaced therein. I have argued thus far that the cemetery attempted to defuse exilic memory. It is to the poets we must look for a more explicit rendering of the trauma of migration, and its link to another set of displaced memories, that of the Palestinian past.

## On the Corner of Bialik and Tchernichovski: The Cemetery as Literary History

> History begins at ground level, with footsteps.
> —Michel de Certeau, "Practices of Space"

Poetry relating to the Old Cemetery also treats it as an archive, though of a different order, as a dynamic repository of literary history. Instead of the stable, bounded "site of memory" envisioned by Kroll and Leinman, the cemetery in poems by Avot Yeshurun and Dalia Rabikovitch is a destabilizing site that upends the notion of history as a linear progression, especially an unequivocal narrative of redemption. Yeshurun's and Rabikovitch's appreciations of the Old Cemetery qua archive may be illuminated by referring briefly to Michel Foucault's conception of the archive. For Foucault, "analysis of the archive involves a privileged region: at once close to us and different from our present existence, it is the border of time that surrounds our presence, which overhangs it, and which indicates it in its otherness; it is that which, outside ourselves, delimits us."[57] Like Freud's uncanny, the archive's fundamental strangeness is dependent on its proximity and familiarity. The cemetery is thus a kind of "shadow" site, *apart from* and *a part of* the city, underpinning its psychic structure, preserving those less assimilable elements of its history. If the cemetery is this kind of memory site, its literary history also tells how memory is produced and meaning invested, a process necessarily informed and circumscribed by cultural context.

Yeshurun's and Rabikovitch's poems recognize the Old Cemetery's pliability, its fundamental uncanniness. In their poems, the cemetery symbolizes an ambivalence toward the "forgotten" diasporic past, as well as an explicit awareness of what Tel Aviv effectively effaced from the Palestinian landscape. The uncanny's doubling effect is immediately apparent in Yeshurun's "Lullaby for Nordia Quarter." Born in Poland, Yechiel Perlmutter immigrated to Palestine as a young man in

1925, and adopted the name Avot Yeshurun ("the fathers are looking [at us]") after the publication of his first volume in 1942. Many of his Tel Aviv poems describe the psychic rift created by the separation from his family. The poet's sense of European Jewish trauma is intimately related to the psychological and physical traumas of Arabs living in Palestine in the pre-State period, what Yeshurun called "the two shoahs: the shoah of the Jewish people there and the shoah of the Arab people here."[58] In this lyric from *The Syrian-African Rift* (1974), the poet links his personal history to that of one of the city's earliest neighborhoods, Nordia, speaking directly to Tel Aviv, attempting to recover in the city the landscape of the shtetl he has left behind:

"Lullaby for Nordia Quarter"

The Bedouins who came from Poland not
as planned spread out over Balfour
Street opposite Ohel Shem now and on
the slope opposite the sycamores now Nordia.

And they were in tents and in huts (*sukkot*) and they were in shacks.
And a door handle about the width of a door and roofs.
And roofs glided like children and changed.
And summer and winter on Dizengoff Street.

And all about rose up baronic houses,
and the domestic cedar spread out over the shacks.
Tel Aviv holy city, you have no
lullaby. Yesterday, it was.

I walked in you everything by foot,
like a horse eats straight from the earth.
There are times I suffer martyrdom
for every faucet you forgot open.

I walked in you in the town I left.
In your city, in my town.
My city that's behind your back
and myself me, toward you I heft.

I walked in you everything.
Firstly was destroyed the first house.
Secondly was destroyed the second house:
Came a bulldozer kicked at the house.

"As Father bought" friends.[59]
One day I'm there my hand on his shoulder,
and he his hand on your thigh.
So exit all your friends.

And in the city I have no funerals except of
Ahad Ha'am, Bialik, Nordau, who drew
His name on the quarter on his name
For you crushed Nordia as you bruise a testicle.[60]

The poet tries to compensate for his lack of personal memories in his new home, first by creating a "history of footsteps," then by placing Tel Aviv as a kind of palimpsest over the shtetl where he was born. The palimpsest is a spatial-mental structure that represents the uncanny's contiguous overlapping of the familiar—"the town I left"—and the strange—Tel Aviv.[61] This link, perhaps a defining trait of poetry about Tel Aviv, recalls the concluding lines of Leah Goldberg's "Tel Aviv, 1935": "and so it seemed—if you but turn your head—there's the town church floating in the sea."[62] For Yeshurun, funerals of the Old Cemetery's famous occupants represent the culmination of his attempt to "walk in [Tel Aviv] in the town [he] left." The poet claims these highly public funerals as his own private history, the only past to which he has immediate, tangible access. Newspaper accounts of the funerals, especially that of Bialik, suggest they were occasions for enormous public mourning that connected Tel Aviv to Jewish communities all over the world.[63] Likewise, a review of *The Book of the Old Cemetery* states that funerals of ordinary citizens were rather small affairs: it calls the *Book* a "second funeral," for those who did not receive huge, public ceremonies: "After all, people here are strangers to one another." Tel Aviv was no one's hometown; rather it was made up of people from "seventy countries."[64] Thus, Yeshurun bemoans more than his own dearth of memories; it is also the city itself that lacks a past: Tel Aviv has "no lullaby," implying that it never had a childhood because it was built so quickly—"yesterday, it was." The poem describes a problem endemic to any fledgling national enterprise, that is, the lack of convincingly authoritative cultural roots. However, this historical poverty is grasped as a virtue constituting Tel Aviv's "holiness," as opposed to the solidly historical resonance of the archetype of Jewish urban holiness— Jerusalem—a comparison made explicit in the destruction of the "first" and "second" houses, a reference to the ancient destruction of the First and Second Temples in Jerusalem. Moreover, Yeshurun's poem admits the presence of exile in Tel Aviv, including the cemetery's uncanny quality, embracing it along with the city's "poverty." This uncanny version of the Jewish past is all that Yeshurun has access to— as in Shofman's Viennese portrait, the "original Jews" are gone. However, this movement toward a certain kind of memory is complicated by an admission of the equally powerful force of forgetting. In a prose poem from the same volume, the poet describes a lock that had been secured to a local kiosk; during the confusion surrounding the neighborhood's destruction, the key was lost, and the lock remained immovable: "Because of this—it being forgotten—it was very more stronger (*meshum kakh—she-nishkach—hu chazak me-od yoter*)."[65] "Oppenheim's kiosk," and with it the memory of both Nordia and the natural landscape beneath it, has been locked away, protected, preserved: forgotten, perhaps, but "very more stronger." The line's neat rhyme and even meter, its almost biblical parallelism, are at odds with its ungrammatical syntax, a deliberate device that foregrounds the awkwardness of writing verse in Hebrew, and thematizes the exilic presence of Yiddish that so informs Yeshurun's work.[66]

"Lullaby for Nordia Quarter" enacts the demands of personal memory upon collective remembering. If the editors of *The Book of the Old Cemetery* believed the cemetery could somehow replace European cemeteries and their symbolic significance, this poem of over three decades later knows the trauma of destruction and migration to have been too enormous. The poem describes an ultimately irredeemable loss, one for which the collective narrative can offer no compensation; this loss is linked to the fate of Nordia—gradually emptied and then leveled in the 1970s for the construction of Dizengoff Center—and is

*Fig. 2.8* A Hebrew pantheon: Bialik, Ahad Ha'am, and Nordau. Photo by author.

also embedded in a retrospective "thick description" of the land's transformations: the arrival of Bedouins from Poland, the construction of a public hall on Balfour Street (Ohel Shem), and the destruction of sycamores to make way for Nordia.[67] The city in which the poet walks "everything by foot," is revealed as only the most recent layer of historical topsoil. Yeshurun's footsteps trace, however reluctantly, the beginnings of Tel Aviv, and the origins of Hebrew cultural history.

Walking through the Old Cemetery today, it does seem that select elements of Tel Aviv's history, and by extension, the history of modern Hebrew culture in Palestine, have been preserved. The dead carry on a kind of impossible postmortem conversation among themselves, an idealized version of history in which Brenner and his "comrades," who "fell *ba-tsavta*" [in comradely solidarity] still lie *ba-tsavta*, their collective martyrdom almost a rebuke to the social gathering of single stones marking Bialik and other famous cultural figures, clustered together in one section of the yard, almost as if caught forever in another of those photographs typical of the period, in which they sit on a porch, or

*Fig. 2.9* Bialik meets Tchernichovski. Photo by author.

around a cafe table, endlessly debating (Figure 2.8). Indeed, there is the strong sense that history is preserved in this kind of sociability, in argument that is almost Talmudic. The streets surrounding the Old Cemetery are another material signification of these permanently dialoguing relationships. Many of the street names repetitively map and reinforce the cemetery's inner memorialization process—again, in Nora's terms, a kind of "secretion of memory," this time not a "hiding away," but an "emission" or "discharge."⁶⁸ Walking down Trumpeldor, one encounters the poet Saul Tchernichovski, then Bialik, and eventually Brenner, with his unlikely companion, Allenby (Figure 2.9). The link between these urban signs and cultural memory is even more explicitly framed in the book cover of a recent biographical history of the period, depicting the fictional meeting of Brenner, Bialik, and Agnon streets (Figure 2.10). This whimsical street corner illustrates a canonical moment in Hebrew literary history, the product of a retrospective gesture. It also, however, hints at the volatility of this moment, in that it marks an intersection, a place where traffic meets and passes. Its very

*Fig. 2.10* Cover of Chaim Be'er's cultural biography, *Their Love and Their Hate*.

status as a fixed location is defined by movement through and around
it. Similarly, though the Old Cemetery may be perceived as a relatively
static site, projected into the future by the editors of *The Book of the Old
Cemetery*, the memory that fixes it is essentially a symbolic tool shaped
by the concerns of the present. Dalia Rabikovitch's "The Poet's Hope"
from the early 1990s explicitly addresses this issue, and the role of
the Old Cemetery in Hebrew literary history. Bialik's grave, it seems,
remains the touchstone.

What is it with you
young poets
that you write so much about poetry,
and the art of poetry
and the use of materials
so that,
heaven forbid,
the poet's silence shouldn't come
and devastate you.

After all, you've got a cure
that drives away all sorrow:
sitting leisurely at the morning table
covered with a slightly faded oilcloth
and gazing mournfully at the window pane,
until afternoon approaches.
And if you are seized by a sleepiness, don't drive it away,
and don't take lightly the taste of honey and butter.
And don't make of it poems or poetry
and don't make any craft
and if you have any joy,
hide it away for many days,
lest the eye should view it.
For why are you afraid, my dear,
to seize the horns of the poem as it slips away,
and poke its ribs
like a lone Bedouin boy hurries
his tarrying donkey?

After all, the only good that will grow from this,
the best of all possible worlds,
is a single grave they'll dig/negotiate for you,
after great efforts at the mayor's office,
in the cemetery on Trumpeldor Street
sixty meters away
from Bialik's grave.[69]

Like much of Rabikovitch's later work, the language is deceptively
simple—beginning with the casual language of the opening line. The

poem seems to call for a resistance to the "idols" Hebrew culture has made of its poets, yet rests squarely on references to Bialik's work. According to the first stanza, poetry about poetry is the last resort before writer's block, "the poet's silence" (line 8), an allusion to Bialik's infamous long poetic silence once he settled in Tel Aviv.[70] The break into biblical cadence in line 18 recalls the second commandment prohibition on graven images. "Don't make poetry out of this," the poem says, meaning "don't make idols of this comfortable existence, nor believe it ethical material for art"; or perhaps, "don't bother actually writing poems, the pose is what counts." The Bedouin boy—a shepherd—is an archetypal version of the poet, his tarrying donkey, an oblique reference to a messianic age. His appearance also signals the moral failure of the "young poets"—reduced in line 23 to a single "my dear"—who exhibit a lack of conscience—the Hebrew for conscience (*maTZPuN*) etymologically lurking in the warning to "hide away" (*haTZPiNua*) the joy of the poetic craft—as well as a weakness of spirit, implied in the poet's fear of seizing the poem by the horns, as a person of principle would seek sanctuary at the altar: "to seize the horns of the altar."[71] The poem's ingenious construction "to seize the poem (*shIr*) by the horns" is a mere vowel away from the phrase "to seize the ox (*shOr*) by the horns," also an allusion to the afterlife, ox meat being a mythically honored dish. The poet is finally imagined as a kind of Job, whose friends acquire a relative place of honor for him, line 30 carrying the double meaning of "dig" and "negotiate."[72]

The brief appearance of a messianically proactive Bedouin youth, against whose behavior the poets seem particularly inept, must be understood within the representation of two kinds of figures, often related or twinned, in Rabikovitch's work—children and Palestinians. Their images appear throughout two earlier volumes, *True Love* (1987) and *Mother with Child* (1992). The Bedouin shepherd in "The Poet's Hope" is a latter-day version of the female shepherd in "Hovering at Low Altitude," who is unaware of the violent danger that the poem's landscape holds for her, and the boy facing the soldiers in "Stones."[73] The immediate political contexts of those two poems—the Lebanese War and the Intifada—are exchanged in "The Poet's Hope" for the broad sweep of Hebrew literary history and its ostensible origins in Tel

Aviv. The shepherd's metaphorical presence does not necessarily evoke a prior physical Arab presence in Tel Aviv, but operates in a more abstract fashion.[74] In a poem from *Mother with Child*, Rabikovitch paraphrases a couplet from Leah Goldberg: "How can we sing songs of Zion / when we have not yet heard?" a question that itself evokes Psalms 137. The question, particularly in Rabikovitch's sharpened revision, goes to the very core of modern Hebrew culture: what kind of culture emerges from an ancient, messianic drive of homecoming, that is itself deaf to the land's other voices? What did Hebrew culture ignore in order to establish itself as that confident constellation of streets radiating out from the Old Cemetery and Bialik's grave?

Despite an implicit promise of the world to come, the poem ultimately maintains that the most a poet can hope for is a permanent resting place sixty meters distant from this grave.[75] The "cemetery on Trumpeldor"—no longer designated by the honorific "old," but by a simple geographic reference—is envisioned as the physical arena in which relations between a literary center and its margins are marked and re-marked as time passes and canonical "intersections" shift within changing cultural and political climates. The number sixty recaps the poem's fluctuating stance vis-à-vis the "headstone" of Hebrew literary authority. How close to the center is sixty meters? What constitutes a place of honor in a graveyard that no one visits? On the one hand, sixty is associated with Solomon's temple, sixty *amot* being one of its chief measurements.[76] But sixty also brings to mind expressions such as "a minor amount in sixty" (*batel be-shishim*), that is, a negligible element of minimal influence, and "one in sixty," meaning "a small portion." Most significantly, however, the number sixty marks the distance Hebrew poetry has traveled since Bialik's death in 1934, neatly translating temporal measurement into spatial quantity— years into meters—a transformation that alludes to the cemetery's own spatialized rendering of time's passage. Although Bialik and the other cultural figures buried in the Old Cemetery are now thoroughly dispersed within Israeli culture, the cemetery itself seems to resist this kind of dissemination, representing instead an entombment of modern Hebrew culture's beginnings. With this ossification, the desire for memory that is the desire for roots expressed in 1939 in *The Book of the Old*

*Cemetery* comes full circle, the anxiety of a budding modernist metropolis replaced by a postmodern shrug of ambivalent recognition, in Rabikovitch's ironic formulation, "the best of all possible worlds."

## The Rhyme of History

The minister of tourism's official visit to Tel Aviv in January 1998 led to the following conclusion: touristic marketing campaigns for Tel Aviv would herald beaches, shops, and nightlife as the city's primary attractions. The historic districts received some attention, and the Old Cemetery itself this brief mention: "Leaders of the Jewish community from before and following the establishment of the State are buried in the Cemetery, which is at present poorly maintained. It could be turned into a touristic site, as is the custom in European metropolises."[77] It seems that Europe is still the reference point; furthermore, though the cemetery is now maintained in considerably better fashion than before, it still remains largely ignored in the city's public consciousness (Figure 2.11).

An interesting exception is the recent theatrical production of Eldad Ziv's *A Matter of Life and Death*, a play set in the Old Cemetery. Though the script seems unfinished, and too often falls into a kind of coarse, buffoon-like humor more appropriate to a television sitcom than to a production of the National Theater, the play poses important questions about Israeli identity and Hebrew culture. The story hinges on the cemetery's reputation as a trysting site for students from the high school across the street. A teacher arranges to meet a student in the cemetery, and they encounter the spirits of some of its inhabitants—Bialik, Meir Dizengoff (the city's first mayor), and Tchernichovski among them—themselves out for an evening stroll to appreciate the carob tree blossoms. Bialik first appears on stage looking annoyed and holding a condom; the effect is both comic and ironic for anyone familiar with Bialik's love poetry and its sense of failed eroticism. The play's main narrative concerns the fate of the cemetery's *galmudim* (anonymous or orphaned ones), people of all ages who were buried in this national pantheon, but whose identity has been erased with the passage of time. The famous believe that the galmudim's presence, their ignorance of their own past, is

*Fig. 2.11* A plaque describing the Old Cemetery's historical significance—"The First Cemetery" in Hebrew and in English—discarded in a corner next to burial stretchers. Photo by author.

ruining the cemetery's good name. The play thus confronts the ostensible inventors of Hebrew identity with their disaffected, disinherited heirs. As the play concludes, however, what appeared to be fixed categories are reversed. Bialik complains to Tchernichovski: "We have no history, we've only got rhymes," revealing their claims to fame and identity as tenuous and fabricated.[78] However, the galmudim were not necessarily buried anonymously; what leaves them bereft of identity is the fact that no one has bothered to maintain their graves. The difference between the galmudim and the pantheon, therefore, is not a matter of actual deeds, but of memory. These orphans are, in a sense, emblematic of Tel Aviv's problem with the past, and with memory. However, the Old Cemetery represents an even deeper kind of amnesia than the one thus far discussed concerning its diasporic roots. The cemetery's establishment not only predates that of Tel Aviv itself; it is contemporaneous with the creation of Abdel Nabi, a Moslem cemetery built in roughly the same area as the Trumpeldor Cemetery, and upon which the Tel Aviv Hilton now stands.

Abdel Nabi was founded for the same practical, hygiene-related reason as the cemetery on Trumpeldor: both spots were, at the time, relatively desolate locations well north of Jaffa, ideal for burial of the city's cholera victims. For decades, Abdel Nabi was an important element of Tel Aviv's profile. In some senses, it occupied a much larger and more obvious piece of the local scenery than did the Trumpeldor Cemetery. A study from 1926 of then current land use in the city, compiled in connection with the Geddes Plan, shows Abdel Nabi as an enormous site, measuring 34,338 square meters, or 1.06 percent of the total land in Tel Aviv, as compared to 9,375 square meters and 0.3 percent for the Trumpeldor Cemetery.[79] Located on a bluff just north of Frishman Street, next to the neighborhood of Mahloul, the cemetery is mentioned in many early descriptions of the city's developing beachfront. It later appears as a fixture in classic memoiristic accounts of the city as a symbol not only of the author-protagonists' youth, but of the inevitable erosion of the city's own idealistic facade (see Chapter 5).

However, beyond these straightforward empirical citations, and the sentimental fictional depictions, there is very little documentation concerning Abdel Nabi in historical writing about Tel Aviv, despite its considerable presence on the city's early physical plane. (The cemetery itself was under the domain of the Waqf—the religious authorities in Jaffa—but the land immediately below it leading down to the sea was administered by the Tel Aviv Municipality.[80]) When mentioned at all, it is usually referred to as "the Moslem cemetery" and treated almost as a natural landmark, a geographic reference point for commercial and residential seaside development. Indeed, this kind of mute visibility generally characterizes sites associated with pre-1948 Arab settlement, to the degree that they enter Israeli-Jewish public discourse at all.[81] At the same time, the cemetery was ostensibly absorbed into the natural beauty of Tel Aviv's beachfront, especially in the 1940s, as it began to suffer from physical neglect after being cut off from the Arab community in Jaffa. Its very "wildness" constituted its value as part of Tel Aviv's sole natural resource—the seafront. These evaluations of the cemetery are consistent with early Hebrew culture's prevailing view of Arab society in Palestine—simultaneously emulated for its "natural" connection to the landscape and denigrated for its "primitiveness."[82] Much of the cemetery was destroyed or built over during the construction of the Hilton in 1965.[83] The remaining small collection of tombstones, surrounded by a high stone wall, sits in the middle of a recreation area called Independence Park, today one of the city's most active gay pickup sites.[84]

A number of letters scattered in different files in the Tel Aviv Municipal Archives give us some sense of Abdel Nabi's presence in the daily lives of Tel Aviv's early residents. A letter from 1925 calls "the high straight bluff that essentially begins with the Moslem cemetery and continues up to the Yarkon . . . the most beautiful spot in the area." However, what "should be the prettiest spot on the entire beach—this place is becoming ruined." The concerned citizen complains of construction work that is tearing apart the dunes: "Soon there won't remain even a trace of this beautiful beach."[85] Another letter insists that "the high hill behind the Arab cemetery in the north" be put to practical use:

> A lovely wind blows healthy air, a place like this I have not yet met in Tel Aviv. I wonder very much why this spot stands unused?! If the municipality hasn't purchased it, it should! Immediately and without waiting a single moment, because this place is the only place in Tel Aviv that is appropriate for hospitals (Hadassah) [and] sanatoriums.[86]

Later correspondence from the 1930s and 1940s indicates a rise in awareness of the increasingly politically contested nature of the land. One letter requests that a guard be assigned to the cemetery, to protect it from gangs of youth who were the cause of some damage.[87] Another letter, from 1939, translated from the German, describes the vandalism and desecration of graves:

> In the Arab cemetery, which previously had been under armed guard, the gate that had been closed by foliage has now been destroyed. Young men carouse among the graves and many graves have already been damaged. One tombstone has even been removed and now rests beside the grave. A sense of piety demands that everything immedi-

ately be returned to its place, before the Arabs sense anything, because this desecration is likely to arouse certain sentiments, and justifiably so. *We too are especially sensitive to the desecration of graves.* The guard must be put there throughout the Sabbath, in order to stop the many strollers who pick flowers there. A prohibition in the newspapers is too dangerous because the Arabs might read the announcement. Perhaps the prohibition should be announced in schools. In any case, the destruction must be stopped *immediately*. Perhaps the residents living near the gate will take the supervision upon themselves [emphasis added].[88]

For the writer of this letter—Bella Heyman, a relatively new resident of Tel Aviv—the desecration of Abdel Nabi brought to mind the contemporaneous destruction of European Jewish cemeteries, a prescient evocation of Yeshurun's "two shoahs." Finally, the following letter, from David Zilman, paints a vivid picture of how Abdel Nabi had become the site of complex, typically urban social encounters.

As I was walking near the Moslem cemetery on the seashore bordering the neighborhood of Mahloul, I came upon the following scene:

On one of the flat graves lay a half-naked young woman, dressed only in a bra and underwear and next to her sat a young man, also on the gravestone.

I approached this woman and asked how would she react if she saw Arab women lying in such a state on the graves of Jews? Her answer was that the cemetery was currently not in use.

On the roof of the house used to prepare the dead, young men were climbing about with terrible shouts with no sense of respect for the sanctity of another religion.

When I entered this building, I couldn't believe my eyes. In a corner, one boy sat using the place as a toilet.

I therefore suggest that you put a guard there, at least on Saturdays, in order to protect against the desecration of another religion during these times.

I chose not to go to the papers with this only out of political reasons.[89]

Zilman identifies the woman as Jewish, perhaps through a shared language, though not necessarily Hebrew. The woman's state of undress seems to bother Zilman less than the location of her activity. In an odd expression of kinship, he evokes their commonality as Jews, and reprimands her with the counterexample of Arab disrespect for Jewish graves. The suggestion to place a guard on Saturdays, also found in Heyman's letter, indicates that the cemetery may have become a kind of leisure location frequented by Tel Aviv's residents on the only regular non-working day. While Zilman seems concerned, like Bella Heyman, with avoiding inflammatory incidents in politically tense times, neither question the legitimacy of the cemetery's existence, a holy Moslem site within the boundaries of Jewish urban space. We cannot deduce, on the basis of these letters, some general condition of tolerance of the Arab presence in Tel Aviv–Jaffa; too many well-documented incidents from these years prove the opposite was more often the case.[90] Yet these documents do show that Abdel Nabi was part of the urban fabric—its existence was recorded as part of daily life; it had a place both on the map and in the city's early imagination.

Abdel Nabi exemplifies a general tendency in Hebrew sources to depict Arab places as ruins (*churva*), a "necessary" but obsolete element of the natural landscape.[91] Ruins generally function as a marker of a long ago "golden age"; they represent what landscape historian J. B. Jackson calls an "interval of neglect," following which "ruins provide the incentive for restoration, and for a return to origins."[92] The sculptor Dani Karavan addresses the potential of Tel Aviv's "ruins" in reaction to a plan for commercial expansion upon one of the city's historic districts: "Perhaps we still don't know that the sites belong to us, the citizens of the city. . . . A city that has had its sites and views, its plants and its memories taken from it, loses its identity, stops existing, and becomes a network of roads, parking lots and buildings without logic, an asphalt desert, the shadow of a man."[93] Any such preservation or "return to origins" for Tel Aviv would involve recognition of one of its original sites— a Moslem cemetery. Clearly any genuine recovery or commemorative project in the case of Abdel Nabi would also mean acknowledging the existence of vibrant Arab communities in and around Tel Aviv—mainly, but not solely, in Jaffa (see Chapter 5).[94] Until this "interval of neglect" ends, the cemetery remains cloistered behind a wall studded with

*Fig. 2.12* View of the Hilton Hotel and Abdel Nabi from within Independence Park, 2001. Photo by author.

broken glass to discourage intruders, visible to the eye only from the vantage point of the Hilton's twentieth floor (Figure 2.12).

## The Snapshot Revisited

> Photography must have some historical relation with . . . the "crisis of death" beginning in the second half of the nineteenth century. . . . For Death must be somewhere in a society; if it is no longer (or less intensely) in religion, it must be elsewhere; perhaps in this image which produces Death while trying to preserve life. Contemporary with the withdrawal of rites, Photography may correspond to the intrusion, in our modern society, of an asymbolic Death, outside of religion, outside of ritual, a kind of abrupt dive into literal Death. *Life/Death*: the paradigm is reduced to a simple click, the one separating the initial pose from the final print.
>
> —Roland Barthes, *Camera Lucida*

Barthes's remarks, from his influential meditation on the intrinsic connection between memory and photography, direct us to consider the
difficult location of death in modern times, particularly in a society
such as Tel Aviv that presented itself as adamantly secular. Though not
imbued with explicitly religious meaning, the significance of death may
still be understood in collective, even ritualistic terms, as we have seen
in the examples above—from the civic mourning surrounding Brenner's death and the anonymous yet public ceremony in Baron's story,
to the Zdunska Wola memorial's naming of an entire community, and
the keen awareness of the presence of a Moslem cemetery within the
municipal boundaries of "the first Hebrew city."

Death, according to Barthes, in its modern incarnation, finds itself
in "the image." He argues that this is true in both private and public
realms, in images of his deceased mother as well as Civil War photographs. The photographs from the tombstones of the Trumpeldor
Cemetery are private mementos displayed in a public space; yet they are
not photographs of dead people, in the most literal sense, nor are they
images of Death, in Barthes' terms (Figure 2.13). They are individual
portraits of human beings, and collectively a depiction of life; as a
group they lend the cemetery a sense of being a "living memorial," representing a vibrant community of varied individuals. Many of the
photos are printed on ceramic surfaces, and the images have remained
intact and startlingly clear, revealing precise details of dress and facial
expression. Some images are more abstracted engravings, carved directly into the stone, and they have aged and cracked together. Other
actual photographs are missing, torn or blown away by the wind. The
stone of the *galmud* is necessarily bare of any image recalling a specific
human face. There is no way of knowing for sure, but the photographs
give the impression of being nearly contemporaneous with the date of
death—though they hide whatever physical degradation may have
occurred due to illness or age. Although the cemetery as a whole
possesses a kind of uniformity, these numerous individual portraits create a sense of intimacy and informality among the graves, and between
the cemetery and its visitors.

Cemeteries generally symbolize a bidirectional obligation—
commemorating the past, for the benefit of the future. It could be said

*Fig. 2.13* Collage of individual tombstone cameos. Photos by author.

that Tel Aviv is also anxious in these two directions, uncertain about both its past and its future. As the city expands around it, the Old Cemetery remains a reminder of where the city came from, the tremendous loss involved, and the degree to which mourning remains unfinished. What would it mean for the Old Cemetery to become a true site of memory, not one of forgetting? It would entail remembering, for example, Abdel Nabi. Though not as explicitly a charged or debated a space as is Jerusalem in this regard, the cemetery on Trumpeldor is ultimately an "object" of competing memories.[95] To fully appreciate its meaning, and the history of the city that grew around it, those nameless orphans who confront Bialik—the present generation stripped of a sense of its past—must themselves confront the Bedouin shepherd in Rabikovitch's poem, and the locked layers of forgetting, traced by Yeshurun's footsteps. This process begins in uncovering the

origins of the city's historical self-image. Examination of the heterotopic site of the Old Cemetery, and to a lesser extent its cryptic dop-
pelganger, Abdel Nabi, demonstrates how memories of the Diaspora
and evidence of the Palestinian past form the bedrock of the city's history. Chapter 3 focuses on the adjacent neighborhood of Achusat Bayit
and its central thoroughfare, Rothschild Boulevard. It is through the
depiction and representation of the streets of Achusat Bayit that Tel
Aviv attempted to move forward out of its past, to create its own unique
sense of place.

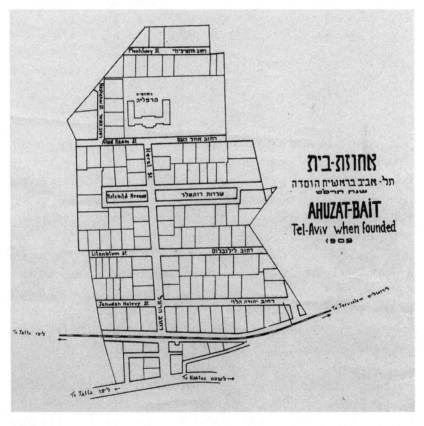

*Map 2.1* Achusat Bayit. Sketch by Avraham Soskin. Avraham Soskin, *Tel Aviv
Views* (Berlin: n.p., 1926).

## Three  Rothschild Boulevard: When a Street Becomes a Monument

> Tel Aviv can't tell very much about her past. She is entirely of the present, all reality, no history.
>
> —Sh. Tchernovitz, *The City of Miracles* (1928)

> The name of a city's streets and squares, the gaps in its very plan and physical form, its local monuments and celebrations, remain as traces and ruins of their former selves. They are tokens or hieroglyphs from the past to be literally reread, reanalyzed, and reworked over time. Images that arise from particular historic circumstances come to define our sense of tradition; they literally manage our knowledge of the historic.
>
> —M. Christine Boyer, *The City of Collective Memory*

The accuracy of M. Christine Boyer's observation regarding the way historical tradition is imprinted upon urban space depends, to a large degree, on the relative experience of the city's residents. Beyond the more explicitly historical sites such as museums, monuments, or specially designated municipal sites, the inscription of history on the plane of the city is neither self-evident nor predictable. Even the reception of these civically sanctioned sites is subject to multiple interpretations. At a minimum, we can say that an individual's memories of his or her own life may be linked more or less strongly to specific sites—a street, a park, a café. Certain kinds of larger, more potentially collective memories may be associated with the unique geographic features of any given city—a river or the seashore, for example—or with constructed sites also particular to that city—a central public park, a landmark building, even a main thoroughfare. New York's Hudson River and Berlin's Unter den Linden are examples of loosely regulated public sites that have become thoroughly enmeshed in the main themes of their cities' pasts, and they are featured as such in cultural representations of the city.

72

A text seeking to describe the city may draw on depictions of these sites as part of a larger reservoir of images that seem mythic in their ability to encapsulate the city's essence. The repeated evocation of such a site, whether in literature, fine arts, or even touristic depictions of the city, furthers the site's monumental character, often without any relation to the site's actual history or its contemporary significance within the city. These texts, however, should be examined as critically as the "tokens and hieroglyphs" in the city's streets; a careful reading of canonical images of the site, as well as the site itself vis-à-vis the evolving plane of the city, will reveal the process through which the site and its significance have become instantiated in the city's collective memory.

Details at the level of the street are one of the ways in which urban space is produced and experienced.[1] Against the background of major movements and events, of landmarks and loud voices, quotidian detail determines the pattern of the everyday, and as such constitutes a kind of history, in the sense described by Roland Barthes in his critique of the *Blue Guide*, the classic guide to French landscape. Barthes notes that "to select only monuments suppresses at one stroke the reality of the land, and that of its people, it accounts for nothing of the present, that is, nothing historical."[2] This chapter seeks to inject some aspect of the "historical" into a reading of Tel Aviv's pre-urban nucleus, the neighborhood of Achusat Bayit, especially the central thoroughfare of Rothschild Boulevard. By "historical" I mean a sense of argument and competing visions of the boulevard as a foundational site in the city's past. The concepts of the "monument" and the "street" provide poles which delineate a provisional poetics of the city—the monument referring to the grand narrative of Tel Aviv's origins, the street referring to the revelation of difference and quotidian detail. As we shall see, these modes of historical consciousness exist in dialectical relation to one another; one never entirely or conclusively eclipses the other; on the contrary each depends on the ever-potential presence of the other. The following pages sketch the development of these two forms of historical thinking about Tel Aviv in early writing and images about the city. An examination of the boulevard itself is first grounded in depictions of the surrounding neighborhood of Achusat Bayit. While this discussion relies partly on historical and touristic texts, it depends largely on the foundational work of three figures intimately associated with the formation of Tel Aviv's popular cultural image: the photographer Avraham Soskin, the painter Nachum Gutman, and the poet Natan Alterman.

## "Even nostalgia isn't what it used to be"

Urban landscape historian Dolores Hayden argues that "the production of spaces begins as soon as indigenous residents locate themselves in a particular landscape and begin the search for subsistence."[3] I would add that the production of *stories* explaining these spaces begins just as quickly; in Tel Aviv, the spaces and the stories about them began nearly simultaneously. As the "first Hebrew city," Tel Aviv was endowed by writers, painters, photographers, and city planners with an image as new, clean, and modern—everything the crowded neighborhoods of Jaffa were not—a city sprung from the sands.[4] Avraham Soskin's famous photograph of the land lottery, where a group of new "shareholders" stands huddled together in the sands, is a carefully staged portrait (Figure 3.1). The angle and perspective of the photo set the horizon on the dunes. There is no sign of the city of Jaffa to the immediate south, nor of the Jewish neighborhoods of Neve Tsedek and Neve Shalom (founded in the 1880s), nor of the Templar settlement Sharona or the extensive Arab agriculture in the form of orchards just to the east. The city is formed ex nihilo—*yesh me-ayin*—despite the protest of the lone figure at the top of the photo who, as legend has it, yelled out "Meshuga'im, eyn kahn mayim!" (You're crazy; there's no water here!). (In a later reproduction of the photo, the figure has been erased, his dissenting presence removed, perhaps by the photographer; he no longer disturbs the unified ring of "pioneers."[5]) This image has become ubiquitous in histories of Tel Aviv, and Soskin himself included it in a 1926 edition of his photographs of the city, with photos of the same sites taken in different years.[6] The "then-and-now" narrative pairs images of bare dunes with the built-up and bustling streets of Achusat Bayit, a contrast meant to engender a sense of wonder and civic pride,

*Fig. 3.1* Establishment of Tel Aviv—Land lottery, 11 April 1909. Soskin Archive, Historical Museum of Tel Aviv–Jaffa.

as well the beginnings of what will become a staple trope in representations of the city: nostalgia for simpler times (see discussion below of Druyanov and Gutman).[7]

Given the technical difficulties and limitations of the trade, as well as the often harsh physical conditions, one can hardly expect smiling touristic snapshots of early Tel Aviv. However, critics have recently begun to argue for a more contextual approach to these photographs, one that would examine both the photographers themselves and their now famous images within the political and social circumstances in which they were produced.[8] The depiction of landscape generally has been critiqued for its hyper-aestheticism and complicity in colonial expansion.[9] Landscape photography of modern Jewish settlement in Palestine utilized a variety of iconographic motifs and often stressed the idealistic quality of human figures in a barren landscape, framed and dwarfed by the sands, often associated with a set of tools, a trade, or building materials.[10] Their postures also accentuate material contrasts between East and West, a mix of European and Mediterranean dress: the children often wear Arab-style headgear while the adults are in suits

*Fig. 3.2* The kiosk on Rothschild Boulevard, 1910. Soskin Archive, Historical Museum of Tel Aviv–Jaffa.

and dresses. In a photograph from 1910, children play in the sand surrounding Tel Aviv's first kiosk, a circular hut with a cap-like, pointed roof topped by a weathervane (Figure 3.2). Although kiosk-style structures were common in European cities by the nineteenth century, they originated in Islamic and Turkish architecture; Soskin's photograph frames the kiosk with the construction of more Western-style structures, including what will become a ubiquitous feature of the landscape of Zionist settlements—the water tower.

The miniature size of the kiosk, with its fanciful, ornamented roof, vis-à-vis the surroundings, resembles the proportions of Reuven Rubin's 1922 *Tel Aviv* (Figure 3.3), one of the earliest paintings of the city, completed shortly after the artist's arrival in Palestine from his native Romania.[11] Tel Aviv, these images suggest, is as new, pure, and spontaneous as child's play. Rust-roofed houses are barely distinguishable from the sand against which they float; the blue dabs marking their doors and windows match the sliver of sea visible at the top edge of the canvas. This edge cuts off the masts of three evenly spaced sailboats, leaving the viewer with almost nothing but a haphazard assortment of cubes. Stare at them long enough and they begin to resemble the early work of Mondrian. Reuven's later Tel Aviv paintings included human

*Fig. 3.3 Tel Aviv* (1922), Reuven. The Rubin Museum.

figures and detailed street scenes, but they all retain the childlike abstraction of this early scene—the confident use of color and simple geometric form that calls into being a city on canvas. In retrospect, Reuven's work, and that of other painters associated with the Tel Aviv or *Eretzyisraeli* (Land of Israel) school, has come to symbolize the same naive confidence with which Tel Aviv was apparently built "off-canvas" as well.[12] Even contemporaneous reviews of their work stressed the role of paintings in the creation of new, "native" Hebrew culture in Palestine.[13] Of course there is also a tremendous amount of instability and ambivalence in the painting: Reuven's houses may have a harmonious, village-like appeal, but they also look as if they might float into the sea, off the canvas, or dissolve into the sand entirely, while the boats are a reminder of the European ports recently left behind. Perhaps the painting's continuing appeal can be traced to precisely this tension: on the one hand, a wondrous belief in the possibility of "making it new," on the other hand an underlying anxiety about the viability of the entire project.

At the very moment of its founding, then, Tel Aviv began to con-struct for itself a coherent narrative describing and explaining the meaning of its origins to its citizens. As time passed, this narrative gained an explanatory power in and of itself, a process typical of the de-velopment of any new city or place, which will naturally create for itself a satisfactory and coherent story about its own foundations. As we have seen in Chapter 2, this desire for authoritative roots coincided with the somewhat contradictory desire to emphasize the city's newness, modernity, and epistemological distance from the Diaspora. Tel Aviv's narrative of its founding and development, as evidenced in a variety of cultural representations of the city, thus shared with other Zionist "master commemorative narratives" both an explicit rejection of the *golah*, as well as an ideologically driven selectivity concerning repre-sentation and interpretation of the past.[14]

The vision of early Tel Aviv depicted in Soskin's photographs and Reuven's painting was also profoundly felt in early writing about the city. Novels set in Tel Aviv regularly mingled the actual streets of Achusat Bayit with fictional circumstance. As early as Y. H. Brenner's *Mikan u-mikan* (1911), writing about the city combined purely fictional characters with famous historical figures and wove details of historical events into an otherwise invented narrative, creating a hybrid genre that reached epic proportions in Agnon's *Tmol shilshom* (1945).[15] The problem of representing Tel Aviv was part of a larger debate concern-ing Hebrew literature's obligation to depict "the truth from Eretzy-israel," in Ahad Ha'am's famous phrasing. Brenner's influential essay "The Eretzyisraeli Genre," while not mentioning Tel Aviv by name, questioned the very ability of literature to authentically depict the essence of so dynamic and newly forming a society.[16]

Israeli novelists inherited—for better or for worse—a powerful set of vividly imagined tropes, anecdotes, and images concerning the city. The relative staying power of the vision of Tel Aviv encapsulated in Soskin's photographs is evidenced in its repeated appearance in later fictional work about the city. Many novelists were also born and raised in Tel Aviv and their fictional writing about the city's "childhood" has a distinctly memoiristic dimension (see Chapter 5). For example, in *The Great Aunt Shlomtsion* (1975), Yoram Kaniuk's novel memorializing pre-State Tel Aviv, the narrator describes a meeting between Aunt Shlomtsion, a figure of almost mythical beauty and difficulty, and her husband-to-be, Nehamiah: It happened on Herzl Street, a place that, he says, "in the eyes of Tel Aviv's residents [was] something singular in Jewish history, a crossroads where 2,000 years of exile met up with the essence of ancient Israel." It was, he continues, a "meta-historical intersection."[17] For the most part, popular versions of the city's past—like Kaniuk's characters—have treated Herzl Street, its intersection with Rothschild Boulevard, and the kiosk at the corner as a "meta-historical intersection," a symbol of social and cultural achievement, and not as simply part of the neighborhood in which people strolled and talked, and watched other people do the same.

The meta-historical narrative of Tel Aviv's simpler past has been overrepresented in art and literature about the city. A measure of its acceptance is the recent installation of an enormous mural in Rabin Square, facing the Tel Aviv City Hall, in honor of the city's ninetieth anniversary. In Nachum Gutman's *At the Beach*, Tel Aviv is built out of the sands by a pair of children who seem themselves to be part of the land (Figure 3.4). Behind them the sea is a playful wash of blue, and Jaffa a mere sketch on the horizon. The two are wholly absorbed in their work, blessed by the rising sun, oblivious to the approach of a serene camel at the scene's right edge. They actually seem to be fashioning a replica of Jaffa, an activity in keeping with Gutman's own express vision of the city's architectonic space, his desire to "lean less on function for its own sake, and focus more on a longing for the East, on getting closer to the nature of the region."[18] The central location of the mural underscores the degree to which Gutman's "naive" drawings and stories about his Tel Aviv childhood have come to constitute a mythology of the city's origins—so much so that the catalog accompanying the recent exhibit called "Gutman's Tel Aviv, Tel Aviv's Gutman" matched Gutman's drawings with photographs from the period, concluding that the artist's "stories of the beginnings of the neighborhood of Achusat Bayit correspond with the reality and historical events of those days."[19]

Gutman's drawings initially appeared in connection with historical writing about Tel Aviv in 1936, as illustrations to Alter Druyanov's *Sefer*

*Fig. 3.4* Nachum Gutman installation in Rabin Square in honor of the ninetieth anniversary of the establishment of Tel Aviv, December 1999. Photo by author.

*Tel Aviv* (The Book of Tel Aviv), the first history of the city. Druyanov took on the project after the death of its original editor, S. Ben Tsion, Gutman's father. In the preface, he makes an interesting admission concerning the book's material sources of information, one that could serve as a warning to future historians of the city: "There were no sources, no preparatory works—nothing."[20] Therefore, Druyanov says, he went straight to the founders themselves, many of whom were still alive and composing their memoirs, and tried to include as much detail as possible concerning the city's beginnings. The result is a kind of montage—equally based on oral history and first-person accounts, and other kinds of documentation that could be found, including journalistic accounts and the copious minutes of discussions held prior to the city's actual establishment. Druyanov writes that he has tried, wherever possible, to give the documents the "right to speak," and has also included numerous illustrations, including Gutman's drawings, which often "explain more than words, written or oral" (xii). Clearly, Gutman's illustrations are far from scientific. The odd thing is that they are included at all in a volume that has been treated as a work of history by subsequent generations of amateur historians and academic scholars alike. To be sure, Druyanov's book contains information that is essential to an understanding of the city's history, but the book is as important for what it says as for how it says it. Part of this "how" has to do with the enormous pull-out maps that accompany the book, which chart the city's physical development in authoritative detail. Gutman's illustrations appear alongside these maps together with Soskin's photographs and statistical tables; all are treated equally as historical documentation. For example, the following description by Druyanov complements two drawings, one of civic guard duty in the city, another of the first street light:

> The artist's eye saw this moment from the first Hebrew city's childhood. . . . A handful of houses, strewn in the desert sand. A handful of people, who were not afraid to cast their flame upon the desert sands, who fled the dirt and filth of the nearby city. And eyes are raised to the new light—"the first electric street lamp"—there aren't many like it, and perhaps there's nothing like it, in the city from which they'd fled. Here, on the lone, new street corner, the new light spreads its bareness over the naked walls and dresses them with a settled charm.[21]

The innocence of the city's early years—its "childhood"—is expressed through the drawings' simple forms; the "light of modernity" no longer wears the romantic guise of a "new dawn" but is embodied here in the very practical fact of an electric lamp, providing both utility and a feeling of safety. The lamp's enlightening presence distinguishes the new neighborhood from Arab Jaffa, "the city from which they'd fled." The "moment" that is seen by the artist's eye, and reinscribed by Druyanov, is chosen for its exemplary qualities, its ability to encapsulate the founders' desires and dreams for their new neighborhood. That Druyanov respected, in a certain sense, Gutman's drawings as historical documents is evidenced by his occasional "correction" of their historical accuracy: in a footnote concerning Gutman's depiction of the city's early publishing ventures he notes "the artist's eye is also subject to amnesia: at that time . . . *Ha-omer* was no longer in existence and

*Ha-moledet* had not yet begun."[22] In fact, Gutman never rendered the city before him "from life . . . , [rather] he only painted his memories."[23] Ultimately what Druyanov's unfortunately truncated version of Tel Aviv's history gives us is a sense of the drama of the city's early years, the minutely choreographed negotiations among the various factions within Jewish society in Jaffa, the new Jewish landowners and their overseas patrons, and the Ottoman authorities. (Though published in 1936, the volume's narrative comes to an abrupt halt with Great Britain's victory over the Turks in 1918.) Druyanov concludes his narrative with the proclamation that as the war came to an end, "so did the final episode of Tel Aviv, the neighborhood; soon after, the story of Tel Aviv the city would begin."[24] In its sentimental tone and use of Gutman's naive drawings, *Sefer Tel Aviv* marks the formal beginnings of what would become an almost obligatory feature of writing about the city— nostalgia. According to literary historian Nurit Govrin, "Longings for the golden sands of Tel Aviv were born with the beginnings of Tel Aviv, and are not only the fruit of her rapid aging from a garden city to a noisy metropolis. The vision of the metropolis was bound up from the start with sorrow over its expected realization."[25]

Indeed, expressions of nostalgia for the Tel Aviv of "once upon a time" can be found as early as 1928, in the following recollection by the poet Ya'akov Fichman. His essay was included in an anthology called "City of Miracles," published on the occasion of the city's twentieth anniversary:

> I remember those days in Tel Aviv as a man remembering the tranquil days of his childhood. Great days, full of sun and quiet and a kind of pure joy, nameless, flavorless, that comes only with the first days. The sea was still far away, and by the time we got to its shore, we would be drowning to death in sand, but its cheerful murmur would fill the entire neighborhood, as if we were in a ship's cabins. . . . In those days the sun-drenched streets burned, with neither shade nor passerby, and when the rumble of a wagon was heard, you would immediately rush to the window, to see what had happened.[26]

Tel Aviv had in fact expanded dramatically beyond its original plan as a garden suburb of Jaffa, particularly after World War I, when its population grew from just under 2,000 to close to 40,000 in the decade

*Fig. 3.5 The Beginnings of Tel Aviv* (1959), Nachum Gutman. Copyright the Gutman Family Collection. Tel Aviv Museum of Art.

from 1918 to 1928.[27] Nostalgia for a time when merely the noise of a passing wagon was an event of consequence lent a sense of longevity to the city, creating the impression of historical roots and permanence. This nostalgia found fertile ground in Gutman's work, especially the images in his 1959 memoir, *A Little Town with Few People in It*, which became a virtual substitute for a genuine and more complicated sense of Tel Aviv's history (Figure 3.5). With the exception of the polemical tone of its final section, the memoir is a gentle reminiscence of days gone by; episodes are related through the impressionable eyes of a young child—the incidents and characters described regarding the city's founding are both unique and emblematic. On the one hand, the author seems to recall in associative fashion the formative scenes of his childhood, which is implicitly understood as Tel Aviv's "childhood" as well. On the other hand, specific episodes and characters are vividly fleshed out, primarily for their paradigmatic value—the first house, the wheelbarrow brigade, the builders, the Arabs—but also because they are what the artist happens to remember. Given this weave of personal memory as exemplary episode, Gutman's memoirs do not read as, nor should they be considered, "history." Neither do they pretend to an exclusive or authoritative tone; in the words of Asher Barash's disclaimer preceding his novel about Tel Aviv during World War I, *Like a Besieged City*, he

> does not intend to depict people and incidents that truly existed, but to paint a general picture of the suburb of Tel Aviv and its mood . . . as the picture was stored in the vision of my memory. Readers who were witness to those and other days are requested not to measure things by their veracity. Their truth is in the degree to which they are poetry. The above remarks are made also by the book's illustrator [Gutman].[28]

Gutman himself makes the point even more explicitly in what amounts to a manifesto for the importance of illustration, published in the journal *Ktuvim* in 1928, a year before the Jewish-Arab riots, which provoked some of his most openly political drawings. In "On Illustration," Gutman outlines the place of the illustrator, and illustration, within the literary work:

> Illustration is not meant merely as a decorative adornment. The illustrator is a partner in the literary work, bone of its bone. . . . Illustration is an organic part of the printed book. Not simply a picture but an integral part of the content. Like musical accompaniment, illustration is the accompaniment to the literary content. Its role is to supplement what isn't said or only hinted at as a leitmotif; it joins passages together, emphasizes moments, determines the frame, and creates the atmosphere of a work. It also brings the book's content closer to life, by giving it a garment and purchase in the reader's imagination. A purchase in fantasy and not hammering it with nails. Because if illustration is exact it will stunt the reader's imagination; the freedom of his thought, its freshness and all of his individual taste will slacken as a result.[29]

The illustration, working with the text, opens a space for the reader in which his or her imagination is free to experience the work according to the reader's "individual taste." Illustration that is overly exact limits the play of fantasy; instead, the images should work more subtly, contributing to the work's atmosphere and accentuating its leitmotifs. Illustration is not meant to duplicate life, but to bring the work closer to it. It is up to the individual reader to supply the final connection, to judge the work by its truth as "poetry," and not for its historical accuracy or veracity. Of course, one could accuse Gutman of playing fast and loose with historical events to suit his artistic temperament. However, it is just this kind of elasticity that allowed for the construction of such a persuasive and monumental version of Tel Aviv's past.

In the illustrations that have come to collectively constitute the myth called "Gutman's Tel Aviv"—the naive version of Tel Aviv erected outside the monumentally modernist City Hall—the city rests under the cheerful gaze of the sun; its industrious residents applaud each new advance in infrastructure—the paving of a road, electricity, running water. Gutman himself seemed to ironize the historical prominence accorded his work in the final section from *A Little Town with Few People in It*. "The Speech I Didn't Give from the Water-Tower (The tower no longer exists and the speech is short)" (Figure 3.6), bemoans the extent to which the Tel Aviv of his childhood—the small neighborhood in which everybody knew each other—is forever gone; this, he concludes sadly in the final pages, is simply Tel Aviv's nature: "in a hurry to change. Its citizens' first houses—erased without a trace. The sycamore trees chopped down. The orchards uprooted. The site of the first Town Committee meeting, mercilessly destroyed."[30] The painter stands with arms outstretched on top of a dotted-line drawing of Rothschild's old water tower. Framing the drawing is an arch-shaped line of text: "This the first, there will be two more; no need to explain why the building is drawn in dots: it no longer exists."[31]

The painter's whimsical position and use of text within the drawing, including several inverted or upside-down letters, are reminiscent of Chagall's Parisian work from before World War I, much of which also includes experimentation with lettering and perspective. Gutman's teetering atop the water tower resembles that of Chagall's atop a

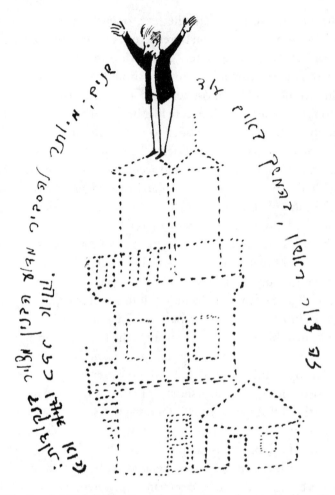

*Fig. 3.6 The Speech I Didn't Give from the Water Tower* (1959), Nachum Gutman.
Copyright the Gutman family.

colorful, childlike model of the Eiffel Tower in *Paris Outside My Window*. Chagall's work in this period accords a prominent place to idyllic, dream-like images of the painter's hometown, Vitebsk, with its small hovels and slanting roofs, and the ubiquitous church steeple. Gutman's work appears to be steeped in the same kind of nostalgia. However, the water tower sketch contains none of the idyllic imagery of a place that has been lost. The artist depicts himself as standing on something that no longer exists, an impresario of an entertainment whose details are fast disappearing; the structure he stands on could collapse at any moment, and he acknowledges his own rootlessness.[32] At best he possesses near-invisible roots—"the small houses, with seventy-centimeter foundations, as prescribed in the city building code—they have additional roots that are much deeper. True, they cannot be seen—but they are there"—a far cry from the radical promise of naive wholeness in his other work.[33] Though they would seem to be entirely different stylists, Gutman's water tower drawing anticipates the fragmented and crumbling city suggested in Avot Yeshurun's late poetry, with its partially collapsed and fragmented words, which are missing a vowel or a consonant: the city in these works is depicted as a work in progress, incomplete, unsubstantial, and likely to collapse. And both Gutman and Yeshurun pointedly address the problem of Tel Aviv's historical memory.

In spite of Gutman's remarks describing the limitations of his drawings as objective historical documents, these images have come to dominate public discourse about the city's history.[34] The prominence of Gutman's drawings in popular conceptions of Tel Aviv is an indication of what occurs as urban topography changes and actual memories of a city's streets and public spaces fade and scatter: "the many voices of the vernacular in particular are stilled as an officially recreated history takes form."[35] Such an officially re-created history is organized repeatedly in guidebooks about Tel Aviv, manuals of civic pride for the resident who wishes to visit that other country called the past. One book states: "It is their civic duty to know their city and its history. . . . The visitor to a city wishing to see its sights without the aid of a guide [book], is like someone in a restaurant ordering a meal without a menu. Both instances involve the danger that the guest is likely to miss the best and most noteworthy."[36]

We cannot overestimate the importance of these guidebooks in an immigrant-dense country like Israel, where most residents were initially as ignorant as tourists. In cities such as Paris, "the ties that bound the city . . . to its history were revealed to the spectator through its architecture . . . [and] 'history' so embodied in the fabric of the city represented an ordering structure enabling each spectator to understand its heroic and virtuous lessons."[37] Tel Avivians, however, apparently needed help in understanding and appreciating the meaning of their own more modest surroundings and monuments of civic pride. The city was thus presented as a kind of artifact to be studied and explored by its residents, in the same way that geography lessons (called either *moledet* [homeland] or *yediat ha-aretz* [knowledge or love of the land]) in school emphasized the importance of firsthand encounters with the landscape.[38] The earliest of these materials about the city were often published in Hebrew, English, and German, to accommodate as wide an audience as possible.[39] Keren ha-yesod (Palestine Foundation Fund) published the pamphlet *Tel Aviv* (1926) and an expanded version, *Tel Aviv: Ir va-em ba-yisrael* (1935), was printed in 40,000 copies.[40] The booklet, which emphasizes the city's creation out of the sands, details different kinds of work and industry and various holiday observances, and describes the integration of Hebrew into daily life, is an advertisement for normalcy and the good life, now available at "European" standards in the Middle East.

These texts of internal tourism in Tel Aviv regularly feature Gutman's illustrations. For example, the *Midrakhon ha-tapuz* or Orange Guide—almost certainly an allusion to Gutman's *The Orange Peel Path* (1958)—published by the Historical Museum of Tel Aviv–Jaffa, tells a story "from Achusat Bayit to Little Tel Aviv." It leads the visitor on the "path of the orange," back to "those good old days" (which even it has the good sense to put in quotes). It stops alongside still-existing structures and explains their former function, and substitutes Gutman's drawings for places that no longer exist, such as the train station. This staple approach follows the path of the orange groves that also no longer exist, back to a circumscribed, iconic vision of Tel Aviv's past.

In the near-seamless triumphal narrative of "building and being built"—the motto on the city's crest, taken from Jeremiah, and mediated through the famous pioneering song—there is an occasional ripple. An example is *The Book of Tel Aviv Street Names*, published in 1944 as a primer for residents who did not know the origins of the names of the city's streets: "there is almost no major personality in Israel for whom a street has not been named; and there is almost no community that symbolizes something in the life of the Hebrew people that does not have a street named for it in Tel Aviv."[41] Initially, the streets in Achusat Bayit were not given official names, but were called various names by early residents. Eventually, however, street names became another way of marking the city as "Hebrew," and the names were often drawn from Jewish history or important figures in contemporary Jewish life. An informational booklet published by the Tel Aviv city police chief in 1925 lists the following streets: Ahad Ha'am, Allenby, Bogroshov, Bialik, Balfour, Bezalel, Gurzenberg, Herzl, Hess, Rambam, Ha-shachar, Yehuda Ha-levi, Lilienblum, Montefiore, Moholiver, Meshutaf, Nahalat Binyamin, Pines, Kalisher, Rothschild, Sheinken.[42] By 1944, however, the city had expanded well beyond Achusat Bayit and contained over 500 streets, and had also acquired another explanatory force for their naming: the epigraph of *The Book of Tel Aviv Street Names*, a chilling variation on Psalms—"If I forget thee O golah, may my right hand lose its cunning"—demonstrates the importance of the Diaspora to the history of Tel Aviv, even as the idea of exile was ostensibly rejected. The book promotes the triumphal narrative of Tel Aviv as "the first Hebrew city," but simultaneously anchors Tel Aviv in the past, in this case, a specifically Jewish, diasporic past. The book, written in the immediate shadow of the war, offers this delineation of what the city could offer its newest citizens, who might have had reservations about its appeal:[43]

> Tel Aviv is the only corner in the world where a person from the nation of Israel can walk in complete security. The Jew knows this natural freedom is no other place in the world, including more enlightened places. Even within the most praiseworthy of metropolises in the golah, the Jew cannot acquire his freedom, except at the cost of diminishing his Jewish image.[44]

An enlarged volume on Tel Aviv streets appearing in 1967 demonstrates how the grid of the city, whose population included a high concentration of survivors, had indeed become a kind of quotidian memorial—the book contains the names of twenty new streets beginning with the word *kehilat* ("community of"), in memory of important Jewish communities in the Diaspora, including Odessa, Budapest,

Bialystok, Brisk, Vienna, Venetsia, Warsaw, Zhitomir, Czernovitz, Lvov, Lodz, Saloniki, Sofia, Poszna, Kovna, Kishniev, Krakow, and Riga.[45]

The role of the Diaspora accorded to the city in *The Book of Tel Aviv Street Names* counters somewhat the triumphal narrative of the city's origins, and complicates the nostalgic version of the city suggested in the use of Gutman's work. This challenge occurs at the micro-level of the street, street signs being one way a city manifests its sense of self. Street signs continue to be an indication of Tel Aviv's relation to the Diaspora. The distance the city has apparently traveled from its one-time promise to commemorate the golah is evidenced in a recent street-sign shuffle on Frug Street. Solomon Frug was a poet who wrote mainly in Yiddish and Russian. On the Tel Aviv street named in his honor, new signs appeared, bearing the name "Prug," misspelled but hyper-corrected in accordance with modern Hebrew rules of pronunciation. (Local residents, including members of a Yiddish organization on an adjacent street, complained and most of the signs have been changed.[46]) Ultimately, it is the friction between this kind of mundane detail and the more iconic yet intimate street life of Gutman's memory that shaped the development of Tel Aviv's historical consciousness. This blend of nascent monumentalism and vibrant detail also characterized another important source of Tel Aviv's early mythology—the poetic personae and landscapes of Natan Alterman's work.


## The Poet and the Street

> The street . . . is the visual image and embodiment of the soul of the people living in the land, and emphasizes the essence of their character.
>
> —Nachum Sokolov, "The Spirit of Tel Aviv" (1934)

No poet's work better embodied Sokolov's dictum than that of Natan Alterman, whose writing about Tel Aviv from the 1930s has come to constitute an important part of the city's mythology of self. Born in Warsaw in 1910 to a Hebrew educator, Alterman grew up in Kishniev and arrived in Tel Aviv at the age of fifteen, completing his education in the city's Herzliya Gymnasium. Alterman's feuilletons about the city originally appeared in the *Ha-aretz* daily from 1932 to 1935, and were later collected in a volume entitled *Tel Aviv Ha-k'tana* (Little Tel Aviv), which was published in 1979 in honor of the city's seventieth anniversary and included early paintings of the city. His first collection of poetry, *Kokhavim bachuts* (Stars Outside; 1938), was both hugely popular with readers and a seminal influence on generations of Hebrew poets for its brilliant imagery, linguistic innovation, and comprehensiveness of vision. The poems, which include a series of odes to an unnamed urban setting, possess a certain affinity with the journalistic work; in a sense, the prose vignettes may be understood as an initial working out of the poetic concerns.[47] However, examining these works together, with an eye to their embedded notions of historical consciousness, also reveals some important, even strategic, differences. Furthermore, given the proximity of their composition, we can find in Alterman's work evidence that these two notions of history—the street and the monument—shape the emergence of the defining poetic persona of modernist Hebrew verse in Palestine, a self firmly rooted in a universal, transcendent landscape that is paradoxically rich in particularistic detail.

We have already seen in Chapter 1 evidence of Alterman's sharp eye concerning the European qualities embodied in the city clock, which he found lacking in the streets of Tel Aviv. At the same time, Alterman rejected the notion of the city's provinciality, despite its village-like intimacy. His prose work details observations made during strolls through the city's neighborhoods: Tel Aviv is both small enough so that he runs into people he knows, and large enough to contain its own "Cité"—an area replete with property speculators and investors of all stripes.[48] Despite Tel Aviv's small size, a "physiognomy" of the city emerges: the city contains types that are identifiable through their attire, language, and body gestures. Alterman's Tel Aviv also contains larger-than-life characters, even some that remind him of figures from world literature (for example, Don Quixote and the moneylender from *Crime and Punishment*).[49] The city's streets in these vignettes are noisy and smelly, a chaotic knot of languages and human interactions.[50] Alterman's journalistic poems of this period, *Tel Aviv Sketches*, also describe a decidedly ordinary urban milieu. In "Legal Assembly," city rhythms flow normally, uninterrupted by military campaigns or political congresses. Instead of waiting for the messiah, "here we wait for the bus."[51] In "Veteran," the city and a citizen encounter one another after a long while and note the changes each has undergone: the citizen's hair has whitened and he is a bit stooped, while Tel Aviv has grown in size and strength; in a nod to the city's polyglot streets, "then, they used to say 'malaise,' now they say 'prosperity.' "[52]

A number of the feuilletons comment explicitly on the importance of a city's historical institutions. In "Hollywood and the City," the poet wryly lauds the existence of a "day-old museum": "A museum is a very important thing. It is a symbol. Testimony to solid foundations and history. . . . More important than its contents is the building in which it is located."[53] In "Memoirs from the Near Future," set in 1975, Tel Aviv even contains an "Old City," just like Jerusalem.[54] Ironically, a writer encountered in this fanciful sketch focuses not on contemporary life, but on the 1930s: writing about the present, he says, is dangerous, and only a great artist can truly capture it. The past, however, "lies before you like raw mute material—get up and do with it what you will." Since the past does not speak, you can "work it like a parrot."[55] The narrator—an Altermanian substitute named Mendel Runfast—observes that nothing has changed, that in his day (the 1930s), people also insisted on writing about the distant past. This futuristic discussion of historical writing suggests that the difficulties posed by the heady uncertainty of Reuven's *Tel Aviv* have become part and parcel of imaginative work devoted to the city. If art is a way of endowing permanence, how does one write about a city that seems to be—in the words of a 1928 observer—"entirely of the present, all reality, no history"?[56] A solution, as we have seen with Druyanov and Gutman, is nostalgia; indeed, Alterman's prose is replete with nostalgic references to the city's early days, including a rhapsodic elegy to what was known as the Casino, a café and dance hall on the beach that was a highlight of Tel Aviv's early social life and a landmark featured in many depictions of the city (Figure 3.7). In Alterman's

*Fig. 3.7* The Tel Aviv "Casino" (Galei Aviv Café), 1920s. Soskin Archive, Historical Museum of Tel Aviv–Jaffa.

whimsical, loving description, the Casino is the only building in Tel Aviv that dared stand in the water, while the rest of the city clung to dry land.[57]

Though the feuilleton form may have done justice to the physiognomy of nineteenth-century Paris, it ultimately did not suit the web of gravity and the commonplace that make up Alterman's Tel Aviv.[58] In a feuilleton entitled "Ir va-em" ("city and mother"—the biblical term for a large city), Alterman makes clear his historical designs for his adopted city:

> One only has to go out into the street and wander to believe that besides politics and economics and Hitler, there are also miracles in the world; and one who dips his feuilleton pen in this whirlpool of life, boiling and churning and fluttering in a bounty of waves, sparks, and flickerings of light and shade, will seem pathetic and ridiculous, like a phlegmatic tourist who wants to capture Niagara Falls with his poor Kodak. . . . The comparison insults me a bit. My self-love pretends to be serious and announces that it does not care

about all the Niagaras in the world, and is ready to write a trilogy of the past, present, and future of Tel Aviv without skipping a single detail and without narrowing the wide canvas even one centimeter.[59]

If "the past, present, and future of Tel Aviv" is construed as a drama of Jewish national redemption against the seemingly more mundane backdrop of "politics and economics and Hitler," one is tempted to understand—in broad fashion—Alterman's first three volumes of poetry—*Kokhavim bachuts* (Stars Outside; 1938), *Simchat Ani'im* (Joy of the Poor; 1941) and *Shirey makot mitsrayim* (Songs of the Plagues of Egypt; 1944)—as just such a historical trilogy. Though addressing universal themes of human relationships, grief, and the persistence of love after death, *Joy of the Poor* also implicitly evokes the turmoil of the war and the approaching Holocaust of European Jewry. *Songs of the Plagues of Egypt* describes ancient Thebes in images that bring to mind contemporary Tel Aviv. It is in *Kokhavim bachuts*, however, that Alterman's most ambitious imaginings for the city are realized. To be sure, there is no critical consensus concerning the identity of the city in *Kokhavim bachuts*. Many of the poems seem to present an almost European space, and their concerns are universal and often mundane. However, read against the historical dilemmas embedded in Alterman's prose, the poems of *Kokhavim bachuts*, in their very namelessness, offer a radical proposal regarding Tel Aviv: the difficulty of writing about a city that seems entirely "present tense," a city that the feuilleton can only attempt to encompass, may in fact be overcome by endowing the relatively new metropolis with a transcendent sense of its own spare roots.

The poems of *Kokhavim bachuts* engage the concerns of the prose work, specifically the city in history. They are an epic account of the city that does not "narro[w] the wide canvas even one centimeter." One poem describes Tel Aviv's origins in the desert's primal strength: as a night storm approaches, the city swears it will remember:

"Hamsin Night"
the wide-eyed openness of this night,
the father's whisper and the strange flame,

the extended hand of her homeland in the wind,
the strength of her unbroken weeping.[60]

The poems achieve some of their timeless, almost mythic quality by not
calling the city by name. Instead, it is assumed that readers will simply
recognize the markings of Tel Aviv's daily existence. The book's third
section consists of a cycle of odes to the city's streets, marketplace,
weather, and people. In "Market Day" typical street scenes are given
iconic status:

I see the majesty of the sycamore on the rise,
the battle of the square—one against a hundred!
I see the wide street, swallowing
a line of buses heavy as tears.

I set out for the market rolling up its sleeves,
I wander between its burning fingers
dizzy from its wine, its head in the heavens,
the fire of the fish-sellers' curses![61]

In "The Birth of the Street," the mere paving of a street takes on
heroic proportions, as the poet himself admits he lacks the words to
match the city's greatness:

For through pain and force [the city's] street is born,
for eternally will her exalted song walk upon it.
I will not be the one to compose words of love to her,
I have not found words
large as she.[62]

By taking for granted the reader's identification with the substance
of the imagery, Alterman grants Tel Aviv a sublime solidity unfelt
in earlier poetry that had focused almost exclusively on the city's
newness and youth. Neither the city's age nor its urban identity is at issue: rather, Tel Aviv is simply a setting within which the eternal drama
of the poet and his beloved unfold, and poems ranging from the folk-
loric ballad to the philosophical lyric may be staged. The city is the site
of longing for some unspecified loss—"For when will we again set out
for the street, / sneaking through its shadows like a tiger" (52)—and

an arena in which nature's cycles serve as a surreal backdrop to the mundane social interactions of urban life:

> Then a great blindness lit up
> the streets and the markets.
> Torrential green skies
> leaned upon the city.
>
> The streets flooded slowly
> mumbling, whispering,
> enslaved to a netted commotion
> of glances and meetings.
>
> Don't dim the light of the past,
> its single flame so weak.
> If it wasn't love,
> it was a lovely fall evening (64).

The passage of time in the city is indicative of both the ordinary and extraordinary: "With neither spectacles nor shade an hour passes in the city" (74). One of the volume's most famous lines—"Even an old sight contains a moment of birth" (37)—contains the quintessential insight into Tel Aviv, a city whose name promises that "spring" (*aviv*) will rise from an "archaeological site" (*tel*). Rothschild Boulevard receives a similarly dualistic treatment in "Boulevard in the Rain":

> It seems—this morning we'll also arrive
> at the last house in the wide pathway
> and there the firmament will stand alone
> and a boy will throw a ball at its feet.
>
> The boulevard is combed with light and rain.
> Speak, greenery, make noise!
> See, my god, with my laughing daughter
> I stroll your main street.[63]

Here the boulevard houses both the sacred and the profane: God's firmament stretches over a children's playground. In its progressive depiction in literary texts, the *bulvar* or "Rothschild" became more than just a symbol of Tel Aviv's past. Rather, it served as a kind of semiotic shorthand denoting different visions of the city, its identity, and its evolution as an urban space.

## The Beginnings of the Boulevard

> The residents of Achusat Bayit apparently saw no need for a public garden in their neighborhood, and if not for an unusual circumstance of necessity, Rothschild Boulevard would not have been created. The highest sand dunes were dumped into the deepest valley. And since this valley, filled with loose earth, could not serve as a place for the building of houses, it was allocated . . . as an avenue of trees, and this was the beginning of Rothschild Boulevard.
>
> —Alter Druyanov, *Sefer Tel Aviv* (1936)

In 1910, a group of residents wrote to the Town Committee (the precursor to the Municipality), requesting that their street be named after Baron Edmund Rothschild, who had sponsored the early establishment of Jewish settlements in Palestine: "We dare believe this act would help bring the Baron and the Zionist movement into closer relation." Their street became, in fact, Lilienblum. Rothschild Boulevard itself was initially called the Street of the People (Rechov Ha-am), and was designed explicitly as the city's first public space, with trees, benches, a kiosk, and an open central area for strolling, a place where its residents could see and be seen (Figure 3.8).[64] The *bulvar*—pronounced with a French intonation—was one of Achusat Bayit's earliest streets, and is featured in numerous photographs from the period as an example of the city's modernity and self-consciousness as an urban space. The neighborhood had originally been planned as a quiet affluent suburb of Jaffa, with one- and two-story single-family homes surrounded by private gardens. This plan, and the landowners' subsequent brief flirtation with Patrick Geddes' garden city model, eventually gave way in the face of an increased demand for housing and commercial development. Urban planning and architectural style reflected the desire to build a city that was both European and the antithesis of Jewish life in the Diaspora, as well as somehow local. Rothschild Boulevard was the site around which many issues connected to the utility and appearance of

*Fig. 3.8* Postcard of Rothschild Boulevard, the "Heart of Tel Aviv," 1920s. Central Zionist Archives, Jerusalem.

public spaces were first debated. The boulevard eventually became the site of the city's earliest examples of International Style architecture, which from the 1930s came to dominate building in Tel Aviv, and later in Israel as a whole (see Chapter 4).[65]

Above all, the boulevard was meant to be a pleasing public space. Despite financial and other practical limitations, Tel Aviv's external aspects were a point of civic pride, and were meant to reflect its modern sensibility. Initial estimations of the city's early appearance were not very encouraging; a typical observation, published in 1922 in the daily *Do'ar ha-yom*, drew on the stereotype of Jews as essentially incapable of aesthetic appreciation:

> In our Hebrew city, there is a large flaw, obvious to any foreign visitor or anyone with an aesthetic sense, and that is the lack of gardens around the houses. Beautiful, large houses stand naked and exposed without any tree or vegetation around them. And these houses bring in a reasonable rent to their owners, who then become wealthy; these same masters, however, are stingy when it comes to fencing and planting a garden; this lack casts a shadow on the residents of Tel Aviv

vis-à-vis outsiders. . . . Anyone who sees the city says "the Jews build great, beautiful houses for the rent income, and not out of a sense of beauty planted within them."[66]

Several American journalists who visited the city in the 1920s were even more frank in their appraisals of the city's ungainliness and dismal external appearance, and directly attributed it to a "Jewish inexperience in building, molding and stabilizing, in giving concrete expression to a social life. For two thousand years the Jews have been literary, liturgical ghosts. They have come to Palestine with their cultural treasury emptied."[67] One called Tel Aviv a " 'soap-bubble city' . . . unsubstantial and impermanent, if stone and cement can bubble from the earth" and especially criticized the houses: "their crass tastelessness, their inharmonious arrangement, the tenement-like structures running down to the sea and ending in the tawdry casino, as bad as any American seaside resort."[68]

Much of the early hopes placed on Rothschild Boulevard were meant to counter these critiques, to prove that Jews could indeed build a public space not only worthy of respect from skeptical visitors from abroad, but one that would be functional and appreciated by its citizens as well. Perhaps these great expectations account for the enormous attention paid to Rothschild Boulevard in narratives of the city's development as an urban space. Its entrepreneurial value was also recognized early on: "Because it was a 'boulevard,' there were those who leaped at the chance to make it a center for soda and ice cream and such things that any person craves in the Land of Israel, with its enormous sea and heat."[69] In retrospect, the boulevard has become an icon of the city's history, a kind of virtual memorial appearing in innumerable literary and pseudo-historical descriptions. S. Yizhar recalls his childhood on Montefiore Street, near the boulevard,

> with its small trees that had difficulty growing because of the thinness of the loose, clean sand, that were planted there precisely because of the thinness of this loose and clean sand, because in that place there had been a large valley before there was Tel Aviv, and the pioneers with their famous wheelbarrows were called for, and they brought sand from the golden sand dunes into that valley and filled it up until the homeowners were afraid to build there because the house that

they had built with what remained of their money might sink into the loose sand, and they decided to plant trees to bind the flying sand to the solid earth.[70]

Drawing on the area's pre–Tel Aviv origins as a dumping ground for sand, the boulevard in Yizhar's memoir is an arena for a mock heroic battle against Tel Aviv's natural elements—the sands that threaten the houses of its residents. This portion of the boulevard contained the city's most extensive landscaping, including rows of sycamores and other trees specially imported from Egypt.[71] Its eventually shaded central passage became the site of Tel Aviv's first "Hyde Park," known as the "parliament of Rothschild," a place of argument, news, and conversation. Its reputation resembled that of St. Petersburg's Nevsky Prospect, whose qualities were memorialized in Gogol's prose. According to cultural historian Marshall Berman, Nevsky Prospect's "essential purpose . . . is sociability: people come here to see and be seen, to communicate their visions to one another . . . as an end in itself."[72] This vivid passage from Alterman's prose captures precisely this kind of sociability:

> Rothschild Boulevard, as is well known, is a meeting place for
> people who don't have a penny in their pocket. Unemployed
> workers, members of the "middle class," looking for some kind of
> class, even less than middle; loafers, gossips, prattlers, the news-thirsty
> and spreaders-of-lies, those dying of curiosity and just plain good
> Jews—all these happened upon Rothschild, a few steps away from the
> flow of the street, like having a "picnic" by the banks of a noisy river.
> Near a tree that was called in the glory days of the place the "tree
> of knowledge," the words of fools and wise men could be leisurely
> listened to. . . . Subject mingled with subject, as did interruption
> upon interruption. Rhythmic, gnashing Bessarabian Yiddish; wide,
> sonorous Polish Yiddish; and Lithuanian Yiddish with large *ahs* and
> expansive *ays*.[73]

Alterman's Rothschild resembles several places: the poet's Eastern European native landscape, where large cities were often bisected by a "noisy river," the biblical Garden of Eden, and a kind of open-air Jewish market, where barter is conducted in vibrant, egalitarian fashion in the lingua franca of Yiddish. It is almost as if the characters had stepped

*Fig. 3.9 Rothschild Boulevard* (1930s), Chaim Glicksburg. Israel Phoenix Association. Co.

out of the Enlightenment fiction of the great Hebrew-Yiddish classicist S. Y. Abramovitch and landed in Achusat Bayit.

Paintings from the 1930s such as those by Chaim Glicksburg and Joseph Kossonogi depict the boulevard's central portion, including the kiosk, accentuating the rows of trees lining both sides and the respite the boulevard could offer from busy streets (Figures 3.9, 3.10). With

*Fig. 3.10 Rothschild Boulevard* (1930), Joseph Kossonogi. Israel Phoenix Association. Co.

their dull, autumnal colors and small, leisurely knots of strollers and bench-dwellers in dark suits, these paintings resemble depictions of European city streets more than anything in Tel Aviv, perhaps a marker of their creators' Parisian training.[74] Unlike Gutman's and Reuven's naive dreamscapes, these paintings offer a fuller, more realistic depiction of the city's developing physical plane. Yet they are also "elsewhere"—in their lush greenery and in their evocation of foreign streets.

The boulevard and its adjacent streets were also featured in many early photographs of the city, particularly in Soskin's enormous catalog of work. As suggested in the above discussion of Soskin's "land lottery" photo, the use of these photographs as historical documents is problematic. However, the images do display a kind of historical consciousness, inasmuch as the frame often suggests an awareness—on the part of both Soskin and his subjects—of the potential historical value of the photograph's site and moment. The photographs often have a staged quality to them; the gravity (and technical difficulty) of taking a photograph creates a sense of "making history": the subjects usually stare unmoving into the camera, into the future. Two later works by Kaniuk and Alterman explicitly poked fun at the performative quality of that period's historical photographs: in the words of Aunt Shlomtsion's cynical and property-speculating father, the Ashkenazim "love to have their pictures taken by Soskin, posing with wheelbarrows."[75] In Alterman's play *Kinneret, Kinneret* (1962), a young photographer is sent by an unnamed Zionist institution to record the life of a group of pioneers in the Jordan Valley. In order to make the picture more naturalistic, he instructs them to bring "spades, rakes, pitchforks, sickles, sheaves, and plows," explaining that he will capture their picture just as the sun rises upon their faces: "it's good for symbolic as well as technical purposes." He is further delighted to discover the presence of a child: "What? A child? . . . Quick, run, get him, put him in the middle. . . . Don't you understand what a *baby* adds to a photo like this??"[76]

Soskin's image from the early 1920s of the Hotel Ben Nachum at the corner of Allenby and Rothschild is a classic example of a photograph of Tel Aviv's historical landscape (Figure 3.11). The building is set in near isolation, at the center of the photograph, displaying to best advantage its centrally defining column and cap, flanked by wings of arched or protruding balconies. Surrounded by a band of white sidewalk, and the well-trampled sand of still-unpaved streets, the structure resembles those in Soskin's other photos from this period: mirage-like, fantastical. The scene is otherwise deserted, save for a blurred figure in the foreground and the silhouette of a child waiting at the *gazoz* (soda) cart in the lower right corner. The photograph stresses the newness of human forms, and of human construction, in this particular landscape.

A photograph taken two decades later by an anonymous photographer from the same position and angle treats the hotel itself as

*Fig. 3.11* Hotel Ben Nachum, Rothschild Boulevard and Allenby Street, 1920s.
Soskin Archive, Historical Museum of Tel Aviv–Jaffa.

backdrop, its outlines overexposed and barely visible through the ficus
and jacaranda branches (Figure 3.12).[77] The intervening years have produced a vibrant street life—small businesses, pedestrians, bicycles, an
overloaded truck. Center stage in this later photo is the idea of image-
making itself: the photographer and his portable equipment—a tripod
and camera with black sleeve, a chair with a screen backdrop. The photograph captures a moment before the image was taken: the photographer fiddles with the screen, the client prepares himself by placing his
hands on his thighs and looking into the camera, while a passerby,
dressed in a curious combination of jacket and what looks like underwear, examines photographs pasted up alongside the camera.

This stretch of Rothschild west of Allenby was filled with photographers and their clients, who took advantage of the shade of the boulevard's relatively considerable foliage. Perhaps the anonymous photographer from 1946 even had Soskin's photograph in mind, so ubiquitous
were Soskin's monumental images of early Tel Aviv. The landscape

*Fig. 3.12* Corner of Rothschild Boulevard and Allenby Street, 1946. Photographer unknown. Central Zionist Archives, Jerusalem.

in the later photograph is dehistoricized to the extent that it purports to record an ostensibly ordinary and repeatable moment. Nonetheless, examining the two photographs together demonstrates the degree to which unregulated public spaces may become monumental, that is "primary elements of the city persisting through time," including "built forms such as the trace of an original street plan, the impression of a city's pre-urban nucleus, or the material evidence of its neighborhoods, streets, brides, arcades." In explaining the architect Aldo Rossi's conception of these monumental forms in the city, Boyer argues that their "mental images impressed themselves on the spectator's or architect's mind; they formed both the memory of each city and created a formal unity out of all its parts. They were the past we still experience in the present, and they enabled us to read the city in a contiguous manner."[78] These forms may be read in both texts and images that document the evolution of urban space, as well as in their physical traces in the city itself.

## The Evolution of a Street Corner

The street corner—Rothschild and Allenby—depicted in the two photographs is a central public site whose history reveals how the production of cultural identity has been represented in Tel Aviv's physical plane. Today the intersection is one of the city's busiest, and many pass through it without noticing the surrounding buildings and landmarks (Figure 3.13). However, traces of an ostensibly minor but revealing historical episode are still observable. In 1922, at Rothschild 32, the Pension Ginosar or Hotel Ben Nachum opened. The building was designed in the "eclectic style" by Yehuda Megidovitch, at the time city

*Fig. 3.13* Corner of Rothschild Boulevard and Allenby Street, 1999. Photo by author.

engineer. Eclecticism, the dominant architectural style in Tel Aviv in the 1920s, was more a search for a style than an actual school; it brought together elements of ostensibly disparate styles in order to fashion an architectural language appropriate to a particular building in a specific site. Gilead Duvshani describes two contradictory pulls of eclecticism in Megidovitch's work—the rational and the romantic—and roots them in the architect's early training and professional experience in Odessa.[79]

Eclecticism's duality seems almost perfectly suited to the construction of the city's first hotel, a building that was simultaneously public and private, and appropriately located at the intersection of a public promenade (Rothschild) and a primarily residential street (Allenby). The building's "public" facade consists of arches facing Rothschild Boulevard's gardens; the openings in its "private" facade resemble those of the neighboring residential buildings on Allenby Street.[80] These two aspects are joined at the corner by stairs, crowned by a dome. The dome itself also represents these two styles—the dense rationalism of the columns topped by the dome's romantic whimsy.[81] The hotel is a ubiquitous element of representations of the boulevard throughout Tel Aviv's early years, including paintings by Avraham Naton and Yehezkel Streichman—both called *The Kiosk on Rothschild Boulevard* (also known as *Rubennko's Kiosk*). Streichman's painting features a sketchily rendered dome floating atop blooming poinciana trees and the smaller cap of the kiosk (Figures 3.14, 3.15).[82]

The hotel was considered enough of a Tel Aviv landmark to be included in a series of postcards dating from the early twenties printed by the German firm Artsenu. The production of city-scene postcards was a way nineteenth-century metropolises defined themselves to the world at large. The postcards typically spotlighted the city's signature spaces and structures, but were either entirely devoid of human figures, or featured human forms in secondary fashion.[83] The first postcards of Tel Aviv were ordered by the Town Committee in 1912; they featured Soskin's photographs and were printed in copious quantities, enough for the city's small population to write several times over to family and friends abroad.[84] A card bearing a photograph of the hotel, dated 26 June 1924, was mailed to Berlin from Tel Aviv by the architect

*Fig. 3.14 The Kiosk on Rothschild Boulevard (Rubennko's Kiosk)* (1937), Yehezkel Streichman. Courtesy of Tsila Streichman.

Alexander Levy to Davis Trietsch, a leading figure in the German Zionist movement.[85] The card is a dense artifact illustrating not only Tel Aviv's evolving self-image, but the strong relation between the new city and European society. The significance of postcards generally lies in their play of text and image, and this card contains a particularly interesting mix of codes on the message side (Figure 3.16). Levy's terse

*Fig. 3.15 The Kiosk on Rothschild Boulevard* (1930s), Avraham Naton. Joseph
Hackmey Collection.

*Fig. 3.16* Postcard from Alexander Levy to Davis Trietsch, 1924. "Write in
Hebrew, Jew!" Central Zionist Archives.

message concerning metal wire samples probably pertains to the building of the "Pagoda," under construction at the time; his German scrawl is bracketed by two lines of printed Hebrew—the Berlin address of Artsenu, and the ideological imperative to write in Hebrew: *Yehudi k'tov ivrit!* (Write in Hebrew, Jew!). Alongside the printed spine dividing the message and address space are written the words "Alexander Levy, Tel Aviv, Palestine." A postal stamp and postmark, in English and Arabic, further complements the card's dizzying semiotic trajectory: printed in Hebrew in Berlin, handwritten in German in Tel Aviv, and mailed back to Berlin from British mandatory Palestine.

The Hotel Ben Nachum featured panoramic views of the sea and the Judaean hills, and modern conveniences such as electricity and phone service.[86] Its opening was marked by the unveiling of a large statue over its entrance by the American sculptor Y. D. Gordon. Three figures—a rabbi and two students—were surrounded by figures of animals, including dolphins and an eagle with outstretched wings. The statue provoked an immediate response from Tel Aviv's religious leaders, who called it a "statue in the Greek spirit," attacking it for its violation of the Second Commandment prohibition of representation of the human body. The statue was viewed as a potential threat to the development of local Jewish art, and a public letter called on the Town Committee to enact a citywide prohibition on statues with human form. It was seen as particularly offensive in light of the fact that the city's new synagogue was under construction a short distance away, on Allenby Street. In fact, the cornerstone had been laid the previous fall.[87] Religious leaders also expressed concern as to what visitors to the city would think: "Here the Jews have statues on their homes just like the other nations."[88]

The statue's unveiling, which had been announced in the papers, provoked this alternative reaction in the daily *Do'ar ha-yom*: the paper commended the impulse behind the sculpture—to beautify Tel Aviv's public spaces. It did not, however, appreciate the aesthetic value of this particular piece.[89] The *rabbanut* appealed directly to the Town Committee, which refused to interfere, replying that it was a private matter.[90] This same reasoning undergirds the committee's responses to many complaints made about various physical aspects of the public sphere, including illegal construction and maintenance, as well as its response to a 1913 complaint about piano playing on the Sabbath: the Town Committee maintained it would not interfere in religious matters concerning private behavior in the home.[91] The sculpture was eventually removed after, it seems, the religious community put some sort of *cherem* (ban) on the hotel.

Across the street at number 29, we find another example of art with its face toward the public sphere—the home of Yitzhak Lederberg, built in 1925 by the architect Yosef Berlin, who designed ten other homes in this stretch of the boulevard between Allenby and Balfour.[92] Its facade is adorned with ceramic plaques by Ya'akov Eisenberg, from drawings by Ze'ev Raban, both under the tutelage of Boris Shatz, the founder of Jerusalem's Bezalel Academy. Shatz's involvement in the creation of Tel Aviv's public face is a brief but particularly interesting chapter in the city's history. With the influx of Polish, largely petit bourgeois immigrants in 1924, building in Tel Aviv was booming.[93] Shatz personally appealed to Meir Dizengoff to commission Bezalel to produce ceramic signs for Tel Aviv's buildings and streets, but his influence is most famously felt in the design of the Herzliya Gymnasium, whose exterior ornamentation reflected Shatz's commitment to a local, Jewish style that drew on ancient Mediterranean motifs. Shatz found a receptive audience in Tel Aviv's most influential citizens, including Dizengoff, who praised the "Hebrew style" of Shatz's solo exhibit at the gymnasium in 1922.[94]

The plaque over the entrance to the Lederberg House bears a larger scene of Jerusalem containing the quote: "Again I will build you, and be built, virgin daughter of Zion" (Figure 3.17). (The same quote was chosen by S. Ben-Zion as a motto for the city crest of Tel Aviv, which was designed by his son, Nachum Gutman.[95]) The other ceramics depict scenes of biblical agricultural activities and are an integral part of the building's architecture, fitting in snugly between porches and windows. (One figure is especially Herzlian.) The scenes were chosen to illustrate the importance of working the land; they are particularly ironic given that the owners of this particular house were not physical laborers. The keyhole shape of the scenes, inviting the viewer to peek inside, further thematizes the owners' desire to be perceived as participating

*Fig. 3.17* Lederberg House, corner of Rothschild Boulevard and Allenby Street, detail of Eisenberg ceramics, 1999. Photo by author.

in this central aspect of national renewal, both a private desire and a shaping force of the public realm.

Both the iconoclastic incident involving Gordon's statue and the Lederberg ceramics provide an interesting context in which to examine public expressions of cultural and religious affinity in the city as well as the degree to which the public sphere was expected to reflect elements of the populace's collective identity and heritage. In fact, they are evidence of the competing visions of Tel Aviv. Both Gordon's statue and Shatz's ceramics adorned private homes yet were perceived as a reflection of cultural identity in the public sphere. They may in a sense be considered Tel Aviv's first public works of art. One raised controversy, the other did not. One was seen as "Greek"—an all-purpose tag word for foreign influence that nonetheless retained a sense of paganism and idol-worship—and the other was praised for its "Hebrew" use of ancient and privileged, local, Jewish tropes. Gordon's statue was eventually removed, apparently to satisfy a community that does not usually receive great play in histories of Tel Aviv—its religious leaders. Given the overwhelmingly secular march of modernity that Tel Aviv is meant to embody, it is perhaps not surprising that this incident receives minor coverage in histories of the city.[96] The ceramics are still in place and are considered an essential part of the city's architectural identity.[97]

Photographs from the 1920s show that, in the middle of the boulevard, between the Hotel Ben Nachum and the Lederberg House, was a third mediating building—a curious structure with Byzantine columns underneath what looks like the minaret of a mosque. It was one of the city's first electric generators, and was designed by Alex Bervald, whose drawings served as the basis of the Great Synagogue in Tel Aviv, with its enormous dome, and who also designed the Technion in Haifa. The cap reflects a desire to utilize "Eastern" or "Oriental" elements, and is meant to resemble the top of a sheik's tomb. (In the 1930s, as construction in the city increased dramatically, Jewish architects considered what could be learned from local Arab architecture, noting that the Arab world had created for itself "eternal monuments," with its palaces and mosques.[98]) Bervald eventually erased the eclectic localism from his work, in favor of the cleaner lines of the International Style in the 1930s, a trend followed by many architects during this period.

Together with Bervald's mosque-style generator, the corner's evolution demonstrates how cultural identity is negotiated in the public sphere. It contains a compact rendering of the spectrum of cultural influences and directions possible in a formative decade in the city's development. Select elements of this decade have been preserved or emphasized; for example, the incident involving Gordon's statue is perceived as a minor episode in histories of the city. Within the context of Achusat Bayit as a whole, however, it provides an interesting site in which to examine the public expression of cultural and religious affinity: What *should* the public sphere reflect? Should public art be Jewish, or "Hebrew," or something else? How was Tel Aviv to compete with the weight of Jerusalem's historical claims? Most importantly, how does a modernist city that prides itself on newness create a sense of an authoritative cultural tradition?

## Rothschild Boulevard Reconsidered

In recent years, Rothschild Boulevard has become the site of numerous public sculptures, often designed as part of the renovation or preservation of its historic buildings. Some of these sculptures explicitly address their historical surroundings; some are merely whimsical. For example, the three plastic figures on the balcony of Rothschild 96—"Introduction: Prologue," by Ofra Zimbalista—seemed to be fixed in mid-song; their postures also suggest a declamation of some sort, recalling the nature of the boulevard as an arena for public discussion. As we have seen in the example of the objections to Gordon's statue, despite Tel Aviv's proclaimed modern, and modernist, intentions, the production of public space was tied to more traditional ideas about visuality in Jewish culture. The Second Commandment is again implied as a standard in a brief discussion of the proper Hebrew term for "memorial" that appeared in the official Municipality bulletin from 1950. The authors favored the use of the term *yad* over *andarta* because the latter is related to the Greek word *andreyus*, deriving from *anor*, which means "a human being." Given that the statues in Tel Aviv are not of human figures, the name *andarta* is not appropriate; instead they should be called "commemorative statues," or *yad*.[99] (In Levinsky's utopian novel, discussed in Chapter 1, we even find the problem anticipated: "There are no pictures or stone statues, you won't see them in any of the Hebrew cities, because the Jews do not realize their heroes in pictures or stone or clay, which are ultimately mute forms. . . . Instead there are numerous beautiful fountains, which purify the air."[100])

*Fig. 3.18 Foundation* (1989), Micha Ulman. Photo by author.

Although monuments encourage an appreciation of the past, as the city develops around them they are likely to be observed in isolation, and only "tenuously linked" to the city as a whole.[101] The Founders' Monument, erected in 1951, stands at the corner of Rothschild Boulevard and Nahalat Binyamin Street, in the place where the water tower had been. Its three levels depict foundational periods in the city's history: the "leveling of the sands," with workers living in tents surrounded by animals; followed by "Tel Aviv's beginnings," the building of the gymnasium, the water tower, and Dizengoff's house; and, finally, Dizengoff Square, with its fountain and the construction of Bialik's house and the National Theater. On the back of the monument are the names of the sixty original "shareholders" of Achusat Bayit.

Micah Ulman's *Yesod* (Foundation) from 1989 is located at the other end of the boulevard, close to the National Theater (Figure 3.18). Ulman's topic is not the human agents of history ("the Founders"), but the process of history itself. The piece is less interested in assessing or delineating origins or personalities than in meditating on the often intangible yet powerful by-products of historical change. Like the Founders' Monument, however, Ulman's *Foundation* also addresses the question of roots, the process through with they are formed, and the relation between what is observable on the surface and what remains buried underneath. Ulman's materials are concrete and soil. The site's play of empty space and filled-in holes is barely visible as one approaches it, and does not seem to be noticed by people walking by and over it. According to Ulman, it is either a place in which a home is built, or the remains of one; either the edge of some subterranean structure which cannot be seen in its entirety, or the "archaeological remains of a house that has been destroyed."[102] It resembles a building after an earthquake that has been covered with dirt (like Ulman's *Sand Day* [1997], in which the artist filled an entire gallery with sand) or the remains of a sunken relic. Ulman himself says "I'm a man who digs."[103] He has dug holes in Arab villages, in Jerusalem and in Berlin, compelling visitors to interact with the work by stepping on or over it. His work engages structural notions of surface and depth, thereby probing the relation between artifact and trace. Ulman's interest in digging and holes grew out of the possibility of whether a hole can be a sculpture, "or in other words: what is the meaning of lack and absence."[104]

One might also ask what it means to dig in a place like Tel Aviv, which has relatively few layers of topsoil to dig through. Perhaps it will serve as an archeological trace for generations to come, who wish to recover and recollect fin-de-siècle Tel Aviv.[105] Together the two pieces demonstrate the evolution of Rothschild Boulevard as a symbol of the city's history. Both the Founders' Monument and Ulman's *Foundation* reflect on the question of roots, and suggest an archaeological model for a future understanding or appreciation of the past. At the same time, they organize for the visitor/viewer different versions of Tel Aviv's past—the Founders' Monument offering a neatly segmented and progressive vision of the city developing organically, almost like the fish and plant life at its base, out of Jonah's Jaffa. Ulman's *Foundation* places Tel Aviv's relatively shallow roots at the center of his project, a notion that is a part of the daily life of Tel Avivians, whether they choose to notice it or not, to walk over it, or pause and reflect.

The kind of activity provoked by Ulman's *Foundation* is eerily anticipated in Ya'akov Shabtai's *Zikhron Dvarim* (Past Continuous; 1977), an epic novel of a crumbling, mid-1970s Tel Aviv.[106] Like Avot Yeshurun's *The Syrian-African Rift* (1974), this "post-utopian" novel implicitly critiques Israel's longstanding Zionist–Labor Party establishment.[107] Both works are part of a larger civic discourse that arose in Israel following the 1973 Yom Kippur War. In their volume *Grasping Land*, anthropologists Yoram Bilu and Eyal Ben-Ari describe the post-1973 break in the following terms:

> The post–1973 war years constituted the critical period in which the Zionist ethos (particularly in its secular-socialist version) began to lose its hegemonic position among wide segments of Israeli society. . . . Against this background, it is not coincidental that the 1970s witnessed the emergence of subversive "counternarratives," which challenged the national myths associated with some of the most prominent sites in the Zionist civil religion.[108]

As with my discussion of Avot Yeshurun in Chapter 2, I am interested in how these counternarratives are inscribed in space, specifically Tel Aviv's urban plane. *Past Continuous* depicts in part an area adjacent to Rothschild Boulevard, the poor and somewhat makeshift neighborhood of Nordia, whose wooden huts authentically denote the rootless condition of its inhabitants' lives. Toward the end of the novel, the anti-heroic protagonist Goldman walks through the remains of this neighborhood of his youth.

> Goldman plodded through the sand and passed the place where the big shack, which had disappeared without a trace, had once stood, skirted the mulberry tree and arrived at the place that had once been the garden in front of Shmuel and Bracha and Grandfather Baruch Haim and Grandmother Chava's shack, which had been demolished like most of the others, but of which the concrete blocks forming the foundation had miraculously remained standing, tracing the floor plan of the shack on the sand. . . . The sand, which had been hidden underneath the floorboards, was now exposed, full of broken glass and china and dead leaves and stems and pieces of coal and scraps of paper borne by the wind, and Goldman bent down and picked up a piece of china and played with it as he went into the second room, which had

once held the big iron bed on which Grandmother Chava had slept
with Grandfather Baruch Chaim and on which they had laid his body
covered with a white sheet, and also a clumsy armchair and a heavy
sideboard bearing a few secular and sacred books. . . . The room was
almost unbearably stuffy and overcrowded, was always full of the smell
of mattresses and down cushions and valerian drops, and although the
walls and ceilings were painted a harsh white, like the front room, it
was never properly lit, but now everything was wide open and daz-
zlingly bright—the broad summer sky stretched above Goldman's
head with its yellow sun, and the castor oil plant, which used to grow
up the side of the shack, penetrated the room with its large leaves, a
fresh purplish green—and Goldman, who stood looking around him
for one more minute, walked through the wall and went on walking
until he came to Dizengoff Street, on the other side of which a giant
bulldozer was busy excavating.

From one day to the next, over the space of a few years, the city
was rapidly and relentlessly changing its face, and right in front of his
eyes it was engulfing the sand lots and the virgin fields, the vineyards
and citrus groves and little woods and Arab villages, and afterwards
the changes began invading the streets of the older parts of town,
which were dotted here and there with simple one-storied houses surrounded by gardens with a few shrubs and flower beds, and sometimes vegetables and strawberries, and also cypress trees and lemon
and orange and mandarin trees, or buildings that attempted to imitate
the architectural beauties and splendors of Europe, in the style of
Paris or Vienna or Berlin, or even of castles and palaces, but all these
buildings no longer had any future because they were old and ill
adapted to modern tastes and lifestyles. . . . And Goldman, who was
attached to these streets and houses because they, together with the
sand dunes and virgin fields, were the landscape in which he had been
born and grown up, knew that this process of destruction was inevitable, and perhaps even necessary, as inevitable as the change in the
population of the town, which in the course of a few years had been
filled with tens of thousands of new people, who in Goldman's eyes
were invading outsiders who had turned him into a stranger in his
own city.[109]

Nordia's small streets and their one-story homes, the surrounding
sands and fields, the eclectic-style castles of Achusat Bayit—none of

these was of any use in the face of rampant land speculation and rising property values. The novel is filled with descriptions of the city crumbling, being chipped away or bulldozed over; Tel Aviv's growth, "like a crazy creature over the sand dunes and the vineyards and the melon patches" (183) causes its inhabitants to feel like strangers in their own town.[110] As the city expands, it erases its semi-agrarian past, into which the now empty Arab villages are subsumed. Shabtai writes from the perspective of a "local son" of the city's political and social elite, and Goldman feels "invaded" by the waves of new immigrants. Shabtai himself claimed to have felt like a refugee in his own hometown,[111] and the resultant anomie is palpable in the novel's extended series of interlocking physical and discursive flâneries: the male protagonists wander throughout the streets, cafés, and apartments of contemporary Tel Aviv, observing the traffic, the crowds along the beachfront and in commercial areas, the intimate interactions in restaurants, in front of private homes, in living rooms. Walking the streets offers an escape from the heat and potential release from dark and depressing interiors; the outdoors seems to offer the possibility of human connection. However, their wandering also reminds them of both the city's general and their own personal disintegration:

> The sense of shame and sin continued to oppress him as he walked along the street glancing from time to time at the girls standing with their little handbags on the corners or in the doorways of the gloomy old buildings, abandoned to neglect and the indifferent process of decay, with their arched windows and doors and the rusty iron grilles with their pretty patterns embellishing the balconies, most of which were in darkness so that it looked as if nobody lived in them and all they contained were broken bits of furniture and dust and cobwebs and evil spirits (162).

As the characters move through the city streets, they sense elements of the past behind the concrete forms of the present; the novel observes the city and their childhood through these memories, as well as those of their extended family. Disparate temporal and spatial situations are woven together in near-seamless fashion, swinging in the breath of a single sentence between ostensibly discrete times and spaces, turning on a whim from the past to the present, in a manner not unlike the flâneur's aimless wandering along the city's streets. Just as the flâneur seems unattached and uninvolved—the ultimate observer, committed to neither a past result nor a future consequence of his actions—the narrative attempts to move in a perpetual present tense, recording the lives of the protagonists, who themselves continually stumble across elements of their past. Their attempts to find comfort in relations in the present are doomed by these old patterns: even after death, Goldman ruminates, "something of the other person remained behind as part of your being forever, and for years afterward the surface of the great ocean of oblivion would be disturbed by various troublesome memories" (74–75). Like the bits of china and glass he encounters in the ruins of Nordia, there is no explicit attempt to give meaning to these material bits of the past—they are simply there to be bumped into and counted.

Dan Miron argues that, more than any specific set of memories, the novel is driven by the "idea of memory"—a metaphysical concept, organizing individual sets of memories into a collective memory, which is attached to a particular landscape during a specific time.[112] However, the workings of memory in the novel are ultimately much less tidy. Memory operates in almost antimodernist fashion, if by modernist we mean the redolence of Proust's madeline, which is soaked in the past and provides comfort to the adult Marcel. There is no comparable moment of grace or transcendence in Shabtai's novel, no instance that even comes close. This absence is painfully obvious in the scene in which Goldman goes through his father's papers:

> Goldman opened the cupboard, which no one had dared to approach as long as his father was still alive.
>
> The cupboard was very clean and neat and tidy: Next to the stamp collection and photograph albums, in which old pictures of fresh young people and a happy family were preserved, there were empty checkbooks from the Zerubavel Cooperative, Anglo-Palestine, and Barclay banks, documents and payments dating back thirty and forty years for all kinds of donations and payments to institutions that for the most part had ceased to exist long ago. Goldman stood looking uneasily at the open cupboard for a moment with remembered fear

and at the same time a strange feeling of proprietorship—all of a sudden everything was in his hands—and then he bent down slightly and rummaged carefully among the papers and documents and found the bankbook and the insurance policy and savings certificates and government bonds, and also an old photograph of his sister and his father's will (173).

In another kind of novel, one more enchanted with the lasting value of images, the photo of his sister Naomi could have symbolized the recuperation of some painful memory of a private event—the death of a sibling—and even offered some insight into his father's experience as well.[113] Instead, Goldman simply flips through this potentially meaningful element of his past along with the other documents. Side by side, in the same untouched chest, items marking a connection to the public sphere—checkbooks and receipts—are stored together with what appears to be a register of similarly arbitrary barter-and-exchange in the domestic realm—younger, fresher, happier families.

Given that the literal meaning of the book's title is "memory of things," these are the "things" of the novel's title, that must be remembered, a process that also entails recycling and reusing: Goldman's Aunt Zippora washed "the clothes that were handed down from child to child, and cut the toes out of shoes grown too small for their owners, and turned old dresses into blouses, and pants into jackets, and tablecloths into dresses" (297). Her actions mark a relation between past and present of interchangeability, of wearing through. Yet the novel's title idiomatically means a memorandum of agreement, or protocol marking a formal, legal relationship. One of the novel's chief preoccupations concerns the relation between these two realms suggested in its title—the private and the public. Just as the "success" or even desirability or feasibility of separating past from present remains an open question in the novel, the individual or private realm is repeatedly examined through the frame of the collective, and is subject to the institutions and events of the public sphere. Ultimately the novel questions the very possibility of describing a private life in a society that is so collectively structured. What constitutes a private life in a society and culture so undergirded by a commitment to collective ideals and experience? If there is no "true" flânerie in the city of one's birth—no escape from familiarity—in what kinds of spaces, through what sort of behavior, can an individual locate and lead a private life?

In the passage cited above, part of an extended, poetic section exploring the cohesion between past and present, Goldman walks back over the remaining block foundations of Uncle Shmuel and Aunt Bracha's home, observing the traces of family life left within: "the sand, which had been hidden beneath the floorboards, was now exposed, full of pieces of broken glass and china and dead leaves and stems and bits of coal and scraps of paper borne by the wind." Goldman attempts, in vain, to give meaning to the remaining bits of past by naming them, noting them, walking over them. According to Tamar Berger, Goldman is ultimately a "failed" flâneur. "Shabtai goes in the wake of these markers in the hope of turning them into signs, of granting them meaning, to resuscitate them and turn them into experience, to give them back their halo—their authenticity and individuality, to stitch them together into a single story. However, the 'things' remain autonomous. Crumbling, disconnected."[114] Goldman's flânerie, and that of the other characters in the novel, is even more fundamentally flawed: there is little anonymity to their walking. Though feeling themselves estranged, they cannot truly "get lost" in the city of their birth. Goldman's passage through the sand in which he stumbles physically over pieces of the past, and tries to describe them, sieve-like, in the net of his present, is an allegory of the narrative's attempt as a whole to remember, to catch the past in the net of the present tense.

The handling of the past in this passage is both archaeological and curatorial—a discovery and an uncovering, as well as an attempt to arrange, align, describe, and explain. Yet the novel as a whole is as much a paean to memory as an exercise in its failure. What the novel does offer us is the boulevard itself, a prosaic antidote to Kaniuk's "metahistorical intersection." Its obsessive, repetitive circling through the streets and along the beachfront deflates the city's monumental narrative of self, exposing the decay, the dirt and debris, and the flimsy arbitrariness of architectural forms, as well as the pettiness and the randomness that make up the lives of its citizens. It is these ordinary and often depressing, even cruel details that remain, embedded in the memories of the characters, and in the city's topsoil. Shabtai makes something enduring, compelling, and beautiful of these details. Rothschild Boulevard has indeed become a monument. If, however, like Ulman, we dig a bit, we can find competing ideas regarding its character; literary memoirs such as *Past Continuous* further unravel the street's symbolic aspect. The boulevard today makes room for expressions of Tel Aviv's official history, as well as its own homegrown ambivalence toward the past.

In this chapter and the preceding one, we have seen how specific sites—the Old Cemetery and Rothschild Boulevard—came to embody key components of Tel Aviv's urban identity as the city grew from an outlying neighborhood of Jaffa to the center of modern Hebrew life in Palestine. For all its unique qualities, however, Tel Aviv shared with other cities features inherent in the creation and expansion of any urban settlement. For example, in writing about Tel Aviv we find a negotiation between the city's public and private spheres, and between its center and the borders that circumscribe it. In the case of Tel Aviv, these ordinary urban conditions were compounded by a concern for a more elusive and intangible sense of Jewishness. As we shall see in the following two chapters, the city's identity as a modern urban space was ultimately complicated both by its loyalty to diasporic forms of Jewishness and by the heterogeneity of the local landscape.

A View from the Balcony: Public and
Private Spaces / Public and Private Selves

> The "public" realm, the realm of the temple or palace has private and
> "mixed" aspects, while the "private" house or dwelling has public
> . . . and "mixed" ones. Much the same may be said of the town as a
> whole.
>
> —Henri Lefebvre, *The Production of Space*

> We are, moreover, a people given to the arts of time rather than
> those in space.
> —Ludwig Lewisohn, "A City Unlike New York" (1925)

Early writing about Tel Aviv takes for granted the notion that space
reflects identity and that identity may be socially produced through the
creation of a certain kind of space. Thus the distinction between private and public space is another way of conceptualizing the ongoing
negotiation of individual and collective identities. Though both
spheres are articulated and regulated by the relation between the
gaze—a singular viewing subject—and the object, persons, or scene
viewed, the junction between public and private spheres is fraught with
the presence of the unseen. Photography is therefore an ideal medium
through which to understand the production and representation of
space in Tel Aviv's early decades. Furthermore, the city's early decades
coincided with a veritable explosion of work by a diverse group of Jewish photographers in Palestine, whose cameras captured the city's development from garden suburb to proto-metropolis.[1] Zionist institutions were also increasingly aware of the ideological power of these
images, particularly in the wake of German migration of the 1930s.
Thus, as the city itself expanded, its photographic representation also
broadened in both scope and influence.

124

As we have seen in the preceding chapter, many of the city's famous
early images are found in Avraham Soskin's photographs. Taken over a
span of several decades, they record events such as the land "lottery"

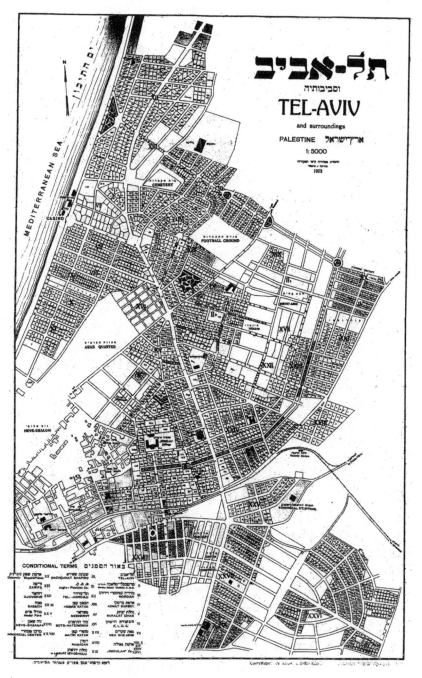

*Map 4.1* Tel Aviv and its surroundings, 1923.

marking the foundation of Achusat Bayit, the cornerstone setting and construction of landmark buildings, celebrations of holidays and other public festivities, and visits of important foreign dignitaries. These photographs of the historical landscape, many of which were sponsored by the Tel Aviv Municipality, and their subsequent use and canonization by later generations of writers and historians, record the emergence of a certain image of Tel Aviv—a bourgeois, gardened neighborhood that became, almost against its will, an economically and socially stratified urban center. However, Soskin also photographed domestic interiors and numerous studio portraits of Tel Aviv's citizenry. This record of other spaces complicates the monumental depiction of space in the city, in which human forms and new construction are framed by an immaculate landscape, as if frozen in some absolute, originary space. These interior images may be read as another indicator of the city's developing identity, both for what they feature and what is absent. Soskin's interiors suggest that the public and the private are produced in relation to one another, and that their very definition intrinsically depends on this relational difference. The process was complicated in Tel Aviv, a city expressly devoted to creating a public Jewish sphere, often out of those very elements that had previously constituted the domestic realm, such as religious rituals and celebrations.

Just as Soskin's historical photographs, together with Gutman's drawings and Alterman's poetry, provided the basis of the discussion in Chapter 3 of Tel Aviv's mythological roots, the first portion of this chapter examines another set of foundational cultural images from the 1920s: a series of interior and studio portraits by Soskin, followed by a group of self-portraits by Reuven. All draw on the conventions of European portraiture and painting, while engaging elements of the local landscape as well as motifs from Jewish traditions. Their focus on the human form, and on interiors or domestic scenes, pulls the attention inward, into the ostensibly private lives of their immigrant-subjects. Yet their status as portraits also offers a glimpse of how this private realm is presented to the public eye. A reading of Reuven's semi-domestic landscape *View from the Balcony* (1924) will provide the chapter's pivotal hinge, on which turns our examination of how this interior, private space is intimately tied to the collective ideals of a nascent public sphere. The chapter's final sections turn outward to examine the flourishing of International Style architecture in the 1930s and photojournalistic street scenes of the 1930s and 1940s. Throughout we will be concerned with noting how otherwise ordinary parameters of the city's public and private facades were believed to intrinsically reflect a Jewish urbanism.

## A Room of Her Own: At Home in Soskin's Studio

> The spaces of femininity operated not only at the level of what is represented, the drawing-room or sewing-room. The spaces of femininity are those from which femininity is lived as a positionality in discourse and social practice. They are the product of a lived sense of social locatedness, mobility and visibility, in the social relations of seeing and being seen.
> —Griselda Pollock, "Modernity and the Spaces of Femininity"

Beginning in the nineteenth century, as work moved out of the home and into the public domain, modern experience was characterized by an increasing "separation of spheres," an ideology that associated women's experience with the domestic realm, and described the public sphere as a primarily male space. The development of this ideology, and the actual conditions pertaining to it, varied in degree and nature, geographically as well as across social and economic groups. Furthermore, to note this gendered conception of the relation between private and public spheres is not to insist that women never operated in the public sphere, or that they were wholly confined to the home; nor does it mean that men had no private life. Although it is true that limitations were placed upon middle- and upper-class women moving on their own in the public sphere, women were also a part of the increasingly industrialized work force. However, the very nature of what came to be considered "modern," especially in the realm of urban experience, depended upon an increasingly sharp and inevitably gendered distinction between private and public realms; one might say this ideology of "separate spheres" was symptomatic of the modern. To the degree that Tel Aviv began as an essentially middle-class garden suburb, Soskin's photograph from the 1910s of a woman reclining, deeply ensconced in the

*Fig. 4.1* "Living Room of Tel Aviv Home," by Soskin, 1910s. Historical Museum of Tel Aviv–Jaffa.

privacy of her own home, reflects this aspiration to be demonstrably modern (Figure 4.1).[2] The room is typical of Tel Aviv's first private homes—fantastical, palatial-looking villas, shaped by both the example of local Arab architecture and an eclectic mix of modern and neoclassical details imported by architects who had studied in Warsaw, Odessa, and St. Petersburg.[3] While the external result was seen as "Oriental," the interiors remained resolutely "European," often merely replicating the material aspects of their inhabitants' previous lives.[4] This high-ceilinged, combination dining room/salon contains an enormous amount of space, especially compared to the more functional units of the 1930s. The wood paneling and heavy, ornate furniture lining and filling the room are broken up by the accoutrements of home—photos of small children and other portraits spotting the walls in slightly haphazard fashion, books resting in a pile on the corner table, bottles of pills, vases filled with flowers, a pair of white lace cloths, candlesticks, a set of glasses, a kiddush cup. Only the Eastern pattern of the tiled floor, partly covered by a thick straw mat, appears local. An art nouveau–patterned cloth covers the large rectangular table, at the very end of which—the center of the photograph—reclines the woman. Dressed in white, she leans her head into one hand, itself propped up by an elbow on the couch arm.

Seated at the far center of the horizon of a wide-angle frame, the woman is technically the photograph's focus. The image grows lighter as the eye reaches her from the rest of the room. Her form is engulfed by the heavy furnishings, swathed in the light, especially as it encroaches upon the whiteness of her dress. The woman is the point at which the photo collapses, nearly dissolves into white. Even her body has begun to fold—only the top two-thirds of her body is visible, or suggested really, in her position on the couch. She is at once enclosed and supported by the room, and also the detail that upsets its harmonious equilibrium. Two chairs have been casually drawn back from table so as not to block the photographer's view of her, or hers of him. The vase of flowers has been moved to the side, apparently for the same reason. These changes in the room's arrangement have almost certainly been made by the photographer, all to get the shot in which the woman appears. What kind of "contract" did the woman share with the photographer? Did he place her on the sofa—a reference to impressionist painterly images of the bourgeois woman—or did she simply not want to get up? Yet there is neither offering nor seduction in her gaze. The woman belongs in the room—like the furnishings, she "fits"—but she also disturbs it: the slightly pained and weary expression, her downturned mouth, is remarkably clear, even at a distance. Except for light pouring through a half-open doorway, and in the outline of a pair of windows above, the room almost entirely effaces the presence of the outdoors. We are told in the caption that it is a room in Tel Aviv in the 1910s, but only the floor tiles offer any solid clue to the room's actual location.

If we treat this photograph as a portrait, then the woman's position and her expression become even more forceful. Portraiture played a special role in Soskin's oeuvre. The sheer quantity and variety of the work recently uncovered in the Labor Movement Archives suggest the photographer was engaged in a kind of social taxonomy of early Tel Aviv, a project bearing some resemblance to *Face of Our Time* (1929) by the German photographer August Sander. Before his death, Soskin

*Fig. 4.2* Family portrait by Soskin, 1920s. Lavon Institute for Labor Research, Tel Aviv.

donated 9,000 glass negatives taken from 1909 to 1933 to the archives; unlike his more well-known images of significant historical occasions, these portraits shot in his studio on Herzl Street depict mostly anonymous individuals from the burgeoning Tel Aviv middle class: portraits of families, couples, soldiers, small children, individually and in groups (Figures 4.2, 4.3).[5] Like Sander's work, these photos display a "social order—a public world of individuals defined through their public roles."[6] If Soskin's studio portraits are any indication, Tel Aviv, and the

*Fig. 4.3* Studio portrait by Soskin, 1920s. Lavon Institute for Labor Research, Tel Aviv.

Jewish community in Palestine generally, respected the power of the photographic image as a means of recording and representing themselves, their achievements, and the landmark events of their lives. The bourgeois character of many of the studio portraits—which often featured European-style backdrops—is itself a striking challenge to a Zionist society that portrayed itself as revolutionary.[7]

Yet despite the avowedly public status of these portraits, indicated by details of dress, background, or props, any notion of a unitary collective identity is upset by the multitude of tiny differences among them, and by the details suggesting a more individuated sense of self. For example, sometimes the backgrounds seem to deliberately upset or contradict the subject's demeanor and dress: a woman dressed in Oriental costume poses before a European landscape (Figure 4.4), or a young couple in simple peasant garb pose in front of classical Greek columns and an ornately framed mirror (Figure 4.5).[8] Again, we might ask what kind of "contract" existed between photographer and subject, and how the photographer's placement of a particular background complicates the subject's presentation. The tension between a socially constructed public self and the lurking presence of an individual, private self constitutes

*Fig. 4.4* Woman in "Oriental" garb, studio portrait by Soskin, 1920s. Lavon Institute for Labor Research, Tel Aviv.

the portrait's primary paradox, and is the source of its ongoing power: "At virtually every level, and within every context, the portrait photograph is fraught with ambiguity. For all its literal realism it denotes above all, the problematics of identity, and exists within a series of cultural codes which simultaneously hide as they reveal . . . its enigmatic and paradoxical meaning."[9]

An anonymous photograph of a woman sitting alone by a table, gazing at a portrait of a child, feels almost like a domestic interior, wherein the photographer had intruded upon a mother looking at a photo of her dead child (Figure 4.6). Yet one hand seems to restrain the other,

*Fig. 4.5* Against a classical backdrop, studio portrait by Soskin, 1920s. Lavon
Institute for Labor Research, Tel Aviv.

as if reaching for something rather than at contemplative rest, and indeed, her eyes are closed, as if she can bear neither the portrait before
her, nor the situation of being photographed. Roland Barthes calls this
kind of disruptive feature a "punctum"—"the detail which attracts or
distresses me" or a "sting, speck, cut, little hole. . . . That accident
which pricks me."[10] In Soskin's interior from 1910, the woman's
expression is that distressing detail. Though she "belongs" inside—in
that the home was seen as a feminine space, more as "a mental map
rather than a description of actual social space"—the privacy of this
room was not meant to bear public scrutiny.[11]

*Fig. 4.6* Woman and child, studio portrait by Soskin, 1920s. Lavon Institute for Labor Research, Tel Aviv.

Soskin's studio photographs trace the seam connecting the private and the public. Produced in a professional studio as part of the public sphere of exchange, the portraits certainly represent something significant about the subject's sense of self to a larger audience. At the same time, they were often intended as private keepsakes of the relationships portrayed—between husband and wife, among siblings or comrades. The portraits are depictions of private selves within the context of an emerging public sphere that was itself expected both to represent and to shape a collective identity—the new Jew. Like Reuven's self-portraits, to which we now turn, they are further evidence that identity is inseparable from its discursive representation.

### Reuven's Self-portraits as a Native

The Hebrew word for self-portrait—*dyokan*—comes from the Greek *dyo* (two) and *eikon* (picture). Perhaps the duality is a reference to the fact that "face" in Hebrew (*panim*) is grammatically plural, suggesting that the face—like the self it both reveals and hides—is multiple and given to change. Reuven's self-portraits are a fascinating and extended exercise in self-invention, an autobiography in which the artist paints himself over and over again, caught in the repeated act of making himself "at home." Though their exact number is unknown, they are numerous enough to have merited an exhibit of their own at Rubin Museum in Tel Aviv; their sheer volume makes them somewhat of an anomaly in local terms.[12] Reuven settled in Tel Aviv in 1922, and from 1922 to 1929 he painted at least eight major oil self-portraits, all of which contain elements of the surrounding landscape; this landscape is often denoted through the use of familiar biblical motifs, while some paintings refer specifically to Tel Aviv's modern structures. Reuven's work generally has been viewed through the prism of European primitivism, a critical frame that works most productively when considering his self-portraits and their referred landscapes.[13] Like his *Tel Aviv* (1922), the portraits reflect stylistic concerns similar to those of his French contemporaries, many of whom sought inspiration in Mediterranean locales (for a discussion of this painting, see Chapter 3). Art historian James Herbert argues that the work of Henri Matisse and the Fauvists simultaneously evoked the *grande tradition* of French painting, embodied in the classical "Latin" themes of the work of Poussin and Ingres, and created a new technique of rusticity whose very form seemed to emulate the peasant lifestyle and its concomitant claims to immediacy and authenticity.[14] The simple, vivid colors and raw brush strokes were meant to represent village life to the sophisticated Parisian palates.[15] Reuven's work also deployed classical (Biblical) motifs within an idealized, local (Mediterranean) landscape; it conflated contemporary realia with myth, in this case achieving a de facto legitimization of the Zionist presence through the invocation of an ancient, privileged setting.

In *Self-Portrait in the Yard* (1925; Figure 4.7) and *My Family* (1926; Figure 4.8), the artist paints himself in two different settings: alone at his easel in the garden, and with his family in a pastoral scene.[16] The tools of his trade—palette and paintbrushes—appear in each painting, as does a goat, a semidomesticated animal whose easy, hand-fed presence is a marker of the painter's own comfort and nativeness. His

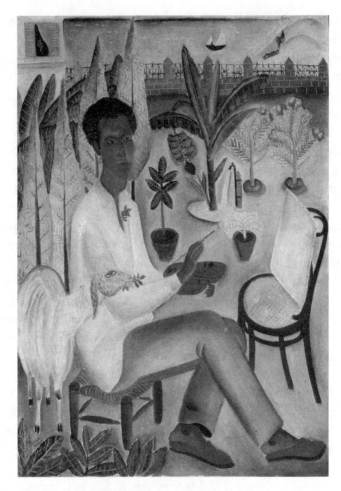

*Fig. 4.7 Self-Portrait in the Yard* (1925), Reuven. Rubin Museum.

familiarity is also signaled through the adoption of casual, local dress, and the wearing of house-slippers. (This dress is explicitly contrasted to the European attire of his mother, sister, and brother in *My Family*, who arrived in Palestine after Reuven.) Most remarkably, Reuven paints his own skin in increasingly darker shades in many of the self-portraits. In this repeated production of his own resemblance to Arab natives, Reuven's self-portraits are an excellent example of what Homi Bhabha has called "colonial mimicry," that is "a desire for a reformed,

*Fig. 4.8 My Family* (1926), Reuven. Rubin Museum. Coll. Tel Aviv Museum of Art.

recognizable Other, *as a subject of difference that is almost the same, but not quite.*"[17] According to Bhabha, "mimicry *repeats* rather than *represents.*"[18] Mimicry is not merely an isolated instance of imitation, but a recurring process in which the self is repeatedly imagined in the guise of the local, until the fundamental difference between the two has dissolved: "mimicry is thus the sign of a double articulation . . . which 'appropriates' the Other as it visualizes power."[19] Reuven was not alone among European Jewish painters in Palestine in his adoption of the Arabs' "visual power."[20] Nachum Gutman, whose myth-making power was explored in Chapter 3, declared that "in the Arab, I saw a direct line of expression, the appearance of our biblical heroes. . . . I loved these Arabs more than the characters of Shalom Aleichem."[21] Constructing the self occurs without an idealized depiction of the Jewish pioneer, or the self in pioneering garb, but directly, though not unproblematically, through the example of the native. This difficulty is represented head-on in *Self Portrait with a Flower* (1922), in which the painter sits against a background of city's first houses, holding an exotic flower in a jar of water, suggesting that the Mediterranean climate may be too harsh for his delicate, European roots. This ambivalence—according to Bhabha, the core of mimicry's discourse—provides much of the emotive power of these early self-portraits.

The duality of Reuven's portraits—his "two-faced pictures"—also structures many of his landscapes of this period and is most evident in their preponderance of windows, balconies, and fences. Though the world outside is never figured as menacing, the light and colors of the new landscape were strange for the artist and took some getting used to. The windows in Reuven's paintings of the 1920s depict a developing relation between internal and external landscapes, between the domestic space of the artist's home/studio and elements of the public domain. According to Gideon Ofrat, these paintings aspire to create a bridge between the painter's private self and the vision of collective experience he senses in the surrounding environment.[22] The gap between interiority and the world outside emblematizes not only the difficulty of adjusting to an alien landscape and climate, but also the tensions between this landscape and the European world left behind, and between a diasporic Jewish culture on the one hand, and the potential of a new, native Hebrew culture, on the other. The spatial division thus also indicates a temporal division, between the immigrant-artist's old and new lives. The fences and balconies in these paintings both divide and integrate, a symbiosis suggested by the fact that similar materials depict both the domestic realm and public sphere. Nature, for example, is both contained in the yard in potted plants, but also outside and elemental in the sea. The objects represented in these paintings have a highly symbolic value whose evolution may be traced in Reuven's work through their placement relative to the window frame, fence, or balcony railing.[23]

*Fig. 4.9 View from the Balcony* (1924), Reuven. Rubin Museum.

Reuven's *View from the Balcony* (1924; Figure 4.9) is a complicated rendition of overlapping and intertwined polarities—indoors and outdoors, private and public, high modern style and arts and crafts, Tel Aviv and Jerusalem, word and image, Europe and the Mediterranean. The painting references biblical texts, modernist painting, and the contemporary institutions of a newly forming secular Jewish culture in Palestine. It displays an idealized proportion of civilization, quasi-nature, and sea, similar to that of Matisse's and Derain's paintings from the south, which "almost without exception, present a vision of town and landscape harmoniously intertwined."[24] The view *from* the balcony, however, is seriously eclipsed by the view *of* the balcony: this latter scene, together with the wrap-around balustrade, occupies a full two-thirds of the painting. The toy-like buildings are dwarfed by oversized camels, while a wagon and donkey await some worker's hands;

the sand-colored landscape flows out from underneath the balcony (we glimpse pieces of houses in between the rails) and ends in a gentle curve of shoreline that haphazardly mimics the line of the balcony. The view from the balcony only barely registers the existence of life elsewhere: the bottom piece of a slip of boat attaches itself incongruously to the top of the canvas.

The center of the painting, then, seems to be the balcony itself. This balcony differs in significant, material ways from the environment outside its borders: its black and white tiles contrast sharply with the natural tone of both the single-story structures and the surrounding dunes. The modest yet patterned surface of the table, suggesting an engraved ledge or Cézannesque cloth, brings the contrast between the fenced-off natural world and the artifice of the domestic sphere into sharper focus. However, the color scheme on both sides of the railing is nearly identical. The two worlds also overlap in the painting's explicitly crafted elements: the woven seat of the chair and the wood box are both manufactured versions of the trees outside. The painting's display of these multiple layers of craft culminates in the canvas itself.

The fruit on the table are particularly evocative cultural markers in Jewish tradition, being members of the seven fruits associated with the biblical Land of Israel. Pomegranates adorned the edges of Aaron's robe in the Book of Exodus and are a common decorative emblem in Jewish religious art. An ancient fertility symbol, the pomegranate also summons a complex network of erotic connotations from The Song of Songs, where it is associated with female sexuality. The *etrog* (citron) is also linked to the Jewish pastoral past, but carries a slightly different register. Strictly a fruit of the male, priestly domain of sacrifice and ritual, the etrog is one of the four special items traditionally offered during the harvest festival Sukkot, a holiday commemorating the transient biblical wandering of the Israelites between Egypt and Canaan. The etrog, part of a required yearly observance, epitomizes the repetitive, cyclical nature of collective memory in the Diaspora. But the painting's ancient, biblical intertext muddles the distinction between exile and homeland. Zionism's return of this diasporic ritual—the etrog—to the Land of Milk and Honey would have it be "a fruit like all other fruits," an ordinary still-life akin to Cézanne's apples. Although Zionist ideology systematically devalued Diaspora culture, *View from the Balcony* suggests something more complicated. The painting questions the very viability and substance of Hebrew culture in Tel Aviv during the 1920s in light of the long-standing vibrancy of European and diasporic traditions. *View from the Balcony* maps a potential relation between European culture, Jewish history, and the local landscape over the liminal realm of the balcony, a location in which the artist's highly individualized self is exposed to, and informed by, the pressures of the public domain's collective vision, during a period in which the public realm is itself undergoing enormous and dynamic change. This fluid and mutually imbricating vision of public and private spaces—and public and private identities—is a hallmark of representations of space in Tel Aviv's early decades.

Chapter 3 discussed the potential challenge posed by Jerusalem's ancient authority to Tel Aviv's developing urban, cultural identity as embedded in the city's public art on Rothschild Boulevard in the early 1920s. We find a similar tension at work in *View from the Balcony*, where the decidedly unripe etrog rests in an olivewood box with the word "Jerusalem" engraved on it, perhaps a poke at Boris Schatz's Bezalel Academy, and its emphasis on religious and decorative art.[25] The presentation of a sliced-open pomegranate facing off with an etrog encased in a ritual box against the background of a secularized, Fauve landscape not only challenged the Bezalel school's vision of the East, but raised the dilemma of art's societal function: what role would the production of fine arts play in a city whose most pressing priorities seemed to be the more concrete work of building homes and paving streets? Should this art emblematize a specific social vision and therefore contribute in some tangible fashion to the national project? Finally, if this is a painting about making culture, then what is the ideal location for this culture? In this case, the intermediary site of the balcony suggests a space both public and private; their propinquity is figured in terms of different forms of cultural and/or religious identification by which Tel Aviv came to be known as a "Hebrew" or "Jewish" city. This intertwined relation between public and private realms suggests an urban space where customs traditionally associated with the private sphere are now idealized in the public realm as a form of new urban collective identity. Early writing about the specifics of Tel Aviv's spatial character focused on the relation of these features to a nascent, native Hebrew culture.

## Intimate Streets: "Where is your Jewish culture?"

> When someone comes and asks you, "Where is your Jewish culture?" you will answer, "What do you mean?" and take him riding through the streets of Tel Aviv.
>
> Marvin Lowenthal, "This Hebrew Renaissance" (1925)

As we saw with the mini-scandal surrounding Gordon's statue on the Hotel Ben Nachum, the appearance and utility of the city's public spaces was hotly debated from the start. By public space we mean those arenas officially designated to fulfill some civic or municipal function; sites that come to constitute the public sphere through daily use— streets, sidewalks, squares or parks; and semi-public areas surrounding private homes such as gardens, balconies, and external facades. The expectations of Tel Aviv as the "first Hebrew city"—the urban realization of Zionist ideology—were most explicitly expressed in the public sphere.[26] As we have seen, an airtight division between public and private domains was neither possible nor desirable. The balcony of Reuven's painting depicts the private sphere as turned outward, toward the public sphere; at the same time, elements of the public realm are domesticated, intimate. Individual interiority is connected to and informed by the forces of the exterior, collective realm. This fluidity is perceived in one account as a consequence of the city's geography, especially in contrast to Jerusalem's "mysterious" mountains. In Tel Aviv, the flatness of the landscape allows everything to be in the open: "In one of your rooms, you still feel as if you are living outside."[27] An article from 1933 notes this dynamic as one of the city's special features:

> Tel Aviv is a street city. People live in the streets, while apartments are nothing but light, transparent, summer dwellings, where every-thing that happens in them is heard on the street. From within, the

street can be seen, and the apartments can be seen from the street. From the street one looks directly into rooms and speaks to those sitting there. There is no boundary between home and street, neither architecturally nor psychologically speaking. A single area, one-dimensional.[28]

The slim difference between public and private space is perceived and constituted by two essential tropes: speech and the gaze. Everything is either exposed through looking or comprehensible through language. The slim "boundary between home and street" is construed—and breached—in both physical (architectural) and metaphysical (psychological) terms. Tel Aviv's streets are understood as extensions of the domestic realm, and this familiarity is explicitly connected to the city's "Jewish" qualities. Accounts from the 1920s note that in Tel Aviv "even the street cleaners are circumcised" and "Jewish policemen, unarmed, keep order and regulate the traffic."[29] It is the city's Jewishness that seems to create an instant feeling of intimacy:

> Everything seems so familiar to me, so dear to my heart, that I cannot believe I haven't seen it before. And the names on so many of the houses . . . are also known to me. Here lives Levontin from the bank, here lives Mordechai Ben Hillel Ha-cohen, here lives Zhagorodski, and so on. I don't think there is another place on earth where so much Jewish education and so many Jewish intellectuals are mixed together as in Tel Aviv.[30]

Although it would later be called a "Hebrew" city, Tel Aviv is referred to early on as *di yidishe vunder-shtot*—the Jewish wonder-city.[31] As early as 1913, David Frischmann admired the fact that Jewish residents of Palestine seemed to have stopped noticing their surroundings:

> The most noticeable trait characterizing Eretzyisrael in the eyes of a stranger on his first visit is the relation between the Jew and the people surrounding him. This relation is neither good nor bad, but simply not felt at all. The Jew there, it seems, has completely forgotten his environment and does not meditate upon it, or think about it at all. We here in the Diaspora must remember each and every moment that surrounds us, and we cannot tear our minds away from it, even for one moment. . . . The surroundings preoccupy us in reality and in

our dreams. . . . Our thoughts and customs and deeds are always
directed externally and we must always take into account every
thought and custom and act in terms of our surroundings. In the
Land of Israel I saw for the first time Jews who had entirely forgotten
that there is a line or some external measure according to which they
must direct their lives. They live their lives, life in and of itself, and
nothing more.[32]

In a retrospective essay, the poet Saul Tchernichovski described the
city in similar terms:

This is, ultimately, the only place in the world that the Jew can be a
Jew, not a Jew as a matter of prohibition or allowance, but simply a
human being called a Jew. Feeling himself a Jew not out of a constant encounter with non-Jews, this is the only place in the world
where a Jew can live without feeling that he is a Jew, without any
need to be aware of it. Like a tree in its forest, a plant on its own
soil, like the Russian peasant from Pozneh, the Frenchman on his
rivers of water, the German from a village in Pomerania. To see the
wide world out of Hebrew eyes without knowing that there are
other eyes. Here—the *sabra* cannot understand what exile is, to
venture out into the entire world from a purely Hebrew point
of view.[33]

Ironically, both of these accounts hold up the Jew's lack of self-aware-
ness as a primary characteristic of the street's Jewish nature. This normalcy is achieved through demographic, political change, and only
subsequently through a substantive cultural revolution.

The use of Hebrew in Tel Aviv's public sphere was seen as a crucial
factor in creating a uniquely Jewish urban space.[34] The Municipality
encouraged shopkeepers to hang signs in Hebrew only, and special importance was paid to the naming of streets:

How close to our hearts are all these names! It's apparently only a
small thing, just names: but the Hebrew sounds of an independent
language are like a balm to the Jew's soul, who everyday sees only
strangeness and is forced to hear the murmurings of a foreign
language. Here one finds a bit of comfort: indeed there is one corner
of the world in which a Jew can honor his revered ones, and read
their names in what he has created![35]

The significance of Tel Aviv's Hebrew street names may seem obvious in retrospect but was not always apparent. Druyanov reports that in early discussions about Achusat Bayit, at least one person suggested that not all names be in Hebrew or Hebraized; rather some should be left in their "diasporic form . . . [because] we came here from the *galut*."[36] Visitors during the city's early years frequently complemented the specifically Hebrew noisiness of Tel Aviv's streets: what was considered in New York the behavior of "vulgar, noisy Jews," was seen in Tel Aviv as evidence of the city's vibrant spontaneity: "The virtue of Tel Aviv is that Jews can be noisy there without hesitation."[37] Even the dogs speak Hebrew: "A dog barked at me in guttural Ashkenazic Hebrew."[38] In fact, only 60 percent of the city's residents spoke Hebrew in 1928, a situation that was compounded by the ongoing influx of immigrants, most of whom arrived with little or no knowledge of Hebrew. A group of gymnasium students calling themselves the Hebrew Defense Brigade organized protests, at times violent, against the use of "foreign" languages in the street: "the 'Brigade' not only called on citizens to speak Hebrew everywhere, but also to remind those speaking in other languages, and even to report bus drivers who didn't address their passengers in Hebrew."[39] The aggressive tenor of the brigade's activities is perhaps indicative of the truly polyglot nature of Tel Aviv's streets. A 1939 account comments on the cultural hybridity arising from this linguistic amalgam: "The Jew in Tel Aviv is mix of Dr. Jekyll and Mr. Hyde, not from a psychological perspective, but from a cultural-national perspective. I said a mix of two but what I really should have said is: a mix of a number of national-cultural images, as many as the languages that penetrate the space of Tel Aviv's streets."[40] This mix of languages betokens Tel Aviv's international cosmopolitan character, as well as its Jewishness, Jewish culture having historically been polylingual. Ironically, Tel Aviv cannot be called a "Hebrew" city, but rather the only "100 percent Jewish city in the world," precisely because so many different languages are spoken there.[41] Natan Alterman's "Tel Aviv Serenade" celebrates his bond to the city in explicitly multilingual terms, embedding Yiddish, English, Russian, German, and Arabic in a lilting ballad form:

You—I got tangled up good with you,
there were no others . . .

like a sail boat to an anchor
I'm tied to you, "tsu dir," "to you" . . .

. . .

I've grown accustomed to escaping
your caresses all the poorer . . .
for all I've received from you—
thank you, "spasiba," "dankeschön."

According to your balalaike tongue,
understand all I bring—
as you like it, "as you like it,"
"alakeyfak," "vi du vilst."[42]

Though no law ever penalized the public use of languages other than Hebrew, theaters presenting plays in other languages were forced to pay an additional tax. The animosity toward other languages found a special target in Yiddish. While the city's cultural, economic, and social life could tolerate the presence of German newspapers, English business correspondence, and French literature, scandal was the word when it came to the screening of the Yiddish film *Di Yiddishe Mame* in 1930. After pro-Hebrew protests marred the first screening, the police were called in and theater owners eventually agreed to show the film without the Yiddish dialogue and singing.[43] This prejudice is also evidenced in official correspondence of the Municipality, which received and responded to letters in Russian, German, French, English, Romanian, and Arabic, often translated as part of official documents. However, records show that a letter from Mr. Lev Rabinovitz of Rishon LeTsion was returned by Dizengoff bearing the following directive: "We herewith return the letter of 4 November written in Yiddish. Please address us in our language ( נא לפנות אלינו בשפתנו )."[44]

Despite official efforts, Yiddish remained a marker of the public sphere's familiarity and intimacy, a fact that is reported, not surprisingly, with more regularity in Yiddish texts about the city. For instance, a text by the Polish-Yiddish writer Der Tunkeler (The Dark One) from 1932 comments on the preponderance of Yiddish in the streets of Tel Aviv. In contrast to his native Poland, the fact that one can speak Yiddish with public officials such as the postman makes even tourists feel at home:

"There are those few who will ask the first question in Hebrew, official, dutifully, simply out of obligation, but they quickly begin to speak Yiddish, and very skillfully."[45] Der Tunkeler is surprised to encounter a policeman who not only recognizes and greets him, but also confesses that when bored around the station, he and the other policemen often read his work.[46]

Der Tunkeler amplifies his perception of the city's monolithic character with the following observation: "In Tel Aviv, even the *shabbes-goy* is a Jew."[47] Made in 1932, this remark could seem at odds with Tel Aviv's evolving image as a site of pantheistic indulgence. That is, beyond the writer's more obvious intention to describe, in the most hyperbolic terms possible, the city's all-encompassing Jewishness, why is there even a need for something like a shabbes-goy—a staple of Jewish religious life—in a city whose major observance of the Sabbath was reputed to be regular beach attendance? Clearly the situation was more complicated than it appeared. On the one hand, no synagogue was included in Achusat Bayit's initial plan; the community's religious needs, like its commercial life, were to be satisfied in Jaffa. (The only building providing public services included in the neighborhood's original plan was the Herzliya Gymnasium, a Hebrew high school established in Jaffa in 1905, devoted to the "secular" study of sciences and the arts.) On the other hand, the modern aspirations of the city's early residents did not always and necessarily mean an aversion to traditional Jewish customs or religious practices. As we saw in Chapter 3, certain normative prohibitions within Jewish law had an impact on the city's evolving public sphere. As Tel Aviv expanded through the addition of both newly founded and established neighborhoods, the regulation of public religious observance became the subject of intense debate. In 1923, negotiations to annex older neighborhoods, including Neve Tsedek, Achva, and Ohel Moshe—all with more traditional populations—nearly collapsed over the city's refusal to mandate public observance of the Sabbath. A compromise was reached in which Saturday was declared the city's official day of rest, on which businesses were to close.[48]

A sampling of documents from the Tel Aviv Municipal Archives reveals some of the issues that shaped ongoing discussion of religious observance in Tel Aviv's public sphere. For instance, an official from a Zionist organization in Poland wished to alert city leaders to the presence of a bad influence: a former resident of his town currently living in Tel Aviv had reported that "most of the city's inhabitants (ninety per cent) eat non-kosher meat and travel and smoke cigarettes in public on the Sabbath. Rabbis do not require a wedding ceremony, which results in most people living with their women not according to the Jewish law, but only on the basis of free love."[49] At the same time, a collection of shop owners from Allenby Street and the Yemenite Quarter complained about a city ordinance requiring them to close their shops at three o'clock on Fridays. Given that most their clientele were workers who themselves did not finish working until that time or later, business suffered.[50] The watering of gardens was also discouraged on the Sabbath and the Town Committee declared that letters would be sent "to all residents requesting again that they not water their gardens on the Sabbath. All those who do water their gardens on the Sabbath will pay a fine the first time [they are caught], and the second time their water will be turned off."[51] These documents evidence, first and foremost, the ordinary workings of a nascent municipality, coping with various pressure groups and grappling with the city's economic and geographic limitations. However, the parameters of an additional ideological dimension may also be deduced, in which the public sphere may—for the first time—be legislated in ostensibly Jewish terms. How would formerly private observances, or even rituals that were articulated by the Jewish community as a whole, find expression in a politically autonomous public sphere? As in all things Tel Avivian, recent diasporic experience provided a key comparative yardstick. Der Tunkeler's observation is therefore telling not only because it suggests the presence of religious observation within an avowedly secular, official mandate. His notion of a Jewish shabbes-goy imports from the Diaspora a sociological structure in which public expression of Jewishness is predicated on difference—the presence of the non-Jew, even in a "100 percent Jewish city." Reporting in *Der Haynt* in the 1920s about his visit to Tel Aviv, Shalom Asch even expressed an ironic nostalgia for the sound "of the name *zhid*. The name had become so dear to me, I was afraid that it would be erased from my vocabulary."[52]

The importance of ethnic and religious difference is also evident, though perhaps less obviously so, in what were the most vibrant and spectacular public displays of a new Jewish urban culture in Tel Aviv: the annual Purim processions and balls. Begun before World War I, these parades were an expression of national and municipal pride—a Jewish tradition transformed into a national Hebrew holiday that was also a celebration of the city itself. Initially limited to costumed children from different schools, after the war the processions—known as *adloyada*—took on a more citywide format, with various groups contributing thematic floats and organizing other activities (Figure 4.10).[53] Important components in Tel Aviv's developing culture were treated within a general atmosphere of spontaneous merry-making: "We are brothers, we are Hebrews. . . . As the procession approaches Achusat-Bayit, people stream toward it, joining up from all sides and from every alleyway."[54] The floats and costumes often addressed contemporary themes connected to industry and agriculture, or significant political events—for example, the establishment of the British mandate after the war, and the Arab-Jewish disturbances of 1929 and other domestic conflicts.[55] Photographs and newsreels from the period show that the processions, sponsored by the Municipality with contributions of local businesses, were massively attended public events; many of the increasingly elaborate evening balls (*neshafim*), however, were private affairs for ticket holders only, and came under fire from workers' groups for their "decadent" resemblance to European carnivals and their "frivolous" waste of money. Purim celebrations thus reflected the growing economic and social diversity of the city's population—as it expanded from a primarily upper- and middle-class suburb to include workers and other people of limited resources—and the energies these groups expended in securing representation within the city's public sphere. Just as the observers above noted the 100 percent Jewish nature of the city, the Purim processions were, at bottom, an expression of Jewish control over public space on the part of newly established Jewish authorities, flexing their muscles vis-à-vis first Ottoman, and later British, authorities. The

Fig. 4.10 Purim procession (*adloyada*) (1933), Ya'akov Benor-Kalter. Silver Print Collection, Ein Hod.

establishment of these citywide festivities was an attempt to create the semblance of an officially sanctioned public sphere. The stylistic influence of public European carnivals on festivities in Tel Aviv has been noted by the curator Batia Carmiel in her detailed study of Purim celebrations in the city.[56] The following pages explore how the social and political tensions that characterized the European carnival also made themselves felt in the newly developing, and increasingly contested, public spaces of Tel Aviv.

In Europe, the carnivalesque spirit of fairs and parades was often accompanied by violence against the Jewish population, who were excluded from participating by virtue of their dietary restrictions. The topsy-turvy world of the European carnival was a site where subversive tensions were allowed fuller expression than usual; the carnival was a kind of necessary "release valve" during which potentially dangerous sentiments regarding the authorities were vented, often resulting in both random and organized violence against religious or ethnic minorities within the general population.[57] The Jew, a potent and ambivalent symbol of "otherness" within Christian Europe, played a special role in the carnival hierarchy—at once a destabilizing force to be curtailed and controlled, and an ever present and necessary element of the local economy.[58]

At the same time, Purim—a Jewish kind of carnival—had its own "checkered history": as social historian Elliot Horowitz has convincingly argued, "annually venting their hatred of Christianity and its most potent symbols might have been, however far back in the distant past, one of the Jews' principal Purim joys."[59] The festival's "more violent anti-Christian undertones" were often the motivating force behind apologetic calls for reform (even banishment) of the holiday among Jewish enlighteners.[60] Celebrations of Purim in Eastern Europe, including the Purim *shpil*—a dramatic presentation based on the biblical Book of Esther—were also an occasion for Jews to dress up like their neighbors, and even to manifest the "saber-rattling" swagger and bravado of Cossacks, a form of mimicry that was really a way of enunciating difference. Unlike the carnival, therefore, "the laughter of Purim [targeted] . . . precisely that alien culture whose customs the celebrant adopts in his feasting and drinking."[61]

This paradoxical web of memories concerning diasporic Purim celebrations and the broader context of the carnivalesque infused observance of the festival in Tel Aviv. Diaspora-flavored costumes were noticeably absent, though, and inspiration was more commonly drawn from local habits of dress, including the *kefiya* (headscarf) and long-sleeved cotton robes.[62] Thus the whole idea of carnival—of a public parade of Jews dressed like other people—in a space characterized as "100 percent Jewish," carried with it a multiple charge: the freedom to parade as Jews, and the freedom to parade as "not Jews." Both of these sensibilities are hallmarks, as we have seen above, of the "intimacy" of Tel Aviv's streets, where Jews paradoxically felt most at home by forgetting their Jewishness, a lack of self-consciousness that is a defining trait of nativeness.

Just as the Jews in Europe were nonparticipants in but necessary elements of the carnivalesque, non-Jewish spectators played a special role in this delicate and complex articulation of Jewishness in Tel Aviv's public realm. Newspapers related the presence of numerous Arabs at the Purim processions: "It was nice to see hundreds of Arabs with their tarbushes and women covered with veils come to see our 'Holiday of Clowns'" and "many Arabs from Jaffa and from other towns in Eretzyisrael as well as from neighboring lands were in the audience and had come to see the noisy Jewish holiday."[63] A visitor writing in Yiddish made special note of the city's non-Jewish neighbors observing the spectacle:

> Everything that lives and breathes in Tel Aviv is out on the street: moreover, everything that lives and breathes in Jaffa, the entire Arab populace, has come to see the holiday. Every stairway, every balcony was seated with their black-veiled women, and the men with the red fezzes mingle among the Tel Avivians, selling vegetables, sweets, lemonade. . . . They walked among the Tel Avivians, but not with the Tel Avivians.[64]

Another Yiddish text remarks on the presence of both Arabs as well as other "guests":

> And in the corner of the street, stand girls from the German colony Sharona, near Jaffa. The Germans do not have much to do with the Jews, though Tel Aviv has expanded around the wealthy colony of Germans in a wide bow. The elders, the solid German peasants, have not come, but the girls have come to see the Jewish carnival. They proceed along the side, with shocked and frightened eyes, daughters of the North, who have turned up in the land of Christ. They were born here and their eyes have never seen a carnival, but their old grandfathers have told them, from their old home in Turingen, about the old customs, what the Jews practice here as well.[65]

It is perhaps not surprising that Yiddish writers were more likely to note the presence of these non-Jewish spectators who, though numerically insignificant, provided an important audience for the becostumed Jewish revelers, many of whom carried the relatively fresh experience of exclusion from similar European public spectacles, and the threat of anti-Semitism this exclusion often precipitated.[66] Their observations belie the notion that Tel Aviv's "Jewish comfort factor" was maintained by the fact that "here we can look at ourselves in our homes, without a foreign observing eye (*blee ayin tsofia zara*)."[67] Perversely, the presence of a "foreign observing eye" reinforces and perhaps even authenticates the Jewish nature of the festivities. The public sphere, no matter how or by whom, is legislated, is always predicated on both looking/seeing as well this crucial display of difference, especially in a realm conceived as "100 percent Jewish." Thus Purim festivities had a multivalent meaning: as Horowitz notes, in Europe "a verifiable 'internal' Jewish meaning would not exclude an additional (hostile) message directed toward the Christian environment."[68] Purim celebrations in Tel Aviv were refashioned by a newly ascendant Jewish elite with pretensions to municipal, and national, sovereignty; the "violent anti-Christian undertones" that once characterized festival observance were replaced by pointed critiques of British policies, including the White Paper's restriction of Jewish immigration in 1930.

In addition to these more explicit public expressions of Jewishness, both religiously and secularly conceived, certain ordinary elements of the city's appearance were associated with Tel Aviv's distinctiveness as a Jewish city, especially in contrast with generally prevailing perceptions of Jaffa.[69] Foremost among these concerns was the city's sanitary conditions. Cleanliness was also related to a division between public and private domains, and to "an anxiety about the strength of boundaries between the two, about making the imagined space of 'the home' impervious to the *stink* of the unwashed and so to the contamination of their diseases."[70] In the case of Tel Aviv, this apprehension was expressly connected to life in Jaffa, and then "eliminated" by the building of Achusat Bayit. In this respect, Tel Aviv resembled other European-founded suburbs adjacent to already existing cities in the

JAFFA, KING GEORG'S AVENUE.                         ‫יפו, רחוב המלך ג'ורג'.‬

*Fig. 4.11* The road from Tel Aviv to Jaffa. King George Boulevard, 1920s. Originally named Jamal Pasha Boulevard (1915), it is now known as Jerusalem Boulevard. Silver Print Collection, Ein Hod.

Middle East. The desire for improved living conditions comparable to
European standards of urban life led to the establishment of many new
suburbs and towns alongside Middle Eastern ports.[71] The need for a
new neighborhood was particularly keenly felt by Jaffa's Jews in the
wake of increased immigration and a subsequent housing shortage.
However, Achusat Bayit was distinguished from the start not by its
geographical remove from Jaffa—another common characteristic of
European suburban settlement in the region—but by the exclusively
Jewish nature of its population and the Zionist rationale ultimately un-
dergirding its establishment and growth (Figure 4.11).[72] The suburb's
ostensibly unique features were all tied, somewhat arbitrarily, to its
Jewishness—as if the modernist imperative to "make it new" carried a
subtext of "make it Jewish."

Sanitation reports from August 1921, just months after Tel Aviv was
granted independent municipal responsibilities, show that most of the
local markets and surrounding residential streets suffered from a lack of

proper drainage in both private yards and commercial spaces, and garbage often lay piled up in the streets.[73] These conditions were further exacerbated by the establishment of "tent neighborhoods" in the city from 1921 to 1925, to accommodate new immigrants and refugees from Jewish neighborhoods in Jaffa, who had left after the May Day disturbances in 1921.[74] Poor sanitary conditions even served in this period as a pretext for the incorporation of some quarters into the city proper.[75] Concerning the tent neighborhoods, we find a report from an Arab doctor from Jaffa to the British authorities: "I wish to point out a paradox and this is the present mind of the Tel Aviv Community with regard to sanitary problems, the great majority come from Europe and demand ideal sanitation yet [there] remains a minority generally poor or destitute who live . . . to the detriment of the Community at large."[76]

Kitchens and bathrooms of private homes were also subject to city inspection. In anticipation of the 1925 visit of Balfour, Mayor Dizengoff set up a committee of engineers, policemen, and sanitation department officials to visit private homes, report on their internal and external condition, and make suggestions for improvement. Follow-up visits would ensure that residents had implemented the necessary changes.[77] The fact that private homes were seen as a space that could be regulated or monitored by the city adds yet another dimension to the idea of Tel Aviv as a place where "there is no boundary between home and street, neither architecturally nor psychologically speaking."[78] Documents in the Municipal Archives reveal an ongoing concern with the appearance of houses and their surrounding yards. Laws obligating homeowners to plant trees in front of their homes were passed, and property owners also bore partial financial responsibility for maintenance of the land immediately surrounding their homes. According to Druyanov, many building regulations were not closely followed by new residents who came from small towns in Europe, where they were either unaware or dismissive of local building ordinances.[79] However, an indication of the proprietary feeling of some early homeowners in Tel Aviv is found in an internal police report from 1921, in which a citizen lodged a complaint against then-mayor Dizengoff for violating public garden laws by riding his horse in a prohibited area.[80]

This attention to and regulation of Tel Aviv's public sphere should be seen not only within the context of building a city whose material conditions were to approximate the European homelands of the residents. A preoccupation with the public sphere (and also, as we have seen, the intimate tie between public and private domains) are crucially bound to abiding notions of Jewishness and space and to doubts regarding the ability of Jews to design an aesthetically pleasing cityscape. Tel Aviv's ugliness was generally accepted and commented upon by visitors and residents alike. The artist Ludwig Lewisohn's backhanded compliment that he was "less offended by the ugliness of the houses in Tel Aviv than I was pleased at the names of the streets which are called after poets," due to the predisposition of the Jews as "a people given to the arts of time rather than those in space," was typical of initial impressions of the city.[81] Lewisohn's comments appeared in the *Menorah Journal*, an English-language American periodical devoted to the development and expression of a "nonsectarian and academic humanist spirit."[82] Other writers in the journal also praised the city's modernity in the 1920s,[83] though it was viewed as spatially at odds with the surrounding landscape:

> Tel Aviv, for all the energy of its spirit and cleanliness of its life and streets, is an architectural monstrosity. With its insouciance, its speed, and its speculation, it can be forgiven; but nevertheless, the simplest of the newer Arab stone houses, such as are to be found near the Bezalel Academy in Jerusalem, would blush deeper than its native red to find itself on Herzl Street, Tel Aviv.[84]

This ugliness was seen not as the result of poor planning or lack of funds but as connected to something more profound, a kind of Jewish spatial deficiency:

> This poverty, one might better admit absence, of architectural distinction, if probed to its source, will reveal for us the whole question of Jewish culture and its content. . . . Behind [the Jewish village], for two thousand years, lies Jewish *inexperience* in building, molding and stabilizing, in giving concrete expression to a social life. For two thousand years the Jews have been literary, liturgical ghosts. They have come to Palestine with their cultural treasury emptied. The argument

for Zionism does not lie in showing that we are a people of gifted individuals, in pointing out our scientists, lawyers, and poets. It lies in Rishon Le-Zion and Petach-Tikvah, which in their sprawling anarchy and ugliness point out how poor we are.[85]

The houses in Tel-Aviv are not beautiful. Some of them are cheap and pretentious and seem to have been built in imitation of the worst period of American domestic architecture. . . . But people from Lodz or Brownsville did not, of course, come here with a new Jewish-Palestinian architecture ready in their minds.[86]

The poet Ch. N. Bialik also commented on Tel Aviv's general ugliness and poor planning and offered suggestions for improvement in his 1932 article "What Should Be Done for the Betterment of Tel Aviv?"[87] While recognizing the limited vision and resources of the city's founders, he believed their mistakes should be corrected for the sake of future residents. In addition to his concern with improving the seafront, he was especially troubled by the city's lack of public green spaces, not only for residents, especially children, but also for visitors from abroad: "The first impression a city makes comes from its degree of green space. There is also a large hygienic advantage to purifying the air." Not surprisingly, Bialik mentions the example of Odessa, whose reputation for beauty stemmed from its wide boulevards and shady trees. He maintains that though thus far Tel Aviv's homes have been built according to individual whims, the result being a hodgepodge of styles, architects should take into account the appearance and style of neighboring buildings, and design accordingly, so that "the general harmony of the street is not spoiled." Again, the norm may be found in the "proper cities" of Europe, and in the enforcement of construction codes, so that strips of land surrounding private homes were preserved for the planting of greenery.

Bialik's article was published just before the building boom of the mid-1930s, a period that in retrospect has been viewed as spanning the single most comprehensive attempt to give the city a unique spatial character. This period also gave rise to a more explicit articulation of the belief that urban space should reflect a new national ethos, and then produce citizens in that spirit.[88] Given that there was little indigenous idea of Jewish space to rely upon, the question as to what form this urban sphere would take remained both open and contentious.

### Ben-Gurion's Kitchen

Tel Aviv found a sort of solution—or at the very least a response—to early criticism of the city's appearance in the International Style, whose clean, functional lines became the city's most well-known physical aspect and led to its moniker, the White City.[89] We begin our discussion of this important period in the city's development with another image of a domestic interior: Figure 4.12 is a far cry from Soskin's "Living Room of Tel Aviv Home," circa 1910. This typical kitchen from the 1930s happens to be in David Ben-Gurion's apartment. Ben-Gurion, Israel's first prime minister, was a centrist-socialist ideologue whose influence on the establishment, institutions, and very fabric of Israeli

*Fig. 4.12* Ben-Gurion's kitchen. Ben-Gurion House Museum. Photo by author.

society remains indelible to this day. His name can be found on streets in every Israeli town, as well as the country's main international airport, and his face and famous shock of white hair grace the fifty-shekel note. His home in Tel Aviv now houses a small museum devoted to his life and work, and much of the apartment's original decor and furnishings—including a large library and study—remain as they were when he lived there. What immediately impresses the viewer of this photograph is that there does not seem to be much to say about this kitchen: its simplicity and relatively austere decor are almost a reproach to any overt description or theorizing. The horizontal window band, a characteristic element of the city's International Style core, is more remarkable for the exacting whiteness of the harsh sunlight barely held back by the short gauze curtain; the Mediterranean coral blue of the cabinets and molding is a color traditionally found in Islamic architecture, where it was believed to provide protection against danger; the simple gas range with three burners typifies the spartan furnishings of many new homes in the city in the 1930s and 1940s; the line of the marble countertop is broken only by a single brown tube snaking down to an external gas connection; the matching series of small, screened circular holes punched toward the bottom of each cabinet is perhaps the kitchen's only obvious ornament; in a row, they are reminiscent of a ship's portholes, another characteristic element of Bauhaus design, but they were also meant to combat the effects of Tel Aviv's notorious humidity on food supplies; the slightly scruffy, faded white tiles are still found in many of the city's older apartments. The prime minister's kitchen contains a calm, yet interrupted, domesticity. At any moment, someone will come in to light a fire, boil water, and prepare some tea. It is both the prime minister's kitchen, and the kitchen of a pair of Polish immigrants, trying to build a new life in the Middle East.

Obviously there is an enormous amount to say about this image, and about Ben Gurion's kitchen, particularly in a social climate that routinely conflated the domestic sphere with the national project. The fact that the room seems to resist interpretation does not absolve or release us from the burden of explaining it. But the room exemplifies the difficulty of talking about the relation of public and private space in a time and place where external events and the facts of landscape had a way of seeping in through even the thickest of curtains. In this image, the local elements of landscape do battle, as it were, with the imposed, imported lines of the Bauhaus; the prime minister's kitchen is a study in determined, plotted domesticity, an attempt to create a home. The kitchen—a far cry from the plush European furnishings of the 1910 image—reflects the asceticism of the pioneer spirit that had come to inform certain sectors of early Tel Aviv, and a certain "anonymity of spirit" that suited the absorption of newcomers by a population who were themselves largely immigrants.[90] If we compare this photograph of the most domestic of interior spaces—the kitchen or "hearth"—to Soskin's interior-qua-portrait, we notice not only the difference, crudely put, between bourgeois luxury and socialist spartanism; Ben-Gurion's kitchen seems more an extension of the public sphere and of the nascent national culture that valued self-sacrifice and a sense of collective purpose.

The International Style eventually dominated Tel Aviv planning and architecture. Its modernist credo seemed an ideal form of physical expression for the newly developing metropolis. Whereas in Europe this erasure of historical references resulted in a "disciplined city of pure form that displaced memory and suppressed the tug of the fantastic," in Tel Aviv the result was the discarding of the eclectic style of the 1920s, with its intentional mix of East and West, local and European.[91] Just as the city seemed to be formulating an integrated building style of its own, reality—the demand for rapid construction—intervened; necessity, in this case, sounded the death knell for invention.

Modernist architecture viewed the landscape as a series of neutral functions to be approached and resolved through its own formal solutions; the focus on climate, for example, served to efface those problematic aspects of the land that were more difficult to assimilate to Zionist discourse—the local population, their customs, culture, and architectural tradition. This rational approach to design and construction represented a kind of internationalizing or "de-localizing" of the landscape, a way of conceptualizing space as neither distinctly Mediterranean nor Eastern, but as simply a set of light and wind conditions. The rise of the International Style, and the eventual rejection of "Oriental" or local architectural inspiration, should therefore be seen against the background of increasing Arab-Jewish political tensions after 1929.[92] Furthermore, "adhering to formal types of high architecture, rather than to a tangible tradition, liberated the Jewish builder from the necessity to comply with any immediate architectural history."[93] The International Style as practiced by Jewish architects in Palestine was an ideal solution for a nation of immigrants with no real architectural tradition.

The subjugation of form to function seemed more than just a perfect fit for Zionism's progressive narrative of redemption; it can also be seen as a kind of oddly appropriate form of Jewish abstraction. In a sense, it was as if Jewish ethics had finally found in the specifics of the International Style a physical form that would not offend the normative, ingrained aversion to aesthetics. I am not suggesting that this is the reason, or even the primary meaning, of Tel Aviv's embrace of what is known in Israeli circles as simply "the Bauhaus"; however, the International Style is now understood by architectural historians as a perfect match for the Zionist project (Figure 4.13), with its strong desire to rationalize and control the Mediterranean landscape. The

*Fig. 4.13 Tel Aviv Expands* (1934), Ya'akov Benor-Kalter. Silver Print Collection, Ein Hod.

austerity of design was an ideal expression of the young, engagé pioneer society. Its clean and simple lines came to be seen as a defining trait of future Tel Avivians—light, untouched by the past, forward-looking, functional. Zionism's adoption of the tenets of the modernist movement resulted in a distinctive interpretation of the International Style. Tel Aviv today boasts the world's highest urban concentration of original Bauhaus constructions, a feature that recently earned it acknowledgment by UNESCO as a World Heritage Site.

As we have seen, the principles of modern urban planning had earlier impressed themselves upon Tel Aviv through the garden city ideal promulgated by Patrick Geddes. The influential Scottish planner was commissioned in 1925 by Tel Aviv's emerging Municipality to design a plan of the city's expanding northern neighborhoods.[94] Traces of the garden city plan are still observable in the city in the patches of green park in otherwise densely built residential areas. The appeal of the Geddes plan quickly faded, however, within the social and economic constraints of the day; urban idealism and green public spaces would eventually have little place in Tel Aviv's real estate market, which was driven by enormous housing demands, as well as a desire for high investor returns.[95]

The decisive moment came in the early 1930s, especially after the rise of the National Socialist Party in 1933, which precipitated a large German immigration; among these immigrants were a considerable number of engineers and architects and, as mentioned above, photographers, who recorded their achievements.[96] Clustered around Arieh Sharon and Ze'ev Rechter and known as the *Chug* or "the Group," these architects rejected the eclectic use of borrowed ornament, just as painters in the Tel Aviv school rejected the Bezalel school's version of a local Jewish style. Capitalizing on the increasing demand for quickly built, cheap housing, they developed a highly functionalist style that sought to allow a decent standard of living to all segments of the population.

Many of these architects arrived in Palestine after having studied and worked in Paris, Berlin, and Belgium, where they were strongly influenced by the ideas of Mies van der Rohe, Le Corbusier, and Walter Gropius. They perhaps faced the ostensibly empty dunes with an expression of absolute astonishment, glee, and fear over their good fortune. The idea that architecture and design could actually engineer a new society must have seemed a tantalizingly real possibility. Their journal, *Ha-binyan ba-mizrakh ha-karov* (Construction in the Middle East), initially contained a pluralistic manifesto published in English, Hebrew, and Arabic.[97] Its stated intention was to provide a forum for professional discussion, given the enormous amount of new residential, commercial, and industrial construction. Soon, however, following an editorial split, the journal changed its name to simply *Ha-binyan* (Construction), in a pointed nod to the ostensibly universal nature of their project, now stripped of any local or regional connotation.[98] *Ha-binyan* is filled with articles on interior design and public space in Tel Aviv, detailing the best orientation for the city's apartments, or calling for "more trees for the Hebrew city."[99] A 1935 illustration details their view of the current state of things in Tel Aviv due to poor planning, and "what could have been done."[100] (See Figure 4.14.) An article describes why Arab architecture could not serve as an example for the "Jewish apartment," and distinguishes between "Arab" and "Jewish" space, the former being both more private, with rooms and a central courtyard, and gendered, with separate spaces for men and women; "Jewish" space, on the other hand, resembled more the European street, with its democratic distribution of rooms and its face turned toward the public. The Jewish architect, moreover, had "no original tradition or past of authentic Jewish construction in the Land of Israel. The Jewish builder brings education and tendencies familiar from the lands of his exile."[101] This disparity between Arab and Jewish architecture is, of course, better understood as the difference between traditional and modern dwellings, especially given the introduction of modernist techniques of planning and construction in Jaffa before 1948.[102] The conflation of "Jewish" with "modern," and of "Arab" with "traditional," is typical of early discourse regarding Tel Aviv's urban distinctiveness. This essentially orientalist paradigm clustered together the terms "Jewish/modern/European" and opposed them to "Arab/primitive/Eastern" without attending to the differences inhering between and among them. For example, as evidenced in the debates surrounding public observance of the Sabbath, many of the

*Fig. 4.14* "What Could Have Been," from the architectural journal *Ha-binyan* (Construction), 1935. Courtesy of Jewish National and University Library, Jerusalem.

older Jewish neighborhoods were relatively traditional. Furthermore, Arab neighborhoods in Jaffa such as Manshiya underwent a partial gentrification contemporaneous to that of Tel Aviv (see Chapter 5).

During the 1930s and 1940s, architects associated with the Chug were the favorites of the Tel Aviv elite; they designed and built about 4,000 new residential buildings, 850 in 1935 alone. Dizengoff Square was constructed in that same year by Genia Auerbach and became a focal point of pedestrian traffic and commercial activity. Engel House (Figure 4.15), located on Rothschild Boulevard, and designed by Ze'ev Rechter, was the city's first structure on columns or *pilotis*; it took Rechter two years to get permission to build it. The area created by this floor of columns was a kind of intermediary space between the public

*Fig. 4.15* Engel House, 1930s. Ze'ev Rechter, architect. Kalter Collection.
Courtesy of Board of Engineers and Architects in Israel and Tel Aviv Museum
of Art.

life of the street and the private homes of the residents. Though partial
construction on the ground floor eventually became more common,
the columns, and the relation they determined between street and
building, became a defining mark of Tel Aviv's central neighborhoods.
The public rooftop was designed for communal functions such as par-
ties and social gatherings, as well as the daily tasks of doing the laundry or simply escaping the heat.

The *me'onot ovdim* (workers' dwellings) are one of the city's more
focused attempts to implement a collective or communal ideal in the
construction of residential areas (Figure 4.16). These small neighborhoods designed by Arieh Sharon were built in accordance with clear
planning principles, taking into account domestic needs and climatic
conditions, for example the arrangement of rooms to take advantage of
the sea breeze and to avoid the harshness of the late afternoon sun
(Figure 4.17).[103] The workers' dwellings were yet another experiment

*Fig. 4.16* Hod Apartments (workers' cooperative dwellings). Arieh Sharon, architect. Kalter Collection. Courtesy of Board of Engineers and Architects in Israel and Tel Aviv Museum of Art.

in creating space that would reflect a new kind of Jew. Ironically, these clusters of once modest workers' housing have become some of the most desirable and expensive real estate in Tel Aviv, because of their central location, sound construction, and private interior common yards.

Though many of these buildings' typifying traits have been altered or muted, they have left their mark on the city to this day (Figures 4.18, 4.19). The typical Tel Avivian downtown street is still characterized by buildings that look more or less like the street in Figure 4.19. Most are built in part or entirely on pilotis, and have gardened spaces beneath; this multilevel effect, together with the enormous variety of open and semi-enclosed balconies, located at different points along the building's facade, creates a free-flowing sense of movement between the buildings and the street. An effective cooling device, the balcony was intended for year-round use—for social gatherings and ordinary domestic chores: "The balcony is the only cool place in the evening hours when the family comes home from work, and it serves as a place for leisure activities during the evening hours in the summer."[104] Both a public stage to be viewed from the street, as well as a

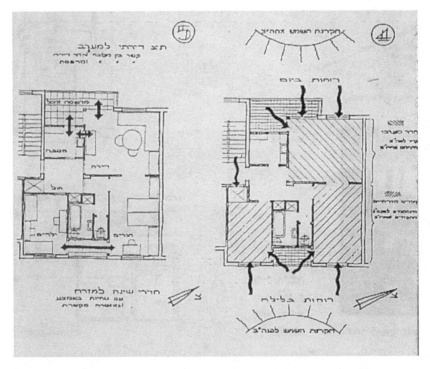

*Fig. 4.17* Sketch by Arieh Sharon showing ideal apartment design for the Middle Eastern climate. *Ha-binyan* (Construction), 1937. Courtesy of Jewish National and University Library, Jerusalem.

semi-sheltered extension of the home, the balcony has become the most enduring physical symbol of Tel Aviv's early dreams of modernity and normalcy. A staple of local urban legend and anecdote, and a central feature of Tel Aviv's image, especially in popular song, the balcony represented a way of thinking about a new relation to space, one where public and private spheres were more interdependent. Tel Aviv poetry of the 1970s featured the balcony as a nostalgic token of a time when the city seemed to possess a more coherent sense of community.[105] The gradual closing of the balconies in many Tel Aviv apartments, through the installation of plastic shutters, can be seen as a symbol of the increasing privatization of Israeli society.[106] The original design had left the area between and behind buildings vulnerable to neglect;

*Fig. 4.18* Mirenborg House, 1935. Pinchas Hit, architect. Kalter Collection. Courtesy of Board of Engineers and Architects in Israel and Tel Aviv Museum of Art.

as the city's population soared, "open space, so precious in the urban situation . . . [was] seen as a mode of separation between the buildings, rather than as useful territory."[107] The "balcony-facing-balcony" effect that had once typified the city was reduced to what one architect has called "plastic slats facing plastic slats."[108] The shutting in of the balconies, usually in order to gain an extra room, also signaled a changed relation to the local landscape (Figure 4.20). A critique from the 1960s described the deleterious consequences of this change:

> The balconies are open, so that it will be open.
> They're closed by plastic, so it will be closed.
> The plastic is gray, so it won't be colorful. . . .
> They bring in air-conditioning, so it won't be hot. . . .
> While the city is built on the shoreline, they built it three kilometers away from the beach, so it wouldn't rust. . . .

*Fig. 4.19* Mirenborg House, 2001. Photo by author.

*Fig. 4.20* Plastic slats: "So they won't say we live in the Mediterranean." Photo by author.

They didn't build interior courtyards, so that everyone could look undisturbed upon our neighbors, who look back at us undisturbed. And so they won't say that we live in the Mediterranean.[109]

If in Reuven's *View from the Balcony* the balcony symbolized a liminal space in which culture partook of both the private and public realms, the closing of the balcony represents not only a privatization of culture, but the exhaustion of an idealized vision of the local landscape as a source of inspiration and materials.

## The Flâneuse of Ben Yehudah Street

> The street becomes a dwelling for the flâneur; he is as much at home among the facades of the houses as a citizen is in his four walls.
> —Walter Benjamin, "The Flâneur"

> To walk is to lack a site.
> —Michel de Certeau, "Walking in the City"

Moving from interiors, through the space of balcony and the public face of the city's architecture, we arrive at the most quotidian and ostensibly democratic of public spaces: the street. Chapter 3 was concerned with delineating the representational power of Rothschild Boulevard, whose iconic presence has shaped Tel Aviv's historical consciousness. Here we begin with a series of images of daily life in the city's streets as a way of supplementing this discussion of how identity is shaped and reflected in the public sphere.

Flânerie is a key trope in modernist writing about the city and has acquired a privileged status in theoretical explorations of urban life. The figure of the flâneur was first formulated by Charles Baudelaire against the background of mid-nineteenth century Parisian arcades, and expanded by Walter Benjamin in conjunction with a Marxist cultural critique involving the same sites nearly a century later. The arcades were commercial structures characterized by a mix of public and private elements, indoor sites with the allure of public exposure and viewing. Part of the flâneur's ambiguous relation with the crowd and the street, what in fact made him quintessentially modern, had to do with this blurring of boundaries between inside and outside: "The crowd was the veil from behind which the familiar city as phantasmagoria beckoned to the flaneur. In it, the city was now landscape, now a room."[110] Making the city strange, and productively so, was the essential gesture of flânerie, considered all the more an accomplishment when achieved in one's hometown. Clearly this kind of behavior posed a difficulty in Tel Aviv, where hard work was ostensibly being done toward the opposite end.

As we have seen, early writing about the city focused, to the point of obsession, on the intimacy of its streets, and the instant sensations of kinship and "at-homeness" Jewish visitors and residents alike seemed to feel. The public sphere was seen not as the stage for an individual exploration of the alienated self vis-à-vis the crowd, but as both a tool for shaping and a reflection of collective values. Yet we can detect in certain representations of street life in Tel Aviv the beginnings of a counter-strain, images of random encounters that reveal the diversity of the city's population, often caught unwittingly in a kind of dioramic display on the city's increasingly busy commercial thoroughfares.

While Tel Aviv's mercantile aspect may today seem obvious, this was not always the case. The opening of stores was the cause of the city's earliest struggle to define itself beyond its initial parameters as a garden suburb.[111] Though Soskin's photographs were primarily an iconic display of a city rising from the sands, views of Tel Aviv's streets of the 1930s and 1940s demonstrated a breathtaking array of available consumer goods and the beginnings of a leisure class who could enjoy it. Films produced during the 1930s about life in the new city included lingering and multiple shots of stores and cafés as well as banks, fire engines, buses and policemen, all examples of how material qualities of life in Tel Aviv could approximate Europe.[112] Alterman the observer-poet notes that the "entire city looks out from display windows, telling of her good taste, her many hues, her amusements and work."[113] Bialik, typically, compares the streets—unfavorably—to "the small village in Poland, with all the tastelessness of store workers who crowd the window with a mix of all kinds of merchandise without any aesthetic feeling."[114] For all this apparent prosperity, the city also contained an underside. A 1940 article from *Ha-poel ha-tsa'ir* describes the relation between the city's seen and unseen aspects:

> Tel Aviv has already succeeded in resembling the metropolises of the world and has acquired for herself two faces, a face turned outward and a face turned inward. Externally well-pressed; spotless, ornamented shop-windows; varied and numerous kinds of lighting; gay parties and carefree, bourgeois entertainments, exacting cleanliness in certain quarters; elegant fashions, society manners, and wasted money; an emerging "society" of upper classes, an absolute and piously observant snobbism. These are the minimal lines of its external image. But within there exist slums and streets that flood every winter; unemployed and hungry walk next to windows that display all kinds of delicacies; abandoned children hatching within their chests a terrible secret, the secret of revenge; deprived of means they roll from lodging to lodging and sleep between dusk and dawn on the city streets . . . and the city's shining achievement is spread like a thin curtain upon this abyss.[115]

Several photos whose subjects turn away from the camera and toward the public display of goods will help us examine the junction between Tel Aviv's "two faces." In front of a large pair of windows on Nahalat Binyamin Street in 1939, a well-dressed woman with a covered baby carriage pauses (Figure 4.21).[116] She examines the tall, smiling mannequins modeling the latest long-sleeved offerings from Paris, while a barefoot young boy in shorts and a cap stands just outside the shop door, peering in. Two women and a man are caught in profile walking past. The women appear to be looking toward the window, the man looks down at the sidewalk. The mannequins are the only figures who face the camera, even seeming to pose for it. In the glass, we can make out the reflection of the awnings and windows of shops across the street and additional pedestrians walking past those shops. The shop's name—Louvre—appearing banner-like in Roman letters twice and once in Hebrew across the top third of the photograph, serves as a kind of bilingual, floating caption, sharpening the sense of display and exhibition represented in the photograph. A photo of Tel Aviv's main shopping district, Allenby, emphasizes the even lines of the street's facade and awnings (Figure 4.22).[117] The figures on the street represent a wide social panorama: a woman with a parasol, a man with a rucksack, an

*Fig. 4.21* Paris meets Nahalat Binyamin Street, 1939. Central Zionist Archives.

Arab in a turban. In the distance, a religious couple—he is bearded and wears an all black suit and hat, she wears a white long dress with head covering—appears with a child in a stroller. Another photo from the same period shows a poorer, older, slightly dilapidated street (Figure 4.23). The photo's three figures all walk away from the camera— two men in dark clothing, looking like manual laborers, and a woman bundled up in black. Several shops ply their wares outside—wicker baskets and furniture, housewares, used clothing, caps and overalls—and a sign advertises currency exchange. The photo's caption, by the German photographer Zoltan Kluger, reads: "Auch das ist Tel Aviv."[118] The use of explanatory captions was typical of the influence of socialist realism, which strove to create "photographic stories" through the depiction of concrete, realistic scenes.[119] Though Kluger was, according to historian Rona Sela, the premier photographer of the Zionist movement in Palestine, his caption seems expressly directed against the normative images of Tel Aviv's civic achievements and economic prosperity.[120] The photograph moves against the grain of most of

*Fig. 4.22* Flânerie on Allenby Street. Central Zionist Archives.

Kluger's work, which was sponsored by Zionist institutions and generally focused on the positive achievements of the *Yishuv* (the pre-State
Jewish community in Palestine).[121] The image utilizes a "diagonal
composition," which, in Kluger's staged photos, expressed a kind of
"upward momentum."[122] Here, however, the figures seem to walk
wearily into nowhere. And unlike the open skies of his studies of the
"new Hebrew pioneers," the sky in this photo is oppressively cluttered
with electric wires, scraggly branches, and the weather-beaten facades
of cramped homes and businesses.

Our final example is a postcard dated 17 March 1927, a personal snap-
shot of a couple standing outside a shop window in Tel Aviv. The handwritten Hebrew message on the back reads: "We had our picture taken
at the Zvulun shop, together with the display window set up for Purim,
Tel Aviv, 17/3/27" (Figure 4.24). The printed insignia of the store beneath the message suggests the photo was produced as a service and
advertisement by the shop. The card is addressed, also in Hebrew, to
an individual in "Berlin, Germany," with no street address. Perhaps the

*Fig. 4.23* "Auch das ist Tel Aviv" (1930s), Zoltan Kluger. Central Zionist Archives.

card, found among the possessions of the addressee, Leo Winitz, was enclosed with a letter. The window display contains mostly dolls, and reflects a building and a tree across the street. This image was ostensibly produced with a specific, personal audience in mind—the receiver of the card, or family and friends of the couple. The photograph, taken around the time of the Purim holiday, marked either a special stroll of tourists, or just an afternoon out, a typical moment on a typical Tel Aviv street. As we have seen, Purim was a time of especially dramatized articulations of Jewishness in the public sphere. Though the photo does not mark any especially historic moment, it is revealing nonetheless for what it tells us about men and women in the public realm.

The man stands outside the shop, wearing a light-colored suit, arms crossed, leaning against a railing in front of the window, looking perfectly comfortable on the street. The woman leans against the door frame, just inside the darkened doorway; her figure is barely visible in her dark coat. Only the white of her legs where they appear beneath the hemline and the white of her face shines. The couple's position, and the

*Fig. 4.24* Purim greeting, 1927. Central Zionist Archives.

partitioning of space by the door and window frame, suggest two separate, related images—one of him on the street, one of her in the shop. As feminist critics have noted, neither Baudelaire nor Benjamin make room for a female figure of difference, for a woman who is free to move anonymously and unimpeded in the city's public sites.[123] The department store, a semipublic space within which women could circulate, occasioned the flâneur's demise and the flâneuse's birth. All of these photos include women as active, equal consumers in the public domain.

The issues raised by probing the relation between public and private space in Tel Aviv are not confined to the city limits, but spill out and define the city's evolving borders, both real and imagined. As a way of concluding this chapter's discussion of public and private space, and introducing the related notions of center and margins that provide the next chapter's conceptual frame, we turn to two texts by the poet Leah Goldberg: an extended reverie on the street from the 1930s, and a later retrospective poem.

Goldberg's arrival in Palestine is commemorated in the poem "Tel Aviv, 1935." Published in 1961 as part of series describing the city's early years, the poem travels what Goldberg calls "the shortest journey":

> The shortest journey is into the past.
> Remember? The cool sea, two boats embracing,
> children on the hill raising torches . . . [124]

According to Goldberg, the experience of Tel Aviv is inevitably inflected by the collective memories of its inhabitants, including images of cities in which they have lived before:

> "Tel Aviv, 1935"
>
> The masts on the housetops then, were
> like the masts of Columbus' ships, and
> every raven that perched on their tips
> announced a different shore [lit., continent].
>
> And the kit-bags of the travelers
> walked down the streets, and the
> language of an alien land was plunged
> into the *hamsin*-days like the blade of
> a cold knife.
>
> How could the air of the small city
> support so many childhood memories,
> loves that were shed, that were stripped
> somewhere?
>
> Like pictures turning black inside a
> camera, they all turned inside out: pure [white]

> winter nights, rainy summer nights of
> overseas, and shadowy mornings of
> great cities.
>
> And the sound of steps behind your
> back drummed marching songs of
> foreign troops; and—so it seemed—if
> you but turn your head, there's your
> town's church floating in the sea.[125]

Like Avot Yeshurun's poetic palimpsests that overlay the shtetl upon the modest homes and narrow streets of Tel Aviv's Nordia neighborhood (see Chapter 2), Goldberg's "Tel Aviv, 1935" treats the physical location of memory, the manner in which culture and history, in the guise of urban space, geography, and even climate, are read into the Tel Aviv landscape. Memories of Europe function like a constant cloud cover over the city. Within the context of the poem's relatively tight formal composition, the local streets are a surreal and slightly off-tilt mix of different languages and cultures. Given the late date of its composition vis-à-vis the year it commemorates, the poem memorializes not only early Tel Aviv, but memory itself. The poem suggests that the spatial passage from Europe to Palestine, like Zionism's temporal distinction between a diasporic past and the present/future of a new national entity, is both blurry and ongoing.

An article by Goldberg published in *Turim* in February 1939 seems to figure in the background of the poem.[126] Reading "This City," a thoughtful and idiosyncratic response to contemporaneous events in Europe, alongside the poem of over a quarter century later further sharpens the poem's delineation of the city's unique/memory's physical parameters. Both texts depict the city as possessing a consciousness that appears to operate almost independently from its citizens. Both place memory squarely at the center of urban experience: walking down the street means remembering; life in one city is inflected with memories of other cities. The space between the article of 1939 and the poem of 1964 allows us to examine how what initially appear as a set of more personal, individual, and detailed memories are eventually cast—in poetry and in retrospect—as a form of national or collective memory.

Goldberg's article opens by contemplating the simple but surprising fact that Tel Aviv has become her home, perhaps a permanent one: "Now you are left to us, the city, and it seems that we won't ever again have to close our eyes to set out on a new road of wandering and carry you on our eyeballs—as a memory." Memories are, in fact, all that remain of other cities she has known:

> I have loved many cities, in different countries, and now the world has grown narrower; they are now closed to me, those cities, as if the door of someone's apartment had closed, leaving him outside, while the key to the "French lock" remains there, in the apartment, inside. But in memory we have borne much.

Goldberg then proceeds to describe, in loving detail and anecdote, the various courtyards she has known. Each is remembered for its particular "music"—"those melodies and their temperament are already in my blood." The courtyard on the banks of the Chapiur sings "I sharpen knives, scissors"; the "music box" of her Lithuanian childhood sings in Russian; and beneath her window in Berlin, a "cheap violin plays a 'Hungarian tune.'" That courtyard is privileged and protected; it is a place of relative safety. As a child, she played there with her non-Jewish neighbor. One courtyard is remembered for the piles of snow melting in spring, another as "a courtyard in a small city in central Russia, just after the revolution." A courtyard in Berlin is recalled as "a box like any box": "as opposed to this, I keep in my heart the memory of a red courtyard across from my windows in a large city on the banks of the Rhine; it was my alarm clock—every morning the deep bells chimed." The courtyards of Rome are remembered by way of Hofmannsthal for their "scent of wet stone." Goldberg concludes: "All these are mine. I took them from the world for myself, as a souvenir, just as one used to take, in sentimental times, the lock of a loved one's hair." These memories of cities in her past—arguably part of the collective submerged memories of Tel Aviv as a whole—trigger a desire to create memories of her current home, memories being an intangible yet powerful marker of attachment and belonging in a new place. Turning her attention to the present, she asks: "However, my city, this city, has no courtyards. What will I take from her, how will I remember her?"

In response, the second half of the article is a lengthy meditation on "the street": "Perhaps I will remember the street. Not a particularly special street, replete with historic memories, dreams of the past, stones that tell stories. There are no such streets in my city, the youngest of all." As we have seen, the proud stress on Tel Aviv's youth and the lack of the burden of a historical past were a mainstay of discourse about the city in its early decades. What is noteworthy in Goldberg's entrance into this discourse is her emphasis on the public space of the street as a future repository for memory's spatial contours, and her abandonment of the more privatized space of the courtyard. Her attachment to Tel Aviv in this article is shaped largely by the forces of the evolving public sphere.

Goldberg explicitly rejects Jaffa's already rich and evocative landscape—including its own courtyards—in favor of Tel Aviv's newness:

Not her exotic borders, the smell of kabob, shishlik and tehina, the suggestive lamps of the mosques of her neighbor Jaffa—none of these will I carry in my memory. I want to remember a simple street, which contains nothing strange or wondrous, a street as I saw it one evening, as it was revealed to me. . . .

I saw the display windows of small shops, the naive, gay, childish lack of taste in the clash of loud colors. People ate their bread in restaurants and city cafés, urban and cynical in their simplicity, declaring to all: "Here you can fill your stomach." There were no curtains on the restaurant windows. The groceries were the prettiest of all—eggs arranged in columns, loaves of brown bread peeping out of colorful "hygienic" paper, the engineered order of sugar boxes. They had something of the cleanliness of a good housewife who loves order, with the gleam of her white apron and shining basket. A village-like touch to the glass containers of milk and yogurt, with a special propriety, the hard cheese in its red hood looked out over the glass. There was in all these some kind of quiet, of wisdom, the beauty of the simplest, most elementary things.

In contrast to the orientalized depiction of Jaffa, Goldberg's "simple street" in Tel Aviv is remarkable for its order, its hygiene, its plentiful supply of goods, its cafés and restaurants open to public view—in short, for its resemblance to the European cities of her past and for its

ability to afford Goldberg the flâneuse a series of sharp, visually compelling images among which she may move anonymously. On the one
hand, her description shares something of the motion and rhythm
of modernist descriptions of large cities such as Berlin, a city that
Goldberg knew and that was, in many ways, the prototype for the modern metropolis. Journalistic depictions of Berlin "represented the urban world as ready-made for browsing. Rich descriptions of cafes,
kiosks, . . . display windows, and street advertisements provided a public roominess that was ideal for the spectator."[127] On the other hand, it
is also clear from her description that she delights in Tel Aviv's small-
ness, the devotion of its physical craftsmen, and even in its relative
provinciality.[128] Her next observation is of a wine shop, whose dimly lit
shelves of bottles and casks contained

> something from the history of all the world's wines and wine houses.
> Something gentile, like the taverns of western Europe, and
> something very Jewish, like the pub on village roads in winter. Two
> old Jews with sidelocks and beards sat next to a lit table, a lantern
> leaking a meager, miserly light. They wore wide-rimmed black hats,
> like those on the heads of Rembrandt's Jews. And their hands—a
> measured movement of quiet deep conversation. In another corner—
> in rebellion against order and rule—was a large pile of dirty sacks and
> overturned pots, and a large crate dumped among them, and on this
> crate—like sacredness amid the profane—two thick books in black
> bindings. *Sforim*—with a penultimate, Ashkenazi accent. The prayer
> book and the *Mishnah*.

The description of the wine shop is almost painterly in its sensual detail, and not only for its reference to Rembrandt. The scene is wholly
taken from "over there"—the "history of all the world's wine houses"
boils down to the easy coexistence of only two distinct types: a gentile
tavern and Jewish village pub. After the extended attention to the
modern hustle and bustle and bright lights of Tel Aviv's streets and after the rejection of Jaffa as a model, Goldberg's eye settles on a darkened interior characterized by the material poverty and spiritual wealth
of traditional Jewish life in Eastern Europe. Yet her final stop is a kiosk
brightly lit with neatly arranged oranges, apples, and bananas, "like a
small oasis in a children's tale. And the fruit's warm color reflected onto

the night, enlivening the street, lending it something of the good scents of groves, and there was a great quiet on the street. Then I loved it very much, and I swore to remember it."

A common feature of depictions of Tel Aviv street life, the kiosk was a source of local color and sound—a cold drink, a radio playing, light in the evening, the brief company of other passersby. For Goldberg, it is the antithesis of the gloomy wine shop, and possesses a fable-like quality. Though Goldberg claims that she will remember Tel Aviv for this simple kiosk, the wine shop, with its particularly Jewish interaction, its mix of sacred and profane, and its strong connection to European culture's view of Jews (via Rembrandt) remains firmly ensconced in her imagination and in her rendition of the local landscape.

At the time of the article's publication, Goldberg had been living in Tel Aviv for four years, perhaps with the growing sense that she would not return to the cities of Europe, whose "doors" were now locked. The weight of these cities on the poet's experience of Tel Aviv is felt in both the article and in the later poem.[129] "Tel Aviv, 1935" is, in a sense, Goldberg's fulfillment of her own promise at the conclusion of her article; it records her memory of Tel Aviv, which is nonetheless irrevocably linked to earlier memories of other places. However, the individual set of memories described in "This City"—the courtyards of houses in which she has lived—are cast in the poem as a set of generalized civic, collective memories. Just as the individual eye carries scenes of remembered cities upon its surface, so the poem's camera records the changing weather of mornings and nights passed in European capitals. The difference between the image of the individual human eyeball and that of the mechanized replication of the camera signifies the transformation of a personal set of memories into a more collective vision. The poem organizes the details of personal experience into the aestheticized order of memory. Unlike the unique and private souvenir lock of hair that symbolizes her memories of other cities, the camera suggests that specific versions of the past have become a product of the public realm.

The poem and the article each record the break of migration in different ways. In the article, the trauma is marked by the text's division into two sections: the first half entitled "Courtyards," the second half entitled "The Street." The poem contains greater psychological insight and a more direct rendering of the magnitude of the trauma: the post-apocalyptic images of the raven, Columbus, and the New World are stripped back to reveal images of the past that are themselves as un-readable as film darkening in a camera. Language and urban space are also experienced differently in each text. The linguistic mix of the ar-ticle provides a Proustian background of music against which Gold-berg savors various childhood scenes. In "Tel Aviv, 1935," however, the immigrants' native tongues are languages of a "foreign land," like cold knives stuck into the local heat. The poem's retrospective point of view poses particular problems in this stanza, in that the poetic speaker seems to refer to her own birthplaces as "foreign." Furthermore, though the word *hamsin*—Arabic for "hot, dry wind"—had become a part of the Hebrew vernacular, its presence adds to the tension be-tween language, landscape, and speaker.

The article's metaphoric space of a locked apartment from which the speaker has been evicted is recalled as a series of empty rooms in the poem. A geographic location of memory that is absent from the article but figures decisively in the poem is the sea, in which the poetic speaker imagines the hallucinatory scene of her town church floating. The im-age is complex and by no means one-sided. Within the poem's cultural universe, it plays a role similar to that of the image of Rembrandt's Jews in "This City." The church represents, of course, both popular and in-stitutionalized anti-Semitism, but also the rich achievements of Euro-pean art. Remembering Tel Aviv means remembering the break—geo-graphical, cultural, and psychological—occasioned by its founding.

In Goldberg's work, the past coexists with the present, just as surely as the spaces of the cities she has lived in are part of her experience of Tel Aviv's streets, if only by virtue of their difference or absence. It is not that the psychic break of migration does not occur; in fact, it is on-going and never fully complete. Her work accepts neither the linear movement of the Zionist metanarrative out of Europe into Palestine, nor the spatial division implicit in this history. Indeed, the "pure" spa-tial representation of Tel Aviv as a "100 percent Jewish city" is con-founded by her introduction of history and the notion of time's passage—even if this distinction is deceptively coded as discrete in her early essay through its division into two parts. Like the work of other women poets, Goldberg's poetry has been critically praised and absorbed into the Hebrew canon by virtue of its "universal" as opposed to "national" aspects—its focus on themes such as love and nature and its stylistic sophistication and integrity. Here, however, Goldberg engages the national metanarrative in which Tel Aviv figures as the site of homecoming and redemption in order to subvert it. This gesture is typical of woman's writing vis-à-vis the enterprise of the nation. In Benedict Anderson's terms, women are always the symbol or image of the nation, a metonym for the land and the people aggregate, but they can never be figured apart from it as agents.[130] Women, therefore, are always the object, but never the subject of national discourse, a situation that presents a special problem for women writers whose work engages the question of the nation.[131] Literary representation of Tel Aviv also inevitably referenced the gendered network of associations within Hebrew literary tradition in which the city is associated with the female body.[132] Biblical sources for this connection range from the appearance of the city as a profligate woman in Lamentations to the ostensibly less charged coinage *Ir va-em* (city and mother), a phrase describing a large metropolis—"mother" to the surrounding area. Thus, for example, Alterman refers to the Tel Aviv in its "age ingrate" as a woman who is "no longer a girl and not yet a madam," stretching the metaphor to ridiculous detail:

> She'll walk about on high heels and she's odd, put on sandals and she's ridiculous; carry a handbag—coquettish, go without—her hands free; she paints herself—a painted girl; no paint—a colorless madam. Her body parts look like they're stuck together, without matching in shape or size. Some have developed early, others are still unripe. She's tall, with the face of a baby, legs are firm but the shape is weak, arms are long but the biceps are thin, the neck is shapely but the shoulders are bony.[133]

This easy substitution of the female body for the city (and more generally "the land") was subverted by the work of Hebrew woman poets, most notably Esther Raab, whose 1929 "Tel Aviv" bemoans the city's "skinny chest," yet challenged the era's normative discourse linking textuality, fertility, and the male poet.[134] Goldberg's flâneuse of 1939, like her retrospective muse of three decades later, also critiques Zionist versions of history—freely traversing both time and space, crossing and recrossing terrain that is otherwise meant to be separate. In Goldberg's work we find a sense of Tel Aviv's developing public sphere but also of the city as a kind of intermediary space defined by both Europe and the Middle East. This awareness of the city's edges, and of the city itself as an edge, is the subject of the following chapter.

## Five

The Edge of Town: Depicting the City's
Periphery as a Way of Naming Its Center

A city and a street have a border and an edge and an identity.
— Doron Rosenblum, *Israeli Blues*

An abandoned washrag hung by itself on the line of the building
opposite, hope rising with a bit of wind and then falling flat again,
lax alongside the rust-eaten gutters, the closed plastic shutters with
their missing slats, a dusty dry planter, protruding air-conditioners,
crooked wires, a giant patch of plaster repair, poor workmanship.
Hatred choked my throat: this whole city is one big transit camp.
North, south, downtown, Bauhaus and the *shmate*, it's all a transit
camp. . . .
— Ronit Matalon, *Sarah, Sarah*

The city is the natural home of difference.
— Richard Sennett, *The Conscience of the Eye*

The preceding chapters have demonstrated how Tel Aviv developed a selective and somewhat ambivalent sense of its historical origins. The same
could be said of the city's fictional representations, which have a relation
not only to Tel Aviv itself, but to each other as well. Just as the city expanded, perhaps unpredictably but with some consciousness of its historical center, so its first epic novel—S. Y. Agnon's *Just Yesterday* (1946)
—had its origins in a slim tale: "Tishrey," which is set in Neve Tsedek, a
Jewish neighborhood founded north of Jaffa in 1887, and was published
in 1909.[1] "Tishrey" traces the bare beginnings and gradual end of a romance between Na'aman and Yael Hayot, whose courtship resembles
that between Yitzhak Kummer, a Galician-born housepainter, and So-
nia in *Just Yesterday*. Agnon himself lived as a young writer in Neve Tsedek from 1908, a member of the neighborhood's small but vibrant Jewish intelligentsia, which included Devora Baron and Y. H. Brenner. The
neighborhood was an important locale in the foundation of secular
Hebrew culture in Palestine.[2] Like his fictional alter ego, Agnon worked

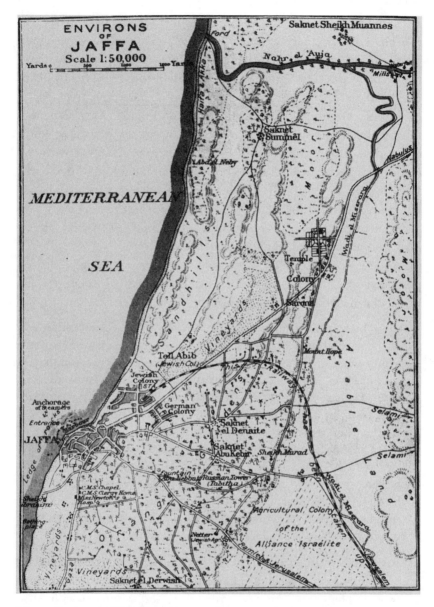

*Map 5.1* Environs of Jaffa, 1917. From *Military Handbook on Palestine* (Cairo: British Admiralty, 1917). Reprinted in Ruth Kark, *Jaffa: A City in Evolution, 1799 – 1917* (Jerusalem: Yad Ben Tsvi, 1990).

as a secretary for local businessmen, bureaucrats, and functionaries, and as a Hebrew tutor.[3] In between "Tishrey" and *Just Yesterday*, Agnon twice revised and expanded the tale as *Giv'at ha-chol*, with the hero's name changed to Hemdat and his poetic ambitions more clearly delineated.[4] All renderings of the life of this Galician-born immigrant display the mix of realism and fantasy characteristically found in Agnon's fiction; this combination presides in extreme fashion in *Just Yesterday*, which concludes with the brutal demise of Yitzhak, whose already active imagination has been further inflamed by rabies and, ultimately, dementia. In "Giv'at ha-chol," the dunes where Hemdat first sees and courts Yael Hayot are called "the hill of love," and it is there that the story ends, with Hemdat caught in a delusional fantasy after they have parted. He remains alone on the hill, haunted by her shadow.[5]

In these works set in Tel Aviv's prehistory, "truth telling" in fiction possessed special significance. In his ruminations, Gurishkin, the fictional chronicler in *Just Yesterday* of the city's protohistory,

> knows that anyone who wants to be a writer has to read and study a lot and expand the scope of his knowledge. Gurishkin had already left behind all his own thoughts and wants only to be the writer of the Land of Israel. A new life is taking shape in the land and it needs its writer. He hasn't yet started writing because he doesn't have a corner of his own, for he lives in a room with three or four of his comrades, and the room is about the size of an egg, and the table is about the size of an olive. And there's no space to spread out paper. And mainly, because he hasn't yet made up his mind whether to write things as they are, that is, to copy from reality, or to make his books novels. On the one hand, his heart inclines to things as they are, for there is no truth like the truth of action, and on the other hand, novels are likely to appeal to the heart and lead to action.[6]

Gurishkin's musings go to the heart of concerns regarding modern Hebrew literature's engaged relation to nationalism and the Zionist enterprise. The phrase "things as they truly are" resonates with Ahad Ha'am's journalistic report of 1891, "Emet me-eretzyisrael" (The Truth from the Land of Israel), which questioned the economic and social viability of Jewish settlement in Palestine. Should literary depictions of the *Yishuv* (the pre-State Jewish community in Palestine) tell "the truth," that is, offer realistic depictions of the challenges of local life; or rather should they seek to challenge readers and inspire them to put down the book and join in the national project? The problem of realism was further exacerbated by both the relative instability of immigrant life and the centuries-old "baggage" of biblical and other depictions of the area as "the Land of Milk and Honey." The issue of oppositional or critical views was even more complex: given the paradoxical combination of flux and gravity that characterized the local landscape, from what physical location is critique possible?

In the 1931 revision of "Giv'at ha-chol," Agnon suggests a solution that will prove productive for later denizens of the city, writers and citizens alike. He locates Hemdat-the-poet between the old world of Jaffa and the as-yet-unrealized city of Tel Aviv; the sites are loosely connected by the train tracks that run through the valley between them:

> If you haven't seen Hemdat, see his room. His room stood in the sands of Neve Tsedek, filled with many windows, one window turned toward the sea, another window turned toward the desert sands upon which the great metropolis of Tel Aviv was being built, and another window turned toward the valley of ghosts through which the train passed, and two windows, which Hemdat kept darkened with green curtains, turned toward the street; he was shorn of the entire world, even of the bustle of Jaffa.[7]

As Tel Aviv is constructed close by, and as Hebrew depictions of the city are themselves "being built," Hemdat's house opens onto those very border expanses that will engage the imaginations of Tel Aviv's writers: the sea, the dunes, the valley to the east with its older Arab and Christian settlements, and Jaffa, whose commotion, even unheard, exists as surely and as steadily as that of the sea.[8] The house's location symbolizes Hemdat's refusal to participate in the surrounding hum of activity, including his budding, romantic relationship with Yael. Despite the relatively liberal social atmosphere, he is torn between acting upon his feelings, a sense of propriety and natural shyness, and the certain knowledge that Yael will prefer to marry someone richer than he. The train's whistle outside Hemdat's windows signals the passage of life that he can only watch. Indeed, the entire enterprise of building Tel

Aviv is represented in the story *alongside* Hemdat's inner turmoil, as incidental and barely a subplot. We hear of the celebrations in honor of the city's founding: "All Jaffa celebrated this great holiday with wine and cakes except for Hemdat, who sits in his room and drinks black coffee."[9] Hemdat, a vegetarian with the smooth hands of a clerk, is a passive antihero. Despite his physical location in Palestine, he resembles the neurasthenic, rootless characters of fin-de-siècle European Hebrew fiction. His disengagement points to the dilemma of writing convincingly about a society that barely exists; at the same time, the idealized autonomy of his house, with its darkened windows that turn toward the street, may be understood as a site not only of withdrawal, but also, potentially, of critique.

The border areas observable from Hemdat's house will change over time: in Hemdat's world, Tel Aviv itself appears as the protean edge of Neve Tsedek, a relative positioning that reverses as the city expands. Shifting boundaries and edges have always been an integral part of urban form, whether the city is created anew or out of previously existing settlements: "The city bounds are not revised lightly, but are not ordinarily frozen in perpetuity. They have to be adjusted as the settlement grows or shrinks through time. Even when there is no actual redefinition, the boundary may subsequently lose some of its significance."[10] In addition to natural borders, other kinds of lines of demarcation evolve through the presence of urban settlement. The history of the cultural landscape is thus the "history of human patterns impressed upon the contours of the natural environment. It is the story of how places are planned, designed, built, inhabited, appropriated, celebrated, despoiled, and discarded."[11] The edges of a city, whether loosely determined through natural phenomena such as waterways or other landscape features, or formalized through walls and gates, have historically signified contact with the world beyond one's home, with a realm of difference, even danger. Though the borders may possess concrete, physical characteristics, the dualistic qualities they represent are invented and easily inverted: what is on "the other side" may be alternately repugnant and desirable. Indeed, what appears to be a site of fixed, differentiated identities is often a fiction. A contemporary Israeli political theorist argues that "the illusion whose name is border always camouflages a world of disorder containing overlapping connections, conflicted loyalties, and identities that cross lines."[12] The border's slippery quality as a signifier of collective identity is particularly problematic in early Tel Aviv, given the city's representation in these years as utterly new.

The imagined relation between center and periphery thus symbolized important aspects in Tel Aviv's emerging identity as an urban center. The very existence of this relation is first and foremost a spatial rendering of temporal longevity, a mark of the settlement's existence and stability over time. This kind of spatial depiction begins relatively early in Tel Aviv's history: the instant there is a kernel of settlement, border areas may also be imagined. Indeed, imagining borders and boundaries became an integral part of defining the city center. The depiction of Tel Aviv's edges was thus a means of delineating the city's cultural uniqueness as "the first Hebrew city." This chapter explores imagined versions of Tel Aviv's actual geographical borders—the largely Arab city of Jaffa, the Mediterranean Sea, and the outlying areas of older Jewish, Christian, and Arab settlement. Each of these regions appeared as either peripheral or even antagonistic to Tel Aviv's evolving city center; at the same time, however, selective elements of each were absorbed into the city's developing identity as an urban hub.

Clearly, all societies delineate boundaries as a way of shoring up what they consider to be their own uniqueness, often in opposition to the surrounding landscape and its inhabitants. Settler societies have a particularly powerful sense of the significance of their frontiers, which may "delineate directions for expansion and growth and provide basic symbols, legends, challenges and myths used for the construction of national identity."[13] Whereas for the Yishuv, and later Israel, this process was more explicit during periods of state-building and the establishment of international boundaries, its seeds can also be detected in Tel Aviv's early decades. The city's first official borders were set by the British Mandatory government in 1921, in the wake of Arab-Jewish riots of that May.[14] The imagining of Tel Aviv's edges was not an entirely innocent process, as actual municipal boundaries expanded after the Jewish-Arab disturbances of 1921, 1929, and 1936, and eventually included the city of Jaffa after 1948. Indeed, the direction of Tel Aviv's expansion toward the seashore was explicitly aimed at curtailing Jaffa's growth.[15] It is important to note, therefore, that although this chapter only indirectly addresses Tel Aviv's actual physical expansion, some version of the process described in fictional, journalistic, and photographic accounts, did happen "on the ground" as Tel Aviv's municipal boundaries extended to incorporate surrounding neighborhoods and to populate the stretches of land in between.[16]

Tel Aviv's gradual expansion and the ongoing tension between the historical center and its margins shaped the city's sense of self. According to a recent history, "different areas within the city's territory— which a short while before had been perceived as outlying districts, isolated and far from the center, where reaching them involved crossing sand dunes—came closer to the center and became an integral part of the city."[17] Descriptions of the city's physical growth engendered a kind of instant nostalgia for a time when Tel Aviv was smaller and more intimate, even if that time happened to be just last year, or even last month; this nostalgia lent a sense of longevity to the city, creating the impression of historical roots and permanence. This, perhaps, is the source of Tel Avivians' notorious nostalgia, even today, for the long-lost Tel Aviv of last year or even last week. However, depictions of the relation between the city's spatial center and its margins also served to articulate difference and critique. Just as history, embedded in the city's streets, buildings, and other physical structures, undermines the confidence of the present, so the periphery, "the vast accumulation of human bodies and low-grade building materials on the edge of the city,"[18] rebukes the center's solidified hubris, revealing its dependence on those very sites it has pushed to the edge. Precisely because these edges were imagined as the location of difference, they were also potential sites of critique.

## Jaffa as Janus

> Her white houses gleam in the hills of sands, and her green citrus groves crown her with fruit trees, and the luster of her sun hovers over her, and the sea breeze blows among her dark cypresses, and the

blue of the sea plays with her sands, a good smell wafts from her
vineyards and from all the other desired trees that desired to settle
in Jaffa.

—S. Y. Agnon, *Just Yesterday* (1946)

If you are a sensitive, curious child in Tel Aviv, you register the terrible
contradiction in which you live. . . . And you are entirely drawn to this
Jaffa. The limestone houses, terra-cotta colors, geraniums in window
boxes. And the mix of the smell of fish with oranges and seaweed.
That sensuality. And for someone who grew up in a city that was entirely "present," a city without time [Tel Aviv], then Jaffa is also all the
past generations. Jaffa is Jonah the prophet. Those towers. The houses
that seem to rise from the sea. But suddenly the shutters are gradually
closed. The green flags are raised. And the crazy sermons in the
mosques. And suddenly it's also the murderous Jaffa.

—Haim Gouri, interviewed in March 2000

In some senses, the city of Jaffa was Tel Aviv's most immediate and
most important edge (Figure 5.1). As we have seen, Tel Aviv was initially conceived as a satellite of Jaffa, one the world's oldest port cities.
With archaeological evidence pointing to human settlement in the area
as far back as 7,500 B.C., Jaffa is the subject of numerous ancient oral
and written traditions.[19] Life in Jaffa during the modern period was
marked by social and cultural heterogeneity, a mix heightened by the
annual arrival of pilgrims and other visitors from within Palestine and
abroad.[20] By the late nineteenth century, the city contained a small
Jewish community dating from the 1840s, a large, well-established
Arab Moslem population, and Christian pilgrims of European and
Levantine origins.[21] In the 1880s, Jaffa's Jewish community began to
distinguish itself from other Jewish urban centers in Palestine, such as
Jerusalem and Safed, by its "atmosphere of modernity, freedom, secularism, and economic enterprise."[22] Beginning in 1887, new Jewish suburbs such as Neve Tsedek and Neve Shalom were established northeast
of the city. Perceived as a place of exotic danger, an orientalized space
against which Tel Aviv defined itself as modern, Hebrew, and secular,
Jaffa would ultimately prove to be Tel Aviv's most problematic, and
most productive, boundary.

*Fig. 5.1* View of Jaffa from the north, 1920s. Silver Print Collection, Ein Hod.

Early twentieth-century accounts of the city by Jewish immigrants focus on three main themes: Jaffa as the wondrous initial point of contact with the Holy Land; Jaffa as a jolting piece of an exotic and terrifying "East"; and Jaffa as a city with mythical and biblical origins. Out of this amalgam of contradictory depictions—Jaffa exalted and desired versus Jaffa denigrated and feared—grew a discourse of "Jaffa as Janus." For the pilgrim-immigrant, Jaffa was the destination, the first site seen when approaching from the sea, an almost unimaginable end to both a personal journey and a more collective sense of vagabondage:

"Jaffa"

But it is not a dream! Here is the sand, here is the shore!
Here a tower peers out at me, peering and declaring:
"At last an end to eternal wandering, here is the end,"
winking at me, all the wall's stones call to me;
and the light-blue sky—the sea lifted above all,
the sea filled with waves of light, lazily swimming . . .
the shore—and how beautiful and exalted, Jaffa—[23]

*Fig. 5.2* Jaffa port (1927), Zoltan Kluger. Silver Print Collection, Ein Hod.

Jaffa was also the primary point of encounter with the local Arab population: given the rocky hazards of Jaffa's port, arriving ships set anchor in mid-harbor. For an additional fee, passengers traveled ashore in small boats (Figure 5.2). A typical immigrant account of the approach of these boats and their handlers describes the Arab laborers "swarming" over the ship like pirates,[24] frightening the passengers with their strange appearance: "dressed in pantaloons as wide as skirts, tarbushes on their heads, barefoot, and bare-chested to the waist, they climbed up the ship's deck."[25] This passage is immediately followed by a description of the chaos of the narrow streets adjacent to the port, with their over-whelming sensory impressions, particularly of noise and smell. Many visitors compared Jaffa with other port cities of the Levant.[26]

Jaffa was often described—in selective fashion—as part of Tel Aviv's "prehistory." Alter Druyanov's *Sefer Tel Aviv*, which became a model for later historical writing about the city, devotes nearly seventy pages to Jaffa's history since ancient times, followed by an additional seventy to the establishment of Achusat Bayit, and nearly three hundred to the city itself, as if Tel Aviv were simply the logical extension of the earlier settlements. This version of Jaffa focused on the city's biblical lineage: the notion that it was reputedly built by Noah's son Yefet, and its men-tion in the Book of Jonah, were cited as evidence of the port's "He-brew" origins. This attention to Jaffa's mythical past highlighted its roots in classical civilization—a ready source of European culture, but notably not part of the East. David Shimonovitz's poem "On the Shore at Jaffa" (1918) includes references to Leda and Neptune, and describes the city as "full of wise men, enthusiastic businessmen, and writers":

> My heart has drawn me to breathe the air of Jaffa,
> perfumed and edifying, spiced with kinds of scents,
> the scent of "Tel Aviv" and revival, the scent of citrons and writers,
> of the sea and of offices, of businessmen and oranges.[27]

Typically, the poem was actually written in Shimonovitz's birthplace, Bobroisk.[28] The forceful collusion of biblical and classical themes is found in Saul Tchernichovski's "By the Sea at Jaffa" (1929), which en-visions the return of pagan powers in the context of the Hebrew revival:

> Oh, land of wondrous gods! For your sake and for mine,
> will that generation of Canaanite trespassers
> be fortified by you and again return to life?[29]

Ya'akov Fichman's "Afternoon in Jaffa" depicts a walk through the city's streets, with a typical mix of market sights, sounds, and smells. However, the city is oddly empty. The muezzin calls but there's no audience:

> Oh, muezzin, it does me good to hear your voice,
> spread over the land, mutely asleep.—
> Like you I too grew accustomed to singing to the wilderness.[30]

Jaffa eventually began to appear as a site of potential violence and danger, particularly after the disturbances of 1921, so much so that the phrase *Yafo, ir damim* ("Jaffa, city of blood") entered the Hebrew lexicon. Some writers found in Jaffa a confounding reflection of their own experiences with prejudice. The poet Eliezer Steinman records a street encounter with an Arab boy and his donkey, in which he notices the boy moving quickly away from him, the Jew; feeling secure in his own city, Steinman recalls "the dread sunk in my bones from my childhood, among the *goyim* . . . the Jew in me prepares his whips: oh animal wearing the crown of the just! Persecuted yesterday, now the bruiser or the bruised!"[31] Whereas in the Purim processionals the presence of Arab spectators is a structural reminder of a certain form of Jewish marginality in European public space, here a position of relative safety leads to a rare—at this time—meditation on the potentially debilitating effects of power. Y. H. Brenner's journalistic "Within the Grove," which describes a similar encounter, has acquired apocryphal status, given its publication shortly before the author's death: "In the dark I lost my way in the dust of the grove's paths at the edge of town. They all belong to the natives, the Arabs. Theirs."[32] He passes three Arabs who refuse to return his greeting, and reflects cynically upon the popular notion that they are actually descendants of the biblical tribes of Israel. Following this, he encounters a young Arab boy employed by one of the men. Entering into conversation with him, he learns, despite the linguistic barrier, something of his family life and working conditions; he feels some connection to the boy—"Lost orphan! Younger brother! . . . Whether we are related by blood or not, responsibility for you lies upon me. It is up to me to open your eyes, to demonstrate human relationships" in a manner beyond politics: "through the touch of the soul . . . from today and for generations . . . and for a long time . . . with no goal . . . no intention . . . except that of a brother, friend, and companion."[33] Brenner's tale bears some resemblance to the imaginary, even hallucinatory, passages of his fictional work: though claiming he speaks no Arabic, he manages to receive—perhaps invent?—details of the boy's life and family as well as the earning practices of other workers. His paternalistic recognition that it is "up to him" to enlighten the Arab and to introduce him to the civilized fellowship of men, typified attitudes toward the local population as primitive and in need of reform. Nonetheless, both Brenner's and Steinman's accounts contain a groping sense of identification with the figure of the Arab— not as an idealized "noble savage," but as an immanent, if troubling, component of their immediate environment.

Jaffa's power as both part of, and apart from, Tel Aviv perhaps explains why it became a privileged trope in later fiction about the city, particularly memoiristic work about childhood. For a number of authors, Jaffa is the site of a political reckoning with their younger selves and with the belief systems of their parents' generation. In a sense, the representation of Jaffa was transformed from the spatial to the temporal realm: once Tel Aviv's physical edge, Jaffa becomes a marker of the city's immediate past. Just as Jaffa was viewed with ambivalence by writers of an earlier immigrant generation, for authors such as Benjamin Tammuz, Haim Gouri, and S. Yizhar, all raised in Tel Aviv, Jaffa figured as a key site of their childhood, at once unspoiled and tainted by primal sin, almost a necessary stage of development to be passed through or overcome. Michel de Certeau uses the phrase "infancies of sites" to describe the essential relation between childhood and "spatial cognition." In reference to Freud's famous realization while watching his grandson play with a spool, making it appear and disappear, he notes that this fundamental differentiation, which Freud compares to the primal separation of infant from mother, also structures our experience of space as adults: "In any palimpsestic site, subjectivity is already articulated on the absence that structures it like existence, and the fact of 'being there,' *Dasein*. To employ space, therefore is to repeat the joyous and silent experience of childhood: it is, in the site, *to be other* and *to pass to the other*."[34]

In the memoiristic work of Tammuz, and especially of Gouri and Yizhar (both of whom were born in Tel Aviv), it is the city of Jaffa—its radical "otherness" and the effects of its subsequent "absence"—that shapes both their psyches and the spatial contours of their remembered childhoods. Tammuz immigrated to Tel Aviv at the age of six in 1924. His story "The Swimming Contest" (1951–52) opens in an idyllic period in the past, probably the late 1920s. The narrator travels as a boy with his mother to visit an elderly Arab woman who had been the mother's patient, in a house in the *pardesim* (orange groves) adjacent to Jaffa. The pair are picked up by a driver with a horse-drawn carriage and taken past the Hasan Beck mosque and through the cacophonous streets of the Manshiya neighborhood at Jaffa's northern edge. Eventually they head into the groves, a site that typified early descriptions of the city.[35] The groves, characterized by a strong mix of attraction and repulsion, are perhaps the best example of the duality that generally informs representations of Jaffa. They are thoroughly local, an integral part of the Middle Eastern landscape, and as such represent the kind of long-lived nativeness that Hebrew culture aspired to achieve. As we saw in Brenner's vignette, they are also a place of both hostility and potential camaraderie. Gideon Ofrat comments on this dual quality of the pardesim in work by painters such as Nachum Gutman: "The *pardes* usually had a doubled mythological face. That is, the good grove and bad grove, an echo of the good forest and the bad forest of European literature."[36] Tammuz's story maps this vision of the grove over time—the "good grove" symbolized in prewar idyll of the traditional Arab home and its extended family; the "bad grove" represented in the narrator's return to the house in the groves as a conquering soldier. The story explicitly recreates a courtyard that no longer exists:

> These days you won't see such a courtyard. If you happened upon a place that had a courtyard like this you find in ruins from the war, piles of rock and wooden planks and spider webs that try to cover the antiquity of things that just yesterday breathed and laughed. In those days a courtyard such as that was filled with life. It was square and surrounded on three sides by a two-story building. Below were the stables and cowshed, and in the yard red and black roosters roamed, their crowing mixing with the neighing of the horse.[37]

The traditional Arab home is depicted on the verge of disintegration, its generations divided by growing nationalism and a sense that the old order is over. At the same time, the house within the grove provides an escape from the city and possesses a solidity and comfortableness unmatched by the boy's own rented apartment. The boy is befriended by the old woman's granddaughter, Nahida, and then loses a swimming competition to Abdul-Karim, a young uncle who engages him in oblique talk of war and peace: "The day you beat me in the pool . . . ," said Abdul-Karim, "will be very bad. For you too, Nahida, it will be very bad. For us all."[38] Years later, the now adult narrator finds himself in Ein Kerem, an Arab village next to Jerusalem, and rents a room in a large house for a couple of weeks. The family and their daily rituals remind him of his stay in the groves of Jaffa, which seems to him now a distant dream. The story's conclusion finds him in 1948, as a soldier fighting in the dunes east of Jaffa. His unit happens upon the same house, and Abdul-Karim is captured while defending it. For a moment, it seems as if the entire political conflict will be resolved by a rematch in the pool. But then Abdul-Karim is led into the grove by other soldiers as the narrator

> undressed and entered the water. It was hot and scummy and it was
> evident the hose hadn't brought water from the well for many
> days. . . . The sound of shooting came from the grove. My heart
> stopped beating. I knew Abdul-Karim had been murdered. . . . After-
> wards I approached Abdul-Karim's body. It seemed as if he had seen
> me moments before, a prophetic vision, as I swam in the pool. His
> face was not the face of a man who had lost. Here, in the courtyard,
> I myself, all of us, were beaten.[39]

As a boy, the narrator had intuited that their swimming contest was more than just a test of physical prowess. As a young man, he begins to comprehend the significance of his own idealized memory of the grove and its inhabitants, the tastes, smells, and sounds that all spell the unattainable permanence of the Arab household. Abdul-Karim's ultimate victory comes as a result of his unbeatable status as native, a condition that appears to remain untouched by the more technical issues of losing a military skirmish or the physical devastation of his homestead. His childhood memory of the house functions like a ruin in the narrator's consciousness, a reminder of a wholeness that is unattainable both for its radical difference as well as its temporal remove.

Haim Gouri was the 308th child born in Tel Aviv. His novel *The Crazy Book* (1972) contains the same litany of sensual detail about

Jaffa found in earlier, more contemporaneous accounts of the city, sharpened by ironic hindsight:

> The taste of moist, sticky stringy Arab *chalvah* in pieces on my lips like a memory. Jaffa of eyes and faces rises and stings me. . . . The Jaffa of domes and mosques rises to sting me. . . . the scent of oranges and fish and seaweed. . . .
>
> And only the sea. And only the sea.
>
> I walk through the city, low winter skies, among Cypriot donkeys, tall, in heat, and caravans of camels continuing the Bible, Damascus caravans ringing their way south. I walk among black carriages and red horses as if at the edge of a dying dynasty. I go to Hasan Beck.[40]

Gouri recalls being both charmed and frightened by the city—"a magical, filthy neighbor to the south of the city of my birth, strewn as if by the hand of fate upon these dunes. Other. Not mine." This attraction is akin to "worshipping the idol of another city, very close, very far." The Jaffa of his memory has been reduced to the images in Gutman's paintings:

> On a caravan sand path . . . goats and bells. A woman walks. A jug. Imitating a famous painting from days of old. Soon the dew will drop upon the Ramadan cannon. Houses that remember a long time. . . .
>
> Spring. Market afternoon . . . scent of spices borrowed from legends. Fragrances taken from a past that has forgotten its beginnings, bananas, onions and oranges.[41]

Jaffa is the site of Tel Aviv's "birth" and the beginnings of his family's local history: "Here, not far, it seems, stood my mother and father after they got off the *Ruslan*, with their belongings, in front of Haim-Baruch's boarding house, or some other boarding house. I walk through Jaffa of just yesterday (*tmol shilshomit*), upon a pure, golden-sanded shore. Pursuing footsteps and an oath of allegiance (*shvuat emunim*)."

Gouri's depiction of Jaffa refers twice to titles of Agnon's Tel Aviv writings (the phrases *tmol shilshomit* and *shvuat emunim*), a comment not only on the importance of Jaffa as a site in his work, but also on the difficulty of writing about the city without reference to its fictional and memoiristic discourse. Above all, Jaffa is the place where violence has an identifiable pattern and history, about which he is repeatedly warned by his mother:

> I go to the Jaffa of sticks and knives, of insane sermons from the mosque. I go to Jaffa. . . . To Jaffa I'm going, the sea and the turrets. . . . Don't go to Jaffa! Don't go to Jaffa! Crazy! They'll butcher you there, don't you know? Crazy! To the Jaffa of 1921, 1929, I'm going, to my fathers dressed in tarbushes and Panama hats and felt bowlers and caps, to my fathers burning with the fire of Ahavat Zion. To my fragile mothers, burning in the sun. . . .
>
> I go to Jaffa. Don't go to Jaffa, crazy! All the shutters are closing. To Manshiya, I'm going. To Ajami. To Abu-Kabir. To Brenner's blood.[42]

Many of these images, and a more extended description of his mother, are conjured in near-identical formulation in a later essay, "The Additional Piece" (1994), in which Gouri reflects on the fictional significance of Jaffa in particular, and Arab culture in general, for his generation:

> Our poets and writers long continued to conjure that world that was no longer contributing their definitive talents to the genre of nostalgia, guilt, and regret. In the landscape of the homeland, the dagger-like hatred of the rioters, the sermons of incitement in the mosques, the cries of the masses in the ruins, and the faces of the murdered in the continuing "disturbances," were always added to the memory of an ancient, picturesque neighborhood.[43]

Gouri's comments point not only to the importance of Jaffa as a trope in the Hebrew literary imagination, but also to its formulaic reification in urban discourse about Tel Aviv. The "versions" of Jaffa I discuss here are exactly that—versions, part of a specific discourse describing an ostensibly unchanging set of characteristics ("Arab Jaffa," "Jaffa, city of blood") against which Tel Aviv could develop its own contrary urban identity. In fact, a similar process of identity formation was also occurring within Jaffan society and in other Arab urban centers in Palestine. The interwar period was characterized by a great influx of largely Moslem migrants from the inland villages to the port cities of Jaffa and Haifa, whose Arab communities were by and large historically Christian. The interaction between these various religious, ethnic, and economic groups resulted in a general redefinition of the social and political contours of Arab society in Palestine.[44]

S. Yizhar was one of the first writers whose work explicitly addressed the moral dilemmas faced by that generation raised on the Labor-Zionist ideology of the pre-State period. "The Prisoner" (1948) and "Hirbat Hizah" (1949) describe the mistreatment of Arabs during the war, and raise both humanitarian and ethical questions about the potentially deleterious effects of power, and the violence that now inevitably characterized Jewish-Arab relations. In *Mikdamot* (1992), the opening volume of a memoiristic series of works, and the author's first extended prose publication in nearly three decades, Yizhar returns to the period before his own birth, recounting his parents' arrival and settlement in Palestine, and then his early childhood: his "first place" is in fact "the color orange, entirely orange, orange-orange, very orange, completely."[45] This solid and undifferentiated expanse, "smooth as a silk robe," eventually gives way to the particulars of the surrounding landscape, the neighborhood of Neve Shalom and the early streets of Tel Aviv. The book details the difficulties of pioneer life, including the new climate and medical problems; this relatively idyllic existence is interrupted by the events of May 1921, the first large-scale disturbances between the Arab and Jewish communities of Tel Aviv and Jaffa and the surrounding neighborhoods. The book's entire second section is taken up by memories of those days, whose events begin to trickle into the boy's home with rumors about "what exactly happened at Beyt Hachalutsim" in Jaffa. Embedded within these events is an extended retrospective description of his mother's arrival in Jaffa in 1908; he imagines her encounter with the local population, at the port and later in the agricultural settlement of Rechovot, which is described as "a small island surrounded by a sea of Arabs, like a world of darkness surrounding a little light":

> Who at home had known about the Arabs? No one ever talked about them. And in the whole abundance of speeches and talk and argument there, in the Volhynia forest on the banks of the Styr, crawling slowly in dark and sated laziness, absorbing quietly, almost indifferently, both

the goats in songs of the homeland as well as the best proofs that only in our land will we find a homeland, while they, the Arabs, were never anywhere for them, not in any arguments, or considerations and of course not in any of those songs, they simply didn't exist—just as camels and donkeys didn't exist in their shaded forest, nor all those prickly wild shrubs, but the wild shrubs themselves were in the songs, they were the very ones, so they said, that we would uproot when we returned to the land and created ourselves a field, all irrigated and all Zionism, and we'll plant new pines that we'll bring from overseas.[46]

Yizhar's narrative trolls the borders between his mother's first-person recollection of her European home and her arrival in Palestine, her son's memory of these impressions, and the events unfolding in Jaffa:

He's a small boy who doesn't understand anything, but he knows there's something not right here. Not when they walk to synagogue and also not in what there is all the time between the neighborhood and Jaffa. Even when there's nothing happening between the Jews and the Arabs, there's always something happening that they try to hide and not speak right about and not admit that something isn't all right here. Isn't this our place? Isn't this their place? Are we pushed into them, or they into us?[47]

Although for the mother the Arabs were initially utterly absent from the landscape and only later "outside of the area, far from here," for the young boy they are always an immediate, adjacent entity, a force that shapes his identity as routinely as the walk to synagogue. If Yizhar's earlier, influential prose evidenced a romantic view of the landscape, "a nostalgia for the world of . . . open spaces,"[48] the memoiristic work of *Mikdamot* admits the formative force of the most primal of spatial divisions, the circumscribed streets of the boy's childhood.

The space of Jaffa in these texts by Tammuz, Gouri, and Yizhar is initially conjured within the context of a mother-child relationship. Certeau again recalls Freud's comparison of a child's development of a sense of space to "strolling in the motherland": "Childhood, which determines the practices of space, then augments its effects, proliferates and inundates private and public space and defaces their readable surfaces, and creates in the planned city a 'metaphorical' city."[49] The "metaphorical city" of Jaffa exists for these writers as Tel Aviv's irreducible southern border; its destruction represents the passage of their own childhood and is also an opportunity for self-censure as adults. The epigraph to this section contains a portion of a recent interview with Gouri, who revisits his childhood experience of Jaffa in almost the same language as in *The Crazy Book*. At the same time, he likens his limited vision of those days to examining a target through the sites of a rifle, with one eye closed for focus:

> And when do you open the second eye? When the danger is passed. . . . And suddenly the picture widens. And you see things you hadn't seen, hear voices you hadn't heard, things you had repressed. And you are filled with enormous pity, pain and regret. . . .
>
> Though it still chokes me sometimes, why didn't I write more? And I ask myself: "That's all you could say?" And at the end of my life I will say to you: No. And I feel bad with this, because I was there, I saw. I saw that the opposition had been broken but still they swept through the city in order to make people afraid, to expel them.[50]

These writers' personal memories overlap with the city's historical memory of its relation to Jaffa, deploying and therefore preserving certain elements of the site's discursive power. At the same time, the periphery of Jaffa and the events of 1948 serve as a matrix of political self-critique, whose temporal and spatial remove allows for some reevaluation of the "metaphorical" city's power (Figure 5.3).

## Tashlich in the Mediterranean

Jaffa in particular, and Palestine more generally, might have been perceived as less strange both geographically and culturally if approached over land, as a contiguous part of a relatively familiar landscape.[51] The sea crossing, the break, the fissure, caused by coming from "over there," is therefore key to the development of Tel Aviv's specific spatial contours. Though other borders may have been more physically malleable, no edge was more given to multiple, even contradictory, meanings than the sea, which was perceived as a defining characteristic of the city, denoting movement, life, freedom, strength, and nature. While undeniably marking Tel Aviv as a city of Mediterranean rhythms, the

*Fig. 5.3* Arab café in Jaffa (1925), Ya'akov Benor-Kalter. Silver Print Collection, Ein Hod.

sea also represented those European metropolises that were the yardstick for Tel Aviv's own urban achievements.[52] For many of the city's early inhabitants, the sea was in fact a reminder of the Diaspora. This equivocal relation to the sea is perhaps most ironically expressed by the fact that many of the city's early neighborhoods were built with their "backs to the sea," instead of along boulevards that opened toward it (Figure 5.4).

Art historian Gideon Ofrat detects this same ambivalence toward the sea and its symbolic value in Israeli painting. In an essay titled "Back Turned to the Sea," Ofrat describes the evolution of the sea's painterly treatment from the 1920s to the 1980s.[53] Although the sea appeared frequently in symbolic form in work from the 1920s (for example,

תל-אביב : ס החיים על שפת הים

*Fig. 5.4* "Back Turned to the Sea." Central Zionist Archives.

Reuven's *View from the Balcony*, discussed in Chapter 4), later painters "didn't need that sea, the sea of immigration."[54] This "sea of immigration" also appeared in symbolic fashion in modernist Hebrew poetry, as we saw in the example of Leah Goldberg's "Tel Aviv, 1935," with its concluding image of her hometown church floating in the Mediterranean. In classic immigration narratives of the period, the sea was purely a place of passage, a means to an end—arrival in the Land of Israel. The story of the sea was thus always a story about the land, even, as Hanan Hever puts it, a "cover story" for the land's troubles. According to Hever, Hebrew poets described the sea as a smooth, conflict-free place, enabling a direct relation to both Europe and a European-flavored Mediterranean past, instead of an actual relation to contemporary Palestinian surroundings. Symbolism was the poetic means through which poets such as Shlonsky "skirted" describing the violence of disputed territory, displacing it with the sea.[55]

In the social realism of early Hebrew fiction in Palestine, the sea was above all the site of physical and national renewal, the birth of the prototypical "new Hebrew," as celebrated in the opening lines of Moshe Shamir's novel *With His Own Hands*: "Elik was born from the sea.

That was what Father used to say when we sat down together for supper on the balcony of the little house on summer evenings."[56] An early journalistic account describes the sea's special powers of renewal in less mundane terms:

> A city that has a sea knows that she is purified. Every day Tel Aviv's residents rise congenially from bathing. Here they make their great *tashlich*. They cast their filth and contamination to its depths, exhaust their excess energy in swimming and play. And it's not only a physical purification. . . . One who strengthens his body in the sea renews his inner spiritual essence.[57]

The writer refers to the ceremony of tashlich, the communal, symbolic casting of sins, often in the form of bread crumbs, into a body of water, on the first day of the Jewish New Year, in anticipation of Yom Kippur, the Day of Atonement. Figure 5.5 depicts the actual ceremony of tashlich in Tel Aviv in the 1920s. The observants are almost all men. Some are markedly religious, wearing beards and more traditional suits; others are clean shaven and in late summer whites. Everyone has a hat of some sort; they read from prayer books as they stand at the water's edge. The photographer, it should be noted, and with him the viewer, stand in the water to get the shot. The construction site in the background suggests the degree to which the city continues to be built even on a holiday. Tel Aviv's seashore, the photograph suggests, is a site of both spiritual and physical regeneration, the sea itself symbolic of the city's sacred and secular aspirations. Jerusalem's historical and religious authority notwithstanding, Tel Aviv too had sacred ambitions. The photo records the sea as the site where two potentially conflicting notions are reconciled—it is the place where *Jewish culture* can be renewed, transformed, reconsecrated as *Hebrew culture*.

Figure 5.6 represents a similar scene, but from the opposite angle; the images are quite different in tone, and it is easy to understand why the first photograph was included in a beautifully produced volume titled *Documenters of the Dream: Pioneer Jewish Photographers in the Land of Israel*. This second image was found uncataloged in a box in a Jerusalem archive, labeled "photographer unknown." In this photograph, women

*Fig. 5.5* Tashlich at the Tel Aviv seashore (1926), Shimon Korbman. Historical Museum of Tel Aviv–Jaffa.

and children are visible among the crowd, which is dwarfed by the surrounding scene; strung out along the edge of the water, with a ship just barely visible on the horizon, they are almost swallowed up by the sea and the pocked, uneven beach behind them. There is no evidence of Tel Aviv's new construction; instead we see the Crusader city of Jaffa silhouetted along the shore. (The loose panorama provides an enormous contrast to the tightly-knit circle of the founding of Achusat Bayit; see Chapter 3.) The not-so-distant but slightly hazy image of Jaffa in the background is matched in the center foreground by a pair of Arabs in traditional garb, one of whom looks directly back at the photographer; together, the city along the coast, and these two figures, effectively, graphically, bracket the broken line of Jewish observants, many of whom seem somewhat disoriented, facing the wrong direction, or more intent on the social, rather than the spiritual, aspect of the ritual at hand. The photograph thus presents a more textured vision of the city's

*Fig. 5.6* Another view of tashlich, 1920s. Photographer unknown. Central Zionist Archives.

social and ethnic composition, and also of the complexity, indeed the relative uncertainty of the entire enterprise.

Concern for the beachfront, and a connection to the sea, were also a matter of popular discourse. Letters in the Tel Aviv–Jaffa Municipality files expressed outrage over the physical condition of the seashore as the city expanded, and tied the question of the seafront's destruction to the very essence of the city's future character. A 1925 letter from a concerned citizen to Meir Dizengoff, the erstwhile founder and mayor of Tel Aviv, protests the ongoing destruction of the seafront, referring to the high bluff of its northern section as "Tel Aviv's Carmel":

> Whose heart wouldn't burst at the sight of hundreds of wild Bedouins standing and destroying these high sands and loading them onto camels and wagons. This is an awful illustration of the level of our cultural relation to the nature surrounding us. There is almost no difference between the wild, strange Bedouin and ourselves who say we want to bind ourselves and our children after us to this place called Tel Aviv.[58]

The passage is an early example of what would become a veritable refrain in Zionist discourse about Arabs' neglect of the land, which ostensibly disqualified them as legitimate, competent caretakers.

The sea was also seen as Tel Aviv's winning attribute as a potential resort, a spa that could compete with the Riviera, a kind of Zionist enterprise of healing, drawing Jews from all over the world to take in the city's therapeutic sea breezes.[59] Dizengoff himself had other ideas. Y. Minor, the architect who designed the poet Bialik's Tel Aviv home in 1925, recalls that

> one day the mayor [Dizengoff] invited me to ride with him outside of town in order to discuss future development possibilities for the city. We rode on horseback and when we arrived at the dunes, Dizengoff waved his hand toward the north in a Napoleonic gesture and said: Here we will build our industrial area. I was thunderstruck. Mr. Dizengoff, I said, don't corrupt this beautiful coast. Tel Aviv should become a resort area for all of Europe. Nonsense, he replied, what do Jews have to do with bathing in the sea? Industry is more important.[60]

Dizengoff's remarks both critique and reinforce stereotypical notions of Jewish life in the Diaspora—a physical weakness suggested by an unfamiliarity with swimming, accompanied by the mandate to develop more productive work habits. Indeed, in the years following Dizengoff's remarks, a site marking this desired industriousness was built at the northern tip of Tel Aviv's coast, near the point where the Yarkon River meets the sea.[61]

The exhibition grounds of the 1934 Fair of the Orient, a World's Fair–style trade fair, attracted 600,000 visitors and displays from over twenty-three countries (Figure 5.7). The fair, whose construction was supervised by the noted Bauhaus architect Richard Kaufmann, symbolized Tel Aviv's pretensions as a budding Mediterranean metropolis, which would serve as a cultural and economic bridge between East and West. Both the fair and the port adjacent to it aspired to make Tel Aviv itself a kind of edge, a point of passage between Europe and the Middle East. Contemporary observers, including Vladimir Jabotinsky, stressed the fair's importance as a showcase for Jewish mercantile achievements—an unsettling claim to make in the interwar period.[62] The giant statue *The Hebrew Worker*, designed by Arieh Al-Hanani, became one of the fair's trademarks. A stylized, denuded figure carrying construction materials on its back, the statue's clean lines and forward stride are a pure expression of Tel Aviv's aspirations as the secular spearhead of a certain

*Fig. 5.7* Fair of the Orient at the Tel Aviv port, 1934. Central Zionist Archives.

vision of modern Jewish life—of Zionism's insistence on self-sufficiency and a resolutely future-oriented profile (Figure 5.8). What remains of the fair and, arguably, the vision it represents is evidenced in the physical deterioration of the site. The statue itself was refurbished in the 1980s; the rest of the former fairgrounds is now home to warehouses, garages, nightclubs, and wholesalers of ceramic tiles and bathroom fixtures. The site's historical meaning, as well the genuine architectural value of its unique Bauhaus constructions, has gone largely unnoticed in the generally rapacious atmosphere of Tel Aviv's real estate market.

The sea continues to mark Tel Aviv both as a Mediterranean city and as a potentially sacred site. These ideas have been taken up and transformed by the city's poets.[63] In a series called *Tashlich* from 1975, Meir Wieseltier describes the sea as the point of embarkation for "refugees from distant cities, people with suitcases, raincoats, buttons."[64] In these poems, Wieseltier questions the place of modern Hebrew culture—now over half a century old—in Palestine, saying "we will never make it from Lod to Beirut" (72). At the same time, in "Sealed in a Bottle," Wieseltier proposes a fragile affinity between the cities of the Mediterranean—"Damascus, Beirut, Tel Aviv. . . . We straggle behind a long historical caravan" (73).[65] While privileging the sea in his work,

*Fig. 5.8 The Hebrew Worker* in the twenty-first century. Photo by author.

Wieseltier nevertheless reminds the reader that something exists on the other side, declaring that "this east bank of the Mediterranean / is hard on poets" (73; note that the area is now defined by a simple geographical direction, no Promised Land.) The series' title, *Tashlich*, necessarily brings the reader to the sea and to the ironic act of casting one's sins toward Europe. Wieseltier's poem defines the city by what it throws away:

"Oh go down go down go down"

Oh go down go down go down
go down Jews to the seashore

the shore of the greenish sea
sweet and sour
that fills the frying pan
your god forged
to make an omelette.

And on the chilled and bored
sand, refreshed by
rows of tiny
tar blooms,

tread in your suede shoes,
inheritance of your forefathers,
which have hardened in dark closets
(like shoes hardened like a walnut)

like walnuts, like shrunken skulls,
like trouble-learned brains,

and ladle out from within the pockets
of your garments
outerware, underwear, revealed and hidden

the crumbs of sinful sticky experience,
baked all year in the body's heat,
it surely won't rise by itself,
though it has wings it won't fly,

and scatter them on the yellowish wave
chewing the sands impotently
caressing their fervor with coolness
and scatter them till the last crumb (90–91).

The poem stages an almost primal encounter at Tel Aviv's edge—its
citizens, sticky with the summer heat, and bereft of any real inheritance
except for some old-fashioned suede shoes, rid themselves of their sins,
only to have them scooped up and nearly thrown back at them by a
capricious chef of a sea god, who seems more intent on making them

sweat than on forgiveness. The poem preserves the formal structure of tashlich, but empties it of any possibility of atonement or purification. Instead we get the banal refuse of a migrant society, the embarrassment of soiled undergarments, and gooey black tar blossoms staining both the shore and the good shoes of Tel Aviv's residents. Wieseltier, considered the Tel Aviv poet par excellence, typically finds redemption in the decay and dirty details of everyday life, at the crumbling edge of the Mediterranean, which is, after all, the only spot offering relief from Tel Aviv's heat. In Wieseltier's work, these two potentially contrary notions of sacredness and locality—what the poet himself refers to as "climate" (*aklim*)—are, if not entirely reconciled, then at the very least, integrated. An uneasy balance between the two is suggested in the disoriented and somewhat distorted poses captured by the photographer Shimon Korbman in a haunting image from his *Tashlich* series, where the late afternoon breeze blows the European dress against the body, and the immigrant-pilgrims muddy their shoes at the very edge of the sea, but turn away from the harsh directness of the sun (Figure 5.5).

## The Villages and the Neighborhoods

> A rumor has reached us that you have dared to organize a German-language cabaret in your hotel, which is located within the bounds of the first Hebrew city. This action harms the goals of our city and its Hebrew face, and we demand that you stop this offense.
>
> —Letter from the Tel Aviv Municipality to the management of the Hotel Ritz, 4 June 1934

On the fifth floor of City Hall, at the end of an unremarkable often smoke-filled corridor lined with rooms issuing permits and documents that regulate private property in the city, one can find the office of the Tel Aviv–Jaffa Municipal Archives. In addition to a small but comprehensive library of publications relating to the city's history, the archive is the gateway to a staggeringly enormous collection of files in the basement; these files, many of which have been computerized by topic, personalities involved, and date, include official correspondence, meeting minutes, pamphlets, maps, memos, and notes connected to the business of running the city over the past eighty years. While this book as a whole makes extensive use of these documents, I would like to comment on them here as a genre, and also on the archive itself and its place in the city.

The archive is free and open to the public; on any given day there are huddled around its several small tables: academic researchers combing the spidery, handwritten onion-skin files of the City Rabbinate, high school students studying the city's cultural history, city clerks researching recent demographics for a neighborhood subject to rezoning, and a grandmother or two, searching for a photograph, or any physical record, of the house her parents bought in 1917 when they arrived from Minsk. The earliest files contain handwritten documents from the 1920s, including official reports from the budding municipality, and letters from proactive, usually irate citizens complaining about some aspect of city life, often their neighbors. The handwriting in the official documents is precise and neat, the signatures delivered with a flourish; the letters range from the formal and accomplished—progeny of the nineteenth-century Yiddish-Hebrew *brivenshteller* (letter-writing guides)—to blunt accusations or requests riddled with spelling errors. In any given file, the documents are stored by date, from latest to earliest, so reading them entails going back in time, observing interactions unfold in reverse, as motivations and intentions are revealed, and different "characters" become involved. As a genre, the letters seem akin to other documents common in Jewish society; the submission of written requests, in Hebrew, for some sort of material or juridical assistance has historically been part of Jewish communities' traditional social fabric. In the Diaspora these transactions took place within a sphere that was itself embedded in a larger civil non-Jewish realm. This was initially the case for the Tel Aviv Municipality, which functioned administratively in semiautonomous fashion, under first the Ottoman authorities and later—with more freedom—the British. Thus some administrative features of the establishment of Tel Aviv hearken back to the traditional structures of Jewish life in the Diaspora.

These letters provide a colorful sense of the period in which they were written—the day-to-day issues and questions that plagued ordinary people. Clearly, though, the letter writers were, to a certain degree, a self-selecting group: those with either knowledge of written modern Hebrew, or access to someone with that skill, who had the inclination to initiate quasi-official dealings with a public institution. Many of the letter writers—even those addressing the most mundane of issues—display an air of self-possession about the city, as if they have a personal stake in its character and feel entitled to express their opinions and have them matter. They also have a very definite view of the parameters and jurisdiction of the "first Hebrew city," as evidenced in the above-cited letter to the Hotel Ritz, written in response to a citizen's complaint about the German-language cabaret. Other letters report on activities that seem salacious—the gathering of Jews and Arabs in the company of prostitutes—or even seditious—a Jewish woman who is a Communist living with an Arab man who was accused of incitement in the 1929 disturbances.[66] Each of these documents represents an individual voice, many of which existed on the city's margins; yet they have been preserved, stored, filed, and itemized in the building representing the center of the city's institutional power—City Hall. Indeed, the mere existence of an institutional archive, an organ expressly devoted to the maintenance of historical records, lends legitimacy and authority to the city; at the same time, however, these very documents reveal the processes through which the city extended its power, and established itself as this authority. They demonstrate that the center is not a given entity but is in fact articulated by its own limits. These peripheral areas—which included older Jewish neighborhoods, Arab villages, and the German Templar settlement of Sharona—upset the city's social, economic, and ethnic homogeneity. They suffered from poor infrastructure and municipal services, and their public face was emphatically not the modernist look of the Bauhaus. These letters provide an important and rare glimpse from the margins of Tel Aviv's self-defined center.

Thus, for example, the neighborhood council of Neve Sha'anan, in a letter dated 15 September 1925, complains that while they are the largest neighborhood in the vicinity of Tel Aviv ("five hundred souls") they have yet to receive basic conveniences such as electricity and paved roads that have been afforded to other neighborhoods. Their repeated requests have been greeted with disdain and indifference (*zilzul va-adishut*).[67] Another letter, dated 5 July 1947, from an "alert citizen" in the same area, indicates that the situation has not improved, and contains a threat to stop paying taxes unless the authorities pay more attention to the neighborhood after election time.[68] The southern areas of the city bordering Jaffa were a particular target of local complaint. A 1930 letter in Arabic from Mohammed Yasin (and a partner of Isaac Eshmerling), an egg merchant from Manshiya, informs authorities about the presence of an illegal bathhouse in the neighborhood and asks that the Municipality send a health official to check on the situation.[69] Residents of Kalisher Street bordering Manshiya complain of the "wild" conditions of local cafés and explicitly address what they perceive as the centers of power: "You who live in the peaceful places of Rothschild Boulevard and the heart of northern Tel Aviv are obligated to pay attention to our terrible situation because we pay taxes just like the residents of the best parts of the city."[70]

There were five Arab villages within Tel Aviv's municipal bounds: Salama, Sheikh Munis, Jarisha, Jammasin, and Summayl.[71] These villages and the German Templar settlement of Sharona founded in 1871 to the east, were perceived as obstacles to Tel Aviv's growth, because of their location and non-Jewish populations. Writers used these peripheral neighborhoods to imagine certain aspects of the city. One account envisioned Tel Aviv's "modern" qualities from the "primitive" perspective of a nearby Arab village:

> Tel Aviv is flooded with electric light. . . . Europe sprayed a spark and it rolled around and landed here. Beyond the gates of Tel Aviv, a dark night clings to the ancient Arab land. . . . A small Arab village sleeps next to the Mediterranean coast. Once in awhile there is an echo of the sound of "Balad Kabir"—the big city—the Jews' city Tel Aviv. At night the city's light is visible—the skies glow. The believers sit on top of tombstones, which have mingled with living quarters, like mixing fresh and dried twigs in a vineyard. They sit and talk about the wonders of the city of the Jews. Their imagination heats up, and truth becomes woven with lies in a single fabric.[72]

A sense of isolation and embattlement is conveyed through the depiction of the city within a landscape whose natural elements seem to bolster the potential danger posed by its human inhabitants: "the purview of the sands was so wide then that at night they would redden with the campfires of the Bedouins on Tel Aviv's border, and during the days of the grape harvest the Arabs of Jaffa would set up their dark tents on the vineyard hills, which surrounded the neighborhood [Tel Aviv] up until Sharona."[73]

The agricultural and architectural achievements of Sharona—especially its generous use of green public spaces—were generally admired, and even imitated, by the Zionist movement in and around Tel Aviv.[74] A memoiristic account recalls the ambivalence associated with this explicitly non-Jewish site:

> Sharona, a readily attainable goal for short hikes, was an entity we didn't know how to categorize. It reminded me of German villages I had known. Farmers' houses within green spaces overflowing with flowers. Sharp-eyed folks also said they even spied pigs in the settlement. Was this realm friend or foe? Those Germans that we fled from, how is it that we encounter them again, here so close by?[75]

The older Jewish settlements of Neve Tsedek (established in 1887) and Neve Shalom (established in 1890) posed a different sort of a problem. On a fiscal level, the absorption of these areas into the city's municipal structure increased the population of Tel Aviv's more indigent social and economic classes.[76] Neve Shalom was described by Rachel Yana'it in 1908 as a "ghetto of the first degree" and "a Jewish village of the Diaspora."[77] Dizengoff viewed the religiosity of these neighborhoods as evidence of their "passive Eastern-ness," as opposed to Tel Aviv's more European way of life.[78] At the same time, the existence of these neighborhoods undermined Achusat Bayit's authoritative status as "first." A relatively clear example of the stability and long-lived nature of these areas is Tsiona Tagger's *Train on Herzl Street* (1924; Figure 5.9). Tagger was born in Jaffa in 1900 to a Bulgarian family and grew up at 3 Rothschild, the first two-story home in Tel Aviv, a house bordered by a vineyard and dunes.[79] While her work generally participates in the jumble of modernist styles—fauvism, cubism, futurism, expressionism—represented in the Eretzyisraeli school, this particular painting has an unusual focus: a train speeding through the canyon between

*Fig. 5.9 Train on Herzl Street* (1924), Tsiona Tagger. Joseph Hackmey Collection.

Neve Tsedek and the German colony, areas that predate Achusat Bayit. Tagger's scene does not represent the singular, instantaneous origins of Reuven's *Tel Aviv* (1922; see discussion in Chapter 3), but a slightly older, more developed setting. The structures in the painting are differentiated by style and size; a continuous human presence is indicated by the bridge and telegraph lines. The painting's dull colors are more naturalistic than the pastels of contemporaneous landscapes by other painters in Tel Aviv. Aside from personal predilection, one way to account for this difference in palette is by recalling the remarks of European-born artists regarding the enormous effect the new Mediterranean light had on their work.[80] Perhaps Tagger, born in Palestine, did not experience this light as strange, a fact particularly evident in her treatment of the sky as patchy, beige, and otherwise unremarkable.

*Train on Herzl Street* evidences the Cézannesque conception of landscape as a composition of geometric forms. These forms—the cylindrical head of the train, the long boomerang-shaped wall, the triangular roofs—have volume and weight, a solidity at odds with the relentless pull of the train's descent and the swift movement indicated by the blur of its wheels. The mix of solidity and movement is most evident in the embankments. The train's motion shapes the earth as it passes, the thick brush strokes pointing skyward away from the tracks. Much of the canvas is taken up by this unevenly painted space, ground that appears to have been ripped open by the tracks. It bears not only the effects of the train's movement; the upward brush strokes suggest the very process itself. Ground that appears to be quite bulky and static is, on closer examination, filled with evidence of motion.

The painting's formal tensions suggest a complicated relation between human presence and natural landscape. Unlike Reuven's houses, which seem perfectly accommodated by the surrounding sands, *Train on Herzl Street* depicts human presence as a violent and disruptive intrusion. The painting offers a more nuanced representation of how human beings live within a landscape—shaping it and living with the consequences of that change. This reading of the painting's unsentimental appraisal demonstrates an acute sensitivity to the effects of urbanism on Tagger's native landscape. Furthermore, her painting's representation of Tel Aviv's older, more outlying districts challenges the idea of Tel Aviv as "sprung from the sands," and forces the viewer to see the city in relation to a previously inhabited landscape.

By way of conclusion, I turn to a pair of short stories, one by Benjamin Tammuz and the other by Devora Baron, that offer delicate depictions of Tel Aviv's geographic center and its periphery. Both stories deploy the ethnic and social specifics of the city's spatial features, especially the contrast between center and margins, to shed light on the psychological growth or dilemmas of their characters. Tammuz's "Sands of Gold" (1950) is in some ways a companion piece to "The Swimming Contest"—both stories feature childhood emersion in an area adjacent to the neighborhood of home.[81] The story follows the restless mind of a bored young boy living in one of the large single-family homes on Rothschild Boulevard or Nahalat Binyamin Street, who fantasizes about a pair of twin playmates who live in "the red house" at the end of the street, past the railroad tracks. Amidst the details of plush domestic furnishings—wool sofa covering and an elaborate glass cupboard containing china—caught between tedium and dreaming, the boy muses that "from the large window you can see the sea at the bottom of the street. From the roof one can even see Jaffa port and its ships."[82] Angry at his mother for making him stay in to prepare his lessons, he suddenly remembers the "sands of gold":

> At the top of road, after you crossed great Allenby Street, you turn and pass over the train tracks and from there left, along the lone sycamores stretched out over the sands. And after them, the wondrous hill and little stream beds and the plowed red clay earth of Sharona. Next to all these was the large red house, a mysterious place from which arose the noise of machinery. Past this stood the twins' house.[83]

The boy "escapes" by way of the porch and makes his way out of the neighborhood, past the iconic markers of the historic city center—the kiosk, gymnasium, and water tower—and pauses for shade within a line of sycamores. Yet even as he wishes for some "real shade," he immediately remembers the twins' house: "the edges of sand and the red house, all stood before him and they are enveloped in far-flung places and a mysterious desire."[84] The passage's precise spatial instructions lead him out of the city into a pastoral, agrarian, yet semi-industrial area. Eventually, he wanders into the groves of Abu-Kabir, adjacent to Jaffa.[85] Resting beneath a tree next to an untended herd of goats, he dozes off three times, waking first to the voice of an Arab shepherd, then to the twins' father's voice, and finally to their mother offering him a slice of bread and cheese. The story ends not with the boy meeting the twins, but with the recognition that the lush quiet of his home lacks something. Wishing briefly that he could live with the twins, he realizes nonetheless that he has been "sentenced to absolute loneliness." The passage between the new neighborhood of Tel Aviv and the surrounding older areas is definitive and meaningful—in town: an ordered domestic setting, the authority of family and society, lessons to do and rules to follow; at the edge of town: exposure to ethnic and social difference, the suggestion of risk or even danger, and a transformative experience of self-recognition.

Devora Baron's "In the Heart of the City" (1948) reverses the direction of Tammuz's story, pulling elements of agrarian margins into the cement-covered center.[86] The story describes an empty lot whose owners are abroad on business. Surrounded, almost choked, by the city's buildings, it has nevertheless absorbed enough sun and rain to become a sort of pastoral refuge. Ironically, an Arab shepherd from a "faraway neighborhood," attracted by the scent of the place, brings his herd into "the urban asphalt whirlpool." Taking up his flute, he plays songs from the time of "his fathers' fathers, before the land was spoiled, when it was still revealed in it fullness and only weeds and fruit-bearing trees grew upon it, as was God's commandment, for human beings and for animals" (300). While the place's abandoned neglect disgusts the city's veteran residents as they ride past in their "bus cages," it brings solace to "the sick man imprisoned on the first floor in the building on the left." For this man, who had been "brought here from the stifling environment of another block of houses," the empty lot represents a place to breathe in the otherwise oppressive city. It reminds him of the greenery of his European childhood—those "gardens of Eden"; unlike the owners of the lot, however, he cannot afford to return abroad for a visit. The man arranges his window shutters to block everything except a view of the lot, and lives in rhythm with its various inhabitants—birds, butterflies, beetles, stray cats who have escaped the cars—"murderous monsters running about the street"—and the grocer's horse, set out to graze in the evening. At the same time, he senses change is imminent. He wakes one morning to find the lot transformed, its greenery torn and uprooted; on the orders of the recently returned owners, workers are turning the place into a parking lot. By evening, cleared and leveled, the lot fills with trucks, motorcycles, taxis: "their headlights all lit, running, breathing heavily, going crazy like a herd of wild animals" (301). The sky darkens with sand and the scent of gasoline:

> The man by his window, in the house on the left, waves his handkerchief feebly. I'm choking, he says, and falls silent, like the helpless and lonely, those who have been entirely abandoned; however, the city veterans, as they pass by on the bus, are satisfied the flaw has been fixed, and the place has become just another part of the city (301).

In the post-Edenic world of Baron's story, the city is trapped under an apocalyptic haze of smog and sand. Like her earlier tale of a Tel Aviv funeral, "In the Heart of the City" presents a morose view of urban life; the claustrophobia of the man's apartment ironically increases as the city expands around him.

Unlike Tammuz's picaresque tale of a boy's self-discovery, a story in which space is the medium through which the "hero" molds his sense of self, moving from the center out into the world's adventure, Baron's story pulls the margins into the center, which is itself viewed by an older man trapped in his own apartment, observing the world through a limited yet self-determined frame—the shutters drawn precisely so as to capture the desired view. An awareness of gender offers a way of accounting for these differences. Drawing on the psychoanalytic insights of Nancy Chodorow's influential study, *The Reproduction of Mothering*, feminist critics have argued that female subjectivity is especially open to multiple affiliations. This more flexible sense of self suggests that spatial relations may also be conceived as more fluid and interrelated. Urban fiction by women writers displays a commensurately permeable sense of space: "Because woman do not separate the sense of self as rigidly as men do, they are more comfortable with seeing the city as mixed and partial, as districts overlapping one another, rather than precise areas."[87] Though Baron's protagonist is trapped in his own home, her story evidences just this sort of porousness, symbolized by the introduction of an agrarian lot into the urban grid of Tel Aviv, a site that itself draws a figure from the edge of town—a young Arab shepherd—whose presence is ignored by the city's bus-riding inhabitants. The lot and its association with this figure from the margins represents a space of difference firmly lodged at the center of town. Furthermore, the power of this space is intuited by a character who appears to be a passive nonparticipant. For readers familiar with Baron's life, this figure, and its embittered agency, is perhaps an oblique reference to the self-imposed confinement of her later years.[88]

Even after settling in Tel Aviv, Baron continued to depict the Diaspora, despite pressures obligating Hebrew fiction to portray national life in Palestine. In discussing Baron's representation of the nation, Orly Lubin describes the juxtaposition of a fragmented, particularistic sense of time—seen through the activities of the female characters—with the more coherent, linear narrative of a national, collective history—symbolized by the male characters.[89] This tension is especially apparent in Baron's novel set in a Jewish émigré community in Alexandria during World War I, *Ha-golim* (The Exiles), where the transition from Europe to Palestine is not conceived as a break between past and present: "on the contrary, there is a continuum, or simultaneity."[90] This temporal synchronicity, which subverts or undermines Zionism's metanarrative of redemption in the Land of Israel, finds its spatial counterpart in "In the Heart of the City," where the city's agrarian borders are drawn into the center, unsettling the city's sense of order and creating a kind of "internal frontier," an "'alien' area within the collective's boundaries into which the core attempts to expand, penetrate, and increase its control."[91] Though the description of the shepherd gestures toward the sentimental, he disappears from the story without a trace, along with any intrinsic connection to the natural landscape. The lot's destabilizing distinctiveness is eventually absorbed into Tel Aviv, becoming "just another part of the city." This erasure of difference is depicted as a brutal—"I'm choking," says the man—but inevitable result of the city's development.

The deployment of space in Baron's story—the way it disrupts and even reverses the firmly constructed alterity of center and edges—resembles the use of time in Leah Goldberg's work about Tel Aviv discussed at the end of Chapter 4. Both women work within the recognizable parameters of early Hebrew writing in Palestine, yet their writing rejects the spatial and temporal structures underlying the Zionist discourse that determines these parameters. Instead, Goldberg's poems and Baron's stories offer a critique; they map a version of the city's spatial contours that recognizes both the contingency of linear, temporal relationships, and the degree to which space is always a product of social, ideological factors.

## A View from the Rooftop

Any examination of Tel Aviv's imagined edges is of course ultimately connected to the larger question of Israel's political borders. Establishing itself as a Jewish or Hebrew city entailed creating or assuming a collective identity for its inhabitants, and making that identity synonymous with specific geographical borders, boundaries that were, in fact, porous and shifting. The border's duality is such that it becomes both a "national icon meant to enlist the identification and utmost loyalty of the people," as well as a frontier to be passed over, "a penetrable space of limbo, which critiques the Cartesian, geometric notions of borders, and therein blurs the differences between 'interior' and 'exterior,' between 'here' and 'there.'"[92] While the space of the homeland was normalized through various forms of educational activity, there was also an "'exoticising' of the border, which strengthened the curiosity and desire for the spaces beyond it. . . . Space became a totem, and the border supplied the taboo."[93] There is a view of Tel Aviv that exposes distinctions between center and borders as fluid and contingent upon the position of the beholder: this is the view from the roof. In the 1930s and 1940s, Yosef Zaritzki painted a series of watercolors from his roof on Galil (later Mapu) Street, just newly built in 1931. The city is presented not from the position of a rooted observer, but from a physically detached, nearly suspended angle. Although the paintings display an almost classical perspective and division of space into neat thirds—roof, city, hills—they became increasingly abstract over the years, with thin lines laid over the barest of washes to indicate the slant of a street, a building's silhouette, or the horizon. Zaritzki's landscapes explore the seam where the city's International Style meets nature. Yet the painter resolutely turns his back on one of the city's defining edges—the sea—and instead gives us panorama after panorama of the hills that would eventually become the eastern suburb of Ramat Gan.[94] This disavowal of the sea is yet another example of how the periphery may be the location of critique; Zaritzki refuses to fetishize the local by deliberately avoiding the sea's symbolic value, a lacunae that distinguishes his work from mainstream Eretzyisraeli art of the period, and prefigures the work of later Israeli artists, who had no "need for that sea, the sea of immigration."[95] In *View from the Roof* (ca. 1940; Figure 5.10), the shadow of the painter appears like a lone actor on the stage, surveying the immediate Bauhaus constructions of his neighborhood.[96] A staircase leaning against the rooftop laundry room suggests an ever-expanding space upwards.

*Fig. 5.10 View from the Roof* (ca. 1940), Yosef Zaritzki. Joseph Hackmey Collection.

The detached quality of these landscapes should not obscure Zaritzki's self-perception as a painter involved in the building of Tel Aviv:

A painter in France or in England rises in the morning and paints and around him stands a city that has existed for hundreds of years, and he neither knows nor wants to know when the road was built and when they put up the house he lives in. Here the painter knows when they built the street and when they built the house, because they were built before his very eyes. He saw when there was nothing and afterwards saw how the house was put up and how the road and the city were built. And so here the painter must also be involved, a partner.[97]

As we have seen, abstraction, and the accompanying pretension to newness and a lack of history, became a defining feature of Tel Aviv's urban landscape. Yet Zaritzki's paintings, despite their abstract quality, are an attempt to capture the city's composition in the moment of its making, to mark in his painting a minutely distinguished historical progression, and as such to grant the city the kind of rootedness experienced by a European painter. In fact, Tel Aviv contains two sites at its very center that endow the city with a genuine sense of place: the village of Summayl and Rabin Square. Each is irrevocably bound up with history; each is tied to events that have left a deep impression on the city and Israel as a whole—the war of 1948 and the assassination of Yitzhak Rabin in 1995. The village and the square, and the events whose traces they contain, provide the core of this study's next and concluding chapter.

## Six

Rabin Square, Summayl, and the Rhetoric
of Walking

> Buildings and monuments are . . . the visible remnants of the past:
> they often outlast the human beings who created them. How these
> structures are seen, treated and remembered sheds light on a collec-
> tive identity that is more felt than articulated.
>
> —Brian Ladd, *The Ghosts of Berlin*

> David Lugasi . . . never knew how much he really loved the Wailing
> Wall until he saw it completely taken apart, stone by stone, and
> loaded onto thirty trucks belonging to his moving and construction
> firm, AA America Shipping and Construction. Until that moment
> the Wall had been a place, just a place. But the Rabin assassination
> changed everything.
>
> —Uzi Weil, "The Man Who Moved the Wailing Wall"

## "How do you get to Rabin Square?"

In January 2000, crowds gathered in Tel Aviv's largest public plaza, Rabin Square—née Kings of Israel Square—located in front of City Hall
and the site of Yitzhak Rabin's assassination on 4 November 1995. The
occasion was a rally in support of continued Israeli occupation of the
Golan Heights. As I walked through the streets closed to traffic, I noticed that people streaming toward the square seemed different from
the usual Tel Aviv crowd. Most of the women wore long skirts; the men
had head coverings and beards; some carried rifles. The refrain repeatedly directed toward me—"Excuse me, where's Rabin Square?"—
marked me as someone local who could help them, and them as non-
Tel-Aviv-residents, as politically and socially distinct from northern Tel
Aviv's largely liberal population. Their walk to the square may have
borne a structural, physical resemblance to the route taken by thou- 229
sands of demonstrators from the Left on other occasions, but it was not
the same walk. It may not have even been the same square that they
were heading toward. Moreover, if Rabin Square is a site that "sheds

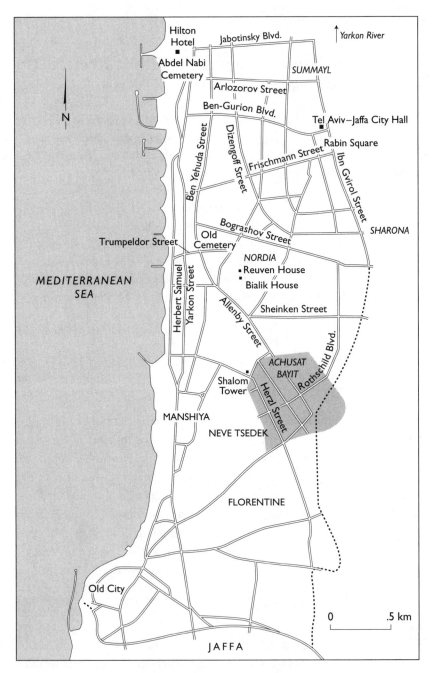

*Map 6.1* Tel Aviv–Jaffa, city center. Places in italics exist in memory only.

light on a collective identity that is more felt than articulated," the assassination and its aftermath revealed just how fully unanimity regarding this identity had come undone, if it indeed ever existed.

Brian Ladd's comments above regarding Berlin—a city whose own urban landscape has recently been the site of intense civic struggle over the city's multilayered past—are meaningful only to the extent that a city's people believe they possess a collective identity and that they can identify and interpret the city's iconic markers of memory. Chapter 3 discussed how the area surrounding Rothschild Boulevard gradually assumed a quasi-iconic status in Tel Aviv's popular imagination. The process of commemoration and history-making surrounding Rabin Square, perhaps the city's most contested "site of memory," was both more complex and more compressed; it is also, in a sense, more explicitly ongoing than the making of Tel Aviv's early history. In thinking about how memory is inscribed in the square, we will have to discard many of the notions of "instant roots" and "invented communities" that informed Tel Aviv's history until 1995. Paradoxically, with Rabin Square, the city gained a site whose memorial cachet seemed transparent but whose meaning would remain fractured and disputed.

"How do you get to Rabin Square?" Answering this question is a simple matter of technical directions—which street to walk down, where to turn. Yet what does the path to Rabin Square signify if one considers the history of the streets and sites passed along the way? Michel de Certeau uses the term "perambulatory rhetoric" to describe walking as a kind of utterance, a behavior that is understood and comprehensible in semiotic terms, like a language, on the axes of selection and combination. Meaning is created by people moving through the space of the city, against the background of physical structures (streets, buildings), and in relation to other possible utterances.[1] The space of the city also necessarily includes some consciousness of its history, whether personal or collective. Walking means "reading" these spaces like a text, on different levels, with attention to form and content, and to figurative and literal effects. So, for example, to get to Rabin Square from the sea, one may go down Ben-Gurion Boulevard, a tree-lined street that is still called by some of the city's older residents by its original name, *Sderot kakal* (Jewish National Fund Boulevard), a reminder of the early years of state-building. One may also walk down Grove Street just north of the square; the street's name marks the fact that there were once orange groves where City Hall now stands. Some of these groves were owned by an otherwise undistinguished Frenchman named Fortles, who sold the land to the municipality in 1926. The grove's small reservoir became a swimming pool, and a zoo was also built on the grounds. A larger adjacent grove was owned by the Felman family, often remembered as pioneers of citrus farming. David Felman, who arrived in Palestine in 1884 and purchased the land from the nearby village of Summayl, died of sunstroke soon after planting the grove. It was managed thereafter by his wife Sarah. Arabs living in the area called the grove *Beyrat Sarah*—Sarah's orchard—while the Jews called it *Beyrat Mazeritch*, after Felman's hometown.[2] Approaching the square from the north, walking down Ibn Gvirol Street (named for the medieval Jewish poet), one crosses Arlozorov Street, named after the Labor movement leader Haim Arlozorov, who was himself the victim of a political assassination in 1933. Like the Rabin assassination sixty years later, Arlozorov's death revealed the intensity of political tensions within Jewish society in Palestine. Two suspects associated with the right-wing Revisionist Party were accused of the murder; one was even identified by Arlozorov's wife, Sima. Two Arab suspects also were arrested, and one apparently confessed to the murder. The Revisionists were eventually found guilty, but the verdict was struck down on technicalities. From the time of the murder in June 1933 to the end of the trial a year later, the streets of Tel Aviv were filled with political unrest and violence, and were frequently the site of clashes between Revisionists and Labor movement supporters.[3]

Chapters 2 and 3 discussed the connection between Tel Aviv's street names and the city's developing identity as a Jewish urban space. However, unlike the older neighborhoods surrounding Rothschild Boulevard, where streets largely recall modern Jewish experience in the Diaspora or life locally during ancient times, many (though not all) of the residential streets surrounding the square refer, in self-reflective fashion, to people, events, and places associated with the history of Tel Aviv itself. Both the square and City Hall at its northern end are relative newcomers to Tel Aviv's downtown core. Originally designated by the

Geddes plan as a public space, construction of the square was not completed until 1965. City Hall, though embraced by many architects as a
singular achievement, is not entirely beloved by the city's residents,
perhaps as much due to its endless bureaucracy as its stern, monolithic
facade and dreary interior corridors. The plaza itself is underutilized on
a daily level—few cross its vast, bare expanse, preferring to skirt around
it on the shaded perimeter streets, and the space has been used mainly
on special occasions: the annual book fair, institutionalized observances of state holidays and, increasingly, political gatherings of both
the Left and Right. In the 1970s, the square became the site of emotional, dramatic speeches by both Likud leader Menachem Begin and
Labor Party leaders against the backdrop of the erosion of Israel's dominant Zionist-Socialist ethos and the eventual rise of Begin's Likud in
1977. Before the Rabin assassination, the square's most salient events in
public memory were the spontaneous celebration of Israel's European
basketball championship in 1977, during which thousands arrived at the
square to celebrate and dance in the fountain in front of City Hall, and
the demonstration in 1982 during the Lebanon War, following the mas-
sacres in the Sabra and Shatila refugee camps in Beirut—dubbed the
"400,000 demonstration," after then-estimates of the crowd's size.[4]
The assassination of Prime Minister Yitzhak Rabin on 4 November 1995
transformed the image of the square in public consciousness; what had
previously been a largely characterless site—a bland, impassive space
that was intermittently filled with the features of whatever national assembly or event happened to be staged there—became irrevocably
linked to one of the defining moments in Israeli history, an event whose
impact continues to be felt and debated across the entire spectrum of
Israeli society.[5]

## The Square as a Site of Memory

"Kings of Israel Square, The Day After"

Remembrance candles in tins cans—
flame after flame like spots
on the tiger

shot in the jungle of his dreams.
His eyes, which almost saw the lamb
living with the wolf, hang suddenly
on the wall of blood
on the way to the heart.

—Ronny Someck

Rabin was killed on a Saturday night and buried the following Monday. Immediately following the assassination, which occurred at the conclusion of a peace rally, the square became a central site of mourning and remembrance. The memorial activities in the square during the week following his funeral—the *shiva* or seven-day mourning period prescribed in Jewish tradition—were spontaneous and characterized by several repetitive rituals: the lighting of memorial candles, a custom previously associated with either domestic remembrance practices or Mizrahi traditions surrounding pilgrimage to saints' sanctuaries; the writing of graffiti on any flat surface that could accommodate it, including the staircase Rabin descended just before he was shot, the exterior walls of the City Hall, the walls of the adjacent parking lot as well as those of the open platform above the lot; the construction of minishrines throughout the square and especially near the spot of the assassination, consisting of flowers, candles, written messages, drawings and photographs of Rabin, and found objects such as bullet casings, models of white doves and a makeshift Ten Commandments inscribed with the words "Thou shalt not kill" (Figures 6.1, 6.2). The combined effect of these rituals produced a dynamic, polyphonic collage of mourning, which appeared to represent the shock and grief of every sector of society. Live images of the square and the crowds of young people who gathered there, sitting in circles of mourning and singing, were continuously broadcast on national television, adding to the sense of a collective, national experience.

The precise spot of the assassination became progressively more organized in its commemorative power. The evolution of the site and its memorial rituals provides an instructive instance of the dialectic between spontaneous and institutionalized memory, and thus another opportunity to examine how "sites of memory" have developed in Tel

*Fig. 6.1* Spontaneous commemoration after the assassination in newly named Rabin Square, November 1995. Photo by Guy Shachar.

Aviv.[6] For example, on the first anniversary of the assassination, the improvised shrine was replaced by an official memorial. Sixteen roughly cut black stones laid at angles to the ground symbolize the rupture in Israeli society caused by the assassination. They are surrounded by a black chain belt, symbolizing the desire for unity. One of the stones is raised higher than the others and bears the inscription: "Here, on this spot, at the conclusion of the Sabbath, 11 Heshvan 5756, 4 November 1995, Prime Minister and Defense Minister Yitzhak Rabin was murdered. Peace is his testament." The inscription appears only in Hebrew,

*Fig. 6.2* Rabin Square with City Hall in the background. 11 Nov. 1995. Photo by Guy Shachar.

as if the site is meant solely for Israelis. The graffiti, which grew thicker as layers of new messages were added, was eventually painted over by the Municipality, despite the objections of some citizens' groups. For a time, a wall was designated by the Municipality as a permissible site for graffiti; it was periodically repainted, thus creating an institutionally sanctioned space for what had previously been spontaneous public expressions of identification or protest.

In 1999, the area was completely redesigned for the fourth anniversary. In place of the rough, vernacular eloquence of the graffiti, informational panels in Hebrew, Arabic, and English present details of Rabin's life, especially his involvement in the peace process (Figures 6.3, 6.4). The site also contains oversized photographs of scenes from the initial mourning period in the square, as well as selected examples of graffiti from this same period, examples of what Michael Feige calls "the commemoration of commemoration." What is commemorated by these images of objects and rituals originally produced in Rabin's memory is not so much the assassination itself, but the memory of it.[7]

*Fig. 6.3* Informational panels at Rabin Memorial, 1999. Photo by author.

The spot of the assassination is covered with a series of metal emblems embedded in the sidewalk, each marking where Rabin and members of his entourage stood when they were approached by Yigal Amir (who is referred to not by name but only as "the assassin"). A plaque containing a legend identifies each person and his position, thus encouraging visitors to enter into an ostensibly unmediated, in situ experience of the assassination.

Discussion of the square's memorial power tends to privilege behavior during the period immediately following the assassination over the later involvement—some would say intervention—of the Municipality, the state, and even the Rabin family.[8] The designer of the site's permanent memorial display, David Tartakover, seemed to agree; his images preserved the graffiti from the initial outpouring, while erasing later additions. This selective gesture is typical of the work of monuments; in their efforts to "concretize heritage in terms of location," they embed time within space, both preserving and effacing, and thus interpreting the past and situating it in the present.[9] We are again facing Nora's qualitative distinction between "sites of memory" and genuine, authentic memorial practice. Both still characterize memorial

*Fig. 64* David Tartakover memorial installation, 1999. Buttons in the sidewalk denote the positions of Yitzhak Rabin, Yigal Amir, and the figures surrounding them at the time of the assassination. Photo by author.

observance of the assassination, especially the cycle of rituals connected with the square that has made it a kind of Israeli Hyde Park, a locus of both spontaneous and planned political debate. Has the assassination in any way, however, made the square a sacred space? On the one hand, sacred space would seem to indicate an extraordinary area distinct from the patterns of daily routine, a transcendent site, impervious to the effects of change. The degree to which this view has become part of general expectations concerning the square is evidenced in the public uproar occasioned by the Municipality's recent announcement of its plans to build a parking garage underneath the site. (The plans are currently on hold, in the wake of discussion in the Knesset about officially declaring the square a national landmark.[10]) Yet urban sacred space also entails another, entirely different set of parameters. Rabin Square houses, after all, the seat of the city's bureaucracy; it is the space around or through which Tel Aviv's residents move in pursuit of fairly mundane matters. With this understated sanctification of everyday life, the square's vitality as a memorial makes it a Tel Aviv site par excellence. Tel Aviv's "holiness," in Avot Yeshurun's terms, derives precisely from the city's earthliness and its embrace of memory as an ordinary matter.[11]

## After Rabin

> Rabin didn't leave a legacy; he left a paradox-riven process.
> —Amnon Raz-Krakotzkin, "Rabin's Legacy:
> On Secularism, Nationalism and Orientalism"

Though some critical insight is gained by viewing the Rabin assassination within the context of other political murders in the *Yishuv*, the event is nonetheless a singular turning point in Israeli history, if only for the stature of its victim and the immediate political consequences. The assassination and its aftermath—including the above-described public mourning, the subsequent electoral victory of Benjamin Netanyahu's Likud Party, and the virtual derailment of the peace process that had begun during the Rabin administration—became a lightning rod for public discourse. What exactly Rabin's murder "revealed" about Israeli society was widely debated, and these interpretations became part of larger attacks on, or defenses of, a whole range of political and social positions. Some argued that the assassination uncovered a deep division within Israeli society, one that divided the country's Jewish population in half:

> Here then lies the true fault line in Israeli society a century after the birth of Zionism. On one side of it stands a community that sees clericalism, messianism, and ethnocentrism as the continuation of the Zionist revolution toward a purer expression of "authentic" Jewish values. On the other stands a community that sees the rejection of modernism, pluralism, and pragmatism as a throwback to the ills that Zionism emerged to cure. These were the two worlds that collided on November 4, 1995.[12]

The columnist Doron Rosenblum viewed the assassination as an attack on Tel Aviv and all it stands for:

> The Rabin assassination may cast a shadow on Rabin's work and even his entire life, just as the fact that it happened in Tel Aviv will perhaps cast a retrospective and retroactive shadow on all the innocence and happiness, secular as well as routine, that has been, and will be, in the city. But that was precisely the intention of the attack . . . to forever muddy the joy of Israeli secularism.[13]

Whether the assassination was seen as an unanticipated shock or the inevitable result of social division and political incitement, whether Yigal Amir's motives were ascribed to religious or nationalist sentiment, or to both, the Rabin assassination marked the end of the "monolithic period of Israeli identity," the shattering of which revealed a mosaic of not entirely compatible identities that had long existed beneath the veneer of the carefully constructed image of "the new Hebrew."[14] The assassination, however, also established the square as a privileged site that was indelibly etched in the memory of Tel Aviv's residents; moreover, the meaning and power of this site reached far beyond the city's municipal boundaries. Rabin Square is Tel Aviv's first overtly national site of memory, a space connected to the assassination's political legacy in a far more profound fashion than Rabin's grave on Mt. Herzl in Jerusalem. In a sense, Rabin Square granted Tel Aviv the kind of symbolic capital previously accorded Jerusalem, and established for the first time a relative parity between the two cities in terms of their authority as historical centers.[15] This is, however, a paradoxical achievement: the square, and by association Tel Aviv, entered the narrative of the nation by virtue of its symbolic deconstruction of this narrative's fragile coherence.

Compared to earlier extended efforts to create a sense of place and historical roots for Tel Aviv, Rabin Square immediately displayed an enormous presence in the city's collective memory, acquiring its new name virtually overnight—a designation effected within collective and individual memories of the Rabin assassination, as well as in daily usage: the square is not only officially called Rabin Square, but is referred to as such by most, if not all, Tel Avivians. This phenomenon may be instructively juxtaposed to the Old Cemetery's abiding absence from official narratives of the city, and from the psychological plane of the city. Whereas the cemetery remains walled-in and seemingly impervious to the vicissitudes of history, the spatial openness of the square corresponds to the idea of contemporary Israeli society as an open and contested site. The differences between the two sites also suggest how radically splintered any idea of a collective national narrative has become in Israel. Though every second of the assassination has been analyzed, and a reenactment of the shooting itself prepared, opinion regarding its significance remains divided.

This division may be starkly observed in attitudes of the younger generation toward the assassination. The tendency to see Israeli society in generational terms, with each wave of youth exemplifying or united behind the national ethos, came to an apex with the Rabin assassination; a new grassroots political movement capitalizing on this notion of the youth's univocal response to the assassination subsequently formed under the slogan "An entire generation demands peace." The media especially focused on the picturesque qualities of the square as a site of mourning, and emphasized what appeared to be the overwhelming response of "the youth of the square" or "the candle youth." In the words of Tel Aviv Mayor Roni Milo, "These last few days, we have been witness to a poignant spectacle that we had never seen before. . . . Youth came and sat and came back here day after day, expressing their grief and ours; and for the sake of all these children, we want tomorrow morning to see a better country."[16] Though perhaps obvious, it bears pointing out that this description applies—almost tautologically—only to those youth who actually came to the square. Subsequent studies have examined the responses of young people to the assassination and discovered diverse opinions, ranging from apathy and disaffection (on the part of recent Russian immigrant youth) to approval and even joy over his murder (on the part of Jerusalem boarding school students from "disadvantaged" areas).[17] Clearly the manner in which youth were affected by the assassination in some way reflected their relation to existing political and societal power structures.

This fractured notion of generation and identity in the wake of the Rabin assassination figures in a number of recent literary works, including Etgar Keret's short story "Rabin Died," a delicate allegory of social and political tensions related through a brief series of incidents involving a cat named Rabin. "Last night Rabin died. A Vespa with a sidecar ran over him. Rabin died on the spot. The driver of the Vespa was seriously injured, and an ambulance came and took him to the hospital. They didn't even touch Rabin, he was so dead, there was nothing to do."[18] In Keret's story, violence is the chief legacy of the Rabin assassination. Yet the incident seems to have no explicit political content; it involves, rather, random violence that explodes suddenly—between strangers who meet as the result of a traffic accident, between police and members of a neighborhood on Tel Aviv's periphery. The story's political context is related obliquely, partly through the characters' names and their implied social and economic status. Rabin is found as a kitten by Tiran and Sini in the square. That same night they meet a girl named Avishag, from an upper-middle-class suburb, who says they should call the kitten Shalom (peace) because "Rabin died for the sake of peace." The initial bones of the encounter suggest a typical, casual meeting in a locale that was synonymous with the spontaneous gathering of youth and their common generational affiliation. However, after Avishag rebuffs Tiran's advances—she already has a boyfriend who is older and a soldier—her own suggestion for a name is rejected because, according to Tiran, "Shalom is a Yemenite name," a reference to Yigal Amir's ethnic origins, which were repeatedly mentioned in accounts and analysis of the assassination. It is precisely their choice of the name Rabin that provokes the later violence with the Vespa driver who was "at first actually nice and apologetic. . . . Only when I explained to him that the cat was named Rabin, only then did he get upset and hit me."[19] Keret's story concludes with a wry account of how the entire situation could have been avoided, an account that parodies similar attempts to "second guess" events leading to the Rabin assassination:

> I thought what would have happened if we hadn't found him [the kitten], how his life would have looked now. Maybe he would have frozen to death but chances are someone else would have taken him home, and then he wouldn't have been run over. Everything in life is a question of luck. Even the original Rabin, if after singing the song of peace instead of coming down the stairs straight from the stage he had waited a bit, he would still be alive, and they would have shot Peres instead, at least that's what they said on the TV. And so if that girl in the square hadn't had a soldier boyfriend she would have given Tiran her number, and we would have called Rabin *Shalom*, and even then he would have been run over but at least it wouldn't have ended in a fight.[20]

In Keret's story, Rabin Square possesses no historic, national significance—it is simply the site of random urban encounters, a place to meet a girl or get in a fistfight. Rabin's murder—the event that introduced Tel Aviv to the history books, and that seemed itself to dramatically alter history—is reduced, retrospectively, in two pages of slight, elliptic yet evocative prose, to the logical outcome of a series of otherwise unpredictable events. The assassination has no larger meaning, and the story appears to offer no grand interpretation; this, in and of itself, is a fairly radical proposition. Though Tiran and Sini scoff at the more normative generational values of Avishag and her soldier boyfriend, they are not simply located outside the national consensus; indeed, they have no identifiable attachment whatsoever to a collective response to the events of 4 November 1995. Instead, their experience of death is both deeply personal and emotional: the story begins with their improvised burial of Rabin-the-cat, during which both cry. Unlike the televised weeping in the square during the week following the assassination, theirs is an intimate demonstration of grief at a private ceremony. The Rabin assassination serves as a loose backdrop against which the story describes a provisional yet determined effort to preserve some notion of individual expression within the public, national domain.

In Alona Kimchi's novel *Susannah ha-bokhiya* (Crying Susannah; 1999), the dysfunctional protagonist's last name is Rabin though she is not, as she insists at various moments throughout the story, "a relation" (*krovat mishpacha shel*). She lives with her mother in the Tel Aviv suburb of Ramat Gan, where they are paid an extended visit by an American cousin, whose enigmatic and sensual presence unsettles Susannah's self-contained interiority. Kimchi suggests that Susannah's isolation is the result of more than simply an inability to form genuine human attachments; the "privacy of her experience" is explicitly linked, against her will, to the larger context of her generation. Unlike her mother, Ada, upon whom she is entirely dependent and who "always has a sense of identification with the state . . . , she has no such sense."[21] Ada sees the state in psychoanalytic terms; following Benyamin Netanyahu's electoral victory in 1996, "Mother says the state is depressed" (190). She also views her friend Nechama's illness in connection with the national malaise (210). Both Ada and Nechama represent, through their personal biographies, politics, and identification with the normative structures of Israeli identity, a societal group that had once been at the center of power. Susannah, however, "doesn't identify with this national depression because, though my name is Susannah Rabin, as I've already noted, I'm not a relation" (190). Though bearing the patriarchal name of the nation, she sees herself, by virtue of her psychological detachment, firmly outside it, and rejects her mother's analysis of her emotional condition in collective terms: "Mother says: 'It's a strange generation.' As usual she snatches away the privacy of my experience, even when it comes to something personal like apathy. I'm part of a generation. An apathetic generation" (195).

Susannah's apathy, however, goes far beyond the generational variety. Her resolute withdrawal from life, from human interaction and any semblance of agency toward her immediate and larger surroundings, provides the novel's emotional center. Her detachment is an extreme version of resistance to any sort of relationship between an individual self and the collective. Her behavior is clearly dysfunctional, in normative terms, but its dimensions simply reflect an attempt to counteract the perverse and enormous pressures of the collective. Feeling trapped by her familial and national past, she retreats to a rarefied inner world whose physical boundaries are her own body. Her eventual path out is also through the body, her brief illicit affair with the cousin, before he disappears from their lives under a cloud of disrepute. The novel ends as Susannah seems at last poised for genuine engagement with the world through her budding development as an artist.

The use of the suburb of Ramat Gan for the novel's geographic setting confirms the evolving notion that Tel Aviv–the-center is defined by the periphery. Susannah moves through a limited repertoire of spaces—the rooms of her apartment, the balcony, the small park next door, the supermarket. Getting to Tel Aviv means a long bus or cab ride, and the city appears initially as a place of escape and freedom. Yet the city offers no spiritual or emotional solution to her isolation: "Tel Aviv's ugly rooftops beneath the pale early summer sky began to take on the delicate orange of sunset. An endless expanse of antennas and solar waterheaters spread before me, as if the city was a slice of the Sargasso Sea, within whose lethal algae thousands of ships had become entangled and sunk" (215). Even tokens of the city's modernity—the familiar rooftop jungle of boilers and wire—seem irredeemably mired in some romantic, primordial past.

The novel's most straightforward and possibly most scathing critique of Zionism comes from the distant periphery, in the figure of the cousin visiting from abroad, or "the guest," as he is referred to throughout the novel. He appears uninterested in politics, but his indifference stems from a recognition of the paradox at the heart of Zionism: "Why did you settle here in this piece of land, speaking this language without understanding that it has no justification, except for those existing in messianic Jewish belief! What is this nonsense—secular Zionism? It's faulty logic!" (194). The cousin simply articulates Zionism's inherent contradiction. While Zionism believed it was destined to succeed in its quest for normalcy, and the "Diaspora Jew" with all his "defects" and fears had been irrevocably supplanted by the *tsabar*—the native Israeli—a much more complex evolution of Israeli identity was underway. In the first place, the Diaspora Jew, as columnist Doron Rosenblum notes, refused to go away, and certain segments of the population viewed Israel as just another Jewish community, except "armed and close to ancestral tombs."[22] Additionally, Zionism as an ideology, in its statist form, never fully reconciled its own nationalist and universalist components, its desire to create a republic both Jewish and democratic. The cousin's remarks expose what he calls Zionism's "faulty logic," its denial of its own ideological roots in religion. This lacunae is also evident, in the view of a cultural critic, in those assessments of the assassination that focus on Yigal Amir's religious background at the expense of his nationalist-Zionist motivations. Amnon Raz-Krakotzkin contends that it "was easier to attack the assassination on the basis of its religious dimension, for its 'man wearing a skullcap,' than on the basis of its nationalistic dimension."[23] (He refers here to a phrase appearing in the informational panels at the memorial site, which originally described Amir as "a Jew wearing a skullcap."[24]) According to Raz-Krakotzkin, depicting the assassination as emanating from purely religious motivations, without noting its nationalist-Zionist dimension, ensures that the debate remains part of the internal dynamic of Israeli Jewish society, thus deflecting the need to consider the peace process

and the Palestinians. While annual journalistic reckonings of the assassination's anniversary regularly note how far Israel has drifted from the
road to peace since Rabin's death, how might reflection upon "Rabin's
legacy," whether in public discourse or the field of cultural production,
be expanded to include an awareness of a broader political context, of
the world outside the square's memorial vertigo?

## Summayl Uncovered

> The internal naming of the city—its squares and boulevards—col-
> lects that text of the nation into its material evidence, so that the
> buildings of the nation are suffused with detail and declaration; the
> central squares of the city amass into a cataract of congealed imagery
> of the nation.
>
> —Stephen Barber, *Fragments of the European City*

I began to describe above how various paths to Rabin Square either
highlight or efface certain aspects of the city's history. If the square,
with its surfeit of memory, has indeed become a "cataract of congealed
imagery of nation," what does this cataract blind the city to? Just a few
short blocks north of the square, on the eastern side of Ibn Gvirol between Arlozorov and Jabotinsky streets, is a small enclave of miniature
structures, clustered behind a high stone wall and beneath a towering
office building. The makeshift small homes are mostly hidden from
street level, surrounded by an oasis of bougainvilleas, date trees, and
low shrubs. Somewhere in this dense assemblage of buildings, which
appear to have been added to and subtracted from over the years, one
might be able to locate a wall or two belonging to a structure from the
original site—the Arab village of Summayl, which was evacuated in
1947 (Figure 6.5).

According the Walid Khalidi, who has prepared a massive volume on
Arab villages in Palestine prior to 1948, Summayl was one of twenty-
three villages in the Jaffa district, five of which were located within
the bounds of the city of Tel Aviv: Salama, Sheikh Munis, Jarisha,
Jammasin, and Summayl.[25] Demographic estimates vary: one survey

*Fig. 6.5* Corner of Arlozorov and Ibn Gvirol streets. Area of the former village of Summayl in lower right corner. August 2001. Photo by author.

put the total population of these villages in 1931 at about 6,000.[26] The primary means of support was derived from agriculture, including orange groves and vineyards. Summayl itself dated from the late nineteenth century. In *Sefer Tel Aviv*, Druyanov describes a map from 1880 that included a gravedigger's path leading from the village to a large sheik's tomb by the sea that later marked the site of Abdel Nabi, the Moslem cemetery founded contemporaneously with the cemetery on Trumpeldor Street.[27] Summayl was annexed to Tel Aviv during the mandate period and as the city expanded around the village, Jewish tenants often rented houses or rooms from Arab landlords. A letter dated 5 November 1944, from a Jewish resident, appeals to the Municipality to ask the village's *mukhtar* to intervene in a dispute between himself and his Arab landlord.[28] At least one letter from the TAMA archives attests to some kind of concerted, joint effort on the part of Jewish and Arab inhabitants to petition the Municipality for improved infrastructure that would benefit the entire population of the village, Jew and Arab alike.[29]

The presence of Palestinian history in Tel Aviv is more felt than seen. A curious thing happens, however, when attempting to locate the former sites of the villages, now largely covered by housing complexes, highways, and parking lots. Khalidi's book provides dry, factual descriptions of the villages, their population and livelihoods, and general notions of where they can be found today: some distance southeast of a certain highway, or currently covered with various kinds of vegetation. As a "guidebook," however, it contains almost no specifics to help find the spot: no addresses and few street names. For example, in Summayl, Khalidi identifies a single abandoned house still standing, formerly the home of Muhammad Baydas, but it is nearly impossible to find this place.[30] A more exact description would entail recognizing the presence of other people who currently live and make their homes there. The end result is a vague guessing game: "Maybe it's that house; no, maybe it's that one." At some point, all the houses on the semi-bluff overlooking Ibn Gvirol between Arlozorov and Jabotinsky begin to look as if they were originally part of Summayl. And this, one suspects, is the point. Given their enormous value as real estate, and the rapid pace of change in the city's physical facade, where buildings and real estate change hands repeatedly, and new restaurants open and close over night, it is incredible that these structures exist at all. Their original owners are long gone, including those Jews who moved in before and after 1948. Somehow, though, this abandonment seems an important part of the site itself, almost as if its relative neglect symbolizes Tel Aviv's blind spot toward this piece of its past. That is, the suppression of memory of the spot is an integral part of its history.

Both Rabin Square and the remains of Summayl are off the grid of Tel Aviv's historic center, and each possesses a distinctly troubled relation to the idea of an urban collective memory. The square, saturated with memory, is the ongoing subject of debate and competing interpretations of "the Rabin legacy." At the same time, the square's memorial site historicizes the assassination, in that it provides a conclusive interpretation of Rabin's life and death, a process that seals the assassination and its aftermath firmly in the past. Summayl is nearly invisible, unremembered and undocumented, and its remains are rarely noticed or traversed by most of Tel Aviv's residents. The village is a structuring absence within the city, representing past events that remain unresolved and therefore, in a sense, ongoing.

Tel Aviv has become, in some ways, the European city it aspired to be. As evidence of this claim, I would point less to the ever-popular Bauhaus construction than to the important role of memory and its absence in the city's physical plane. Like Western and Eastern European capitals alike, Tel Aviv struggles to manage the reverberations of its recent traumatic past, and its cityscape demonstrates a necessarily selective interpretation of this history. Tel Aviv also shares with its European counterparts the imprint of a utopian modernist vision, a radical belief in the ability of space to shape an abiding national or collective consciousness, as well as a growing awareness of the limits of this vision. In Tel Aviv, the sorest test of this vision has been reconciling the complexities of the city's immediate European past with the alien and often hostile surroundings of the Middle Eastern landscape.

## Coda: Tel Aviv, Holy City

> And so it happened that in Tel Aviv, the village that I came from followed me. Tel Aviv accepts this. She understands that certain of her streets and corners are beloved, because they remind us of the past. And when an old house is destroyed, oy, that's not good. Tel Aviv, holy city.
>
> Avot Yeshurun, *Kol shirav*

As we saw in the discussion of his poetry in Chapter 2, much of Avot Yeshurun's work detailed the minor encounters and exchanges of everyday life in his Tel Aviv neighborhood and recorded the city's rapid physical changes. He claimed that, unlike Jerusalem, there is no "heavenly Tel Aviv," that the city exists on earth alone, but this in and of itself constitutes a kind of sacredness. For Yeshurun, the city's holiness consists of its embrace of memory—the memory of its residents' diasporic pasts, as well as the more immediate residue of Tel Aviv's cityscape. Memories of these now decaying neighborhoods appear in Yeshurun's work thoroughly enmeshed in even older memories of his

Polish shtetl. This pervasive connection to the Diaspora is the very substance of Tel Aviv's transcendence. However, the texture of memory in Tel Aviv contains another dimension as well. While Yeshurun's poetic palimpsests overlay the shtetl upon the modest homes and narrow streets of Tel Aviv's Nordia quarter, these same streets bear another, even less visible, set of memories. The poet's sense of European Jewish loss is intimately related to another psychological and physical trauma, what he called "the two shoahs: the shoah of the Jewish people there and the shoah of the Arab people here."[31] This twinned destiny is evoked in his "Lullaby for Nordia Quarter," where he refers to "the Bedouins who came from Poland," and more generally in his highly idiosyncratic poetic Hebrew, which includes elements of both Yiddish and Arabic.[32]

A poem by Aharon Shabtai, published in *Ha-aretz* in February 2002, vividly demonstrates the inextricable connection between memories of Tel Aviv and its early migrant population, and memories of the Palestinian landscape. As we have seen in the fictional and memoiristic work of Ya'akov Shabtai, Haim Gouri, and Yoram Kaniuk, a now aging generation of native Hebrew writers mourns the erasure of the Palestinian landscape they experienced as youth. Shabtai's opening lines recall a lesson in *moledet*, or "homeland studies," a class meant to afford students, many of whom were immigrants, a native sense of their new home. What the adult speaker remembers learning, however, is not the seasonal details of his new surroundings, but a different set of facts about the land before him:

"Our Land"

I remember how,
in 1946, hand in hand
we went out into the field
at the edge of Frishman Street
to learn about autumn.
Under the rays of the sun
slanting through the October clouds
a *fallah* was cutting a furrow
with a wooden plough.
His friend wore a jalabiya

rolled up to his knees
and crouched on a knoll.

The poem's litany of Eastern European surnames and professions is
also presented as indigenous:

Soon we'll meet
in the Tel-Aviv below—
Weinstein the milkman,
and Haim the iceman,
Solganik
and the staff at the dry-goods co-op,
Hannah and Frieda and Tzitron,
and the one-armed man
from the clothing store
at the corner
near Café Ditza;
Dr. Levova
and Nurse Krasnova;
the gentle
Dr. Gottlieb.
And we'll meet Stoler
the butcher,
and his son Baruch;
and Muzikant the barber;
along with Lauterbach, the librarian,
and the pretty dark-skinned lady
from the Hahn Restaurant.
And we'll meet the street-sweeper
Mr. Yaretzky. . . .
For these *fallahin* as well,
and also for the children of the village of Sumel,
who herded goats
on Frug Street,
the heart will make room . . .
For we belong
to a single body—
Arabs and Jews.
Tel-Aviv and Tulkarem,

> Haifa and Ramallah—
> what *are* they
> if not a single pair of shoulders,
> twin breasts? . . . [33]

Shabtai's insistence that they will all "soon meet / in earthly Tel-Aviv (*Tel Aviv shel mata*)" is a distinct rejection of "heavenly Jerusalem" (*Yerushalayim shel ma'ala*), and suggests a new way of conceptualizing the local landscape: *not* as a repository of the past, the metropole qua memorial, but as a dynamic, vernacular invention of its present-day inhabitants. For Shabtai, Tel Aviv's embrace of exile is no longer sufficient; the city must also confront what Meron Benvenisti has called the "buried history" of the land, the Arabic map whose geographical features were erased by the advent of the Hebrew map.[34]

Poetry has generally been an important register of attitudes toward the past within Jewish culture. It may not be where "what really happened" is adequately recorded, but poetry, and in particular the lyric's autobiographical force, has been a crucial site of historical intervention in modern Hebrew culture. Poetry not only preceded history in Tel Aviv; in some ways it preceded, and eventually superseded, the physical existence of the city itself. This is perhaps the ultimate desire of modernist writing vis-à-vis the metropole—to suggest a transcendent, imaginative space built from the ordinary and even profane details of the city down below. In Tel Aviv, this typically modernist enterprise coincided with the national project, thus enabling a kind of blindness regarding the land's actual history; at the same time, modernism's grudging respect for history has allowed for Tel Aviv's special brand of holiness to remain embedded in its streets.

*Appendix*   Selected Poems in the Original
Hebrew

אברהם שלונסקי
בְּתֵל אָבִיב

א

פָּנַי רְחוֹב בְּטֶרֶם עֶרֶב רַד,
הָהּ מִי הִדְלִיקְכֶם, צַהֲבֵי־עָיִן!
עַל מָה הֵבֵאתָ, אוֹטוֹ רֵיק, בְּלִי־עֵת
אוֹרֵחַ זָר אֶל בֵּית־הַיָּיִן?

עַל כְּתָלִים תְּמוּנוֹת־Hackerbrau.
עַל דֶּלְפֵּק — כּוֹסוֹת בְּהִפּוּכָן.
וּבְקֶרֶן־זָוִית שָׁעוֹן נָם,
וְיהוּדִי נִרְדָּם אֶל הַדּוּכָן.

אֲנִי, יְהוּדִי, בָּאתִי סְתָם.
אֲנִי יְהוּדִי, שָׁב הַבָּיְתָה.
עוֹד רֶגַע יִזַּח אוֹטוֹ רֵיק,
וְשָׁבָה דְמָמָה לִכְשֶׁהָיְתָה.

וְשׁוֹפָר נִחַר צָרַח לוֹ,
וַתְּהִי שָׂרֶטֶת בְּעוֹר הַדְּמָמָה.
וְרַק פַּנָּסִים זוֹרְקִים כְּבָר
טַבָּעוֹת צְהֻבּוֹת לָאֲדָמָה.

. . .

ד

רוֹכֵל מְפַהֵק שַׁח עַל קֻפָּתוֹ.
כְּנֶפֶת סַבָּלִים בְּקֶרֶן־הָרְחוֹב.
אוֹטוֹ בֵּן יַתִּיז. גָּמֶלֶת. תִּינוֹקוֹת.
עַרְבִי עִם קוֹף.

צוֹפֶה קִיקְלֹפִּי אוֹרְלוֹגִין הַמִּגְדָּל.
«אָרֶץ» תֵּימָנִי צוֹרֵחַ בְּעֹז.
דּוּכָנִים עֲזוּבִים בְּאַרְבַּע הַקְּרָנוֹת:
גָּוּוֹז!

וְיָמִים עַל יָמִים, בַּטָּלָה, בַּטָּלָה.
עָיֵף אָנֹכִי וְרָעֵב כִּמְעַט.

. . .

ה
טַיָּל אַחֲרוֹן בְּקִרְיַת־לְאַחַר־חֲצוֹת,
מוֹנֶה דְמָמָה פְּסִיעוֹתָיו מִתְּנוּמוֹת.
פַּרְצוּף לֵאֶה לַבָּתִּים הָרוֹבְצִים תַּחְתֵּיהֶם,
וְעֵינֵיהֶם עֲצוּמוֹת.

מָה אֶתְעֶה בָּרְחוֹבוֹת, וְהָרוּחַ מֵאַחֲרַי
מְכַשְׁכֵּשׁ בִּזְנָבוֹ?
וּמָה אֵלְכָה הַחַדְרָה, וְחַדְרִי כְּאָרוֹן
הַמְחַכֶּה לְמֵתוֹ: הוּא יָבֹא... הוּא יָבֹא...


אבות ישורון
שִׁיר עֶרֶשׂ לְשִׁכוּנַת נוֹרְדִיָה

הַבֶּדּוּאִים שֶׁבָּאוּ מִפּוֹלַנְיָה שֶׁלֹּא
כַּמַּתְכֹּנֶן הִתְפַּשְׁטוּ עַל רְחוֹב
בַּלְפוּר מוּל אֹהֶל שֵׁם עַכְשָׁו וְעַל
הַמִּדְרוֹן מוּל הַשִּׁקְמִים עַכְשָׁו נוֹרְדִיָה.

וְהָיוּ בְּאֹהָלִים וְהָיוּ בְּסֻכּוֹת וְהָיוּ בְּצְרִיפִים.
וְיָדִית שֶׁל דֶּלֶת כְּרֹחַב דֶּלֶת וְגַגּוֹת.
וְגַגּוֹת דָּאוּ כִּילָדִים וְהִשְׁתַּנּוּ.
וְקַיִץ נָחֲרַף בִּרְחוֹב דִּיזְּנְגּוֹף.

וּמִסָּבִיב קָמוּ רוֹזְנֵי בָּתִּים,

וְהִתְפַּשְּׁטוּ אַרְזֵי בַּיִת עַל הַצְּרִיפִים.

תֵּל אָבִיב עִיר הַקֹּדֶשׁ, אֵין לָךְ

שִׁיר עֶרֶשׂ. אֶתְמוֹל זֶה הָיָה.


הָלַכְתִּי בָּךְ הַכֹּל בָּרֶגֶל,

כְּמוֹ שֶׁהַסּוּס אוֹכֵל יָשָׁר מֵהָאֲדָמָה.

לִפְעָמִים אֲנִי מוֹסֵר נֶפֶשׁ

בְּעַד כָּל בֶּרֶז שֶׁשָּׁכַחְתְּ פָּתוּחַ.


הָלַכְתִּי בָּךְ בָּעֲיָרָה שֶׁעָזַבְתִּי.

בָּעִיר שֶׁלָּךְ, בָּעֲיָרָה שֶׁלִּי.

אֶת הָעֲיָרָה שֶׁלִּי שֶׁמֵּאַחֲרֵי גַּבֵּךְ

וְאֶת עַצְמִי אֲנִי, כְּלַפַּיִךְ זָרַקְתִּי.


הָלַכְתִּי בָּךְ הַכֹּל.

רֵאשִׁית כֹּל נֶחֱרַב בַּיִת רִאשׁוֹן.

שֵׁנִית כֹּל נֶחֱרַב בַּיִת שֵׁנִי:

בָּא בּוּלְדוֹזֶר בְּעַט בַּבַּיִת.


דְּזַבִּין אַבָּא חֲבֵרִים.

יוֹם אֶחָד אֲנִי שָׁם יָדִי עַל כְּתֵפוֹ,

וְהוּא יָדוֹ עַל יְרֵכַיִךְ.

כָּךְ יוֹצְאִים כָּל חֲבֵרַיִךְ.


וּבָעִיר אֵין לִי לְוָיוֹת אֶלָּא שֶׁל

אַחַד הָעָם, בְּיַאלִיק, נוֹרְדוֹי, שֶׁמְּשַׁךְ

אֶת שְׁמוֹ עַל הַשְּׁכוּנָה עַל שְׁמוֹ

שֶׁמַּעֲכַתְּ אֶת נוֹרְדָיָה כְּמַרַח אֲשֶׁךְ.

דליה רביקוביץ
# תִּקְוַת הַמְשׁוֹרֵר

מַה יֵּשׁ לָכֶם אַתֶּם
מְשׁוֹרְרִים צְעִירִים
לִכְתֹּב כָּל כָּךְ הַרְבֵּה עַל הַשִּׁירָה,
וְאָמָּנוּת הַשִּׁיר
וְהַשִּׁמּוּשׁ בָּחֲמָרִים
וְשֶׁלֹּא תָבוֹא,
חַס וְשָׁלוֹם,
שְׁתִיקַת הַמְשׁוֹרֵר
לַעֲשׂוֹת בָּכֶם שַׁמּוֹת.

וַהֲרֵי יֵשׁ לָכֶם מַרְפֵּא
הַמְגָרֵשׁ כָּל צַעַר:
לָשֶׁבֶת רְוֵחִים לְשֻׁלְחַן הַבֹּקֶר
הַמְכֻסֶּה שַׁעֲוָנִית מְעַט דְּהוּיָה
וְלִתְלוֹת עֵינַיִם בִּזְגוּגִית הַחַלּוֹן,
עַד שֶׁתִּתְקָרֵב שְׁעַת הַצָּהֳרַיִם.
וְאִם תֹּאחַז בָּכֶם תְּנוּמָה אַל תִּגָּרְשׁוּהָ
וְאַל יֵקַל בְּעֵינֵיכֶם טַעַם דְּבַשׁ וְחֶמְאָה.
וְאַל תַּעֲשׂוּ בָּזֶה שִׁירִים וְשִׁירָה
וְאַל תַּעֲשׂוּ כָּל מְלָאכָה
וְאִם תִּהְיֶה לָכֶם חֶדְוַת לֵב,
הַצְפִּינוּהָ יָמִים רַבִּים
לְבַל תֶּחֱזֶה בָּהּ עַיִן.
כִּי מָה אַתָּה נִבְהָל, יַקִּירִי,
לֶאֱחֹז בְּקַרְנֵי הַשִּׁיר הַחוֹמֵק
וְלִדְחֹק בְּצַלְעוֹ
כַּאֲשֶׁר יְזָרֵז נַעַר בְּדָוִי בּוֹדֵד
אֶת חֲמוֹרוֹ הַמִּתְמַהְמֵהַּ?

וַהֲרֵי כָּל הַטּוֹב שֶׁיִּצְמַח לְךָ מִזֶּה,
הַטּוֹב שֶׁבְּכָל הָעוֹלָמוֹת הָאֶפְשָׁרִיִּים,
הוּא קֶבֶר אֶחָד שֶׁיִּכְרוּ לְמַעַנְךָ,
לְאַחַר הִשְׁתַּדְּלוּת בְּלִשְׁכַּת רֹאשׁ הָעִיר,
בְּבֵית הַקְּבָרוֹת שֶׁבִּרְחוֹב טְרוּמְפֶּלְדּוֹר
בְּמֶרְחָק שִׁשִּׁים מֶטֶר
מִקִּבְרוֹ שֶׁל בְּיַאלִיק.


נתן אלתרמן
# לֵיל שָׁרָב

. . .

— אֶת רֹחַב הַלַּיְלָה הַזֶּה הַפָּקוּחַ,
אֶת לַחַשׁ הָאָב וְהַלַּהַב הַזָּר,
אֶת יַד מוֹלַדְתָּהּ הַשְּׁלוּחָה לָהּ בָּרוּחַ,
אֶת כֹּחַ בִּכְיָהּ שֶׁאֵינֶנּוּ נִשְׁבָּר.


נתן אלתרמן
# יוֹם הַשּׁוּק

. . .

אֶרְאֶה אֶת גֵּאוּת הַשִּׁקְמָה בְּעָלֶיהָ,
אֶת קֶרֶב הַכִּכָּר — הָאַחַת מוּל מֵאוֹת!
אֶרְאֶה אֶת הָרְחוֹב הַגָּדוֹל, הַבּוֹלֵעַ
שׁוּרַת אַבְטוֹבּוּסִים כְּבֵדִים כִּדְמָעוֹת.

אֵצֵא אֶל הַשּׁוּק הַמַּפְשִׁיל שַׁרְווּלַיִם,
אֵלֵךְ מִתְנוֹדֵד בֵּין צְבָעָיו הַדּוֹלְקִים
סְחַרְחַר מִיֵּינוֹ, מֵרֹאשׁוֹ בַּשָּׁמַיִם,
מֵאֵשׁ הַקְּלָלוֹת שֶׁל מוֹכְרוֹת הַדָּגִים!

. . .

נתן אלתרמן
## הֶלֶדֶת הָרְחוֹב

. . .

כִּי בַכְּאֵב וּבַכֹּחַ יֵלֵד רְחוֹבָהּ,
כִּי לָעַד יְהַלֵּךְ בּוֹ שִׁירָהּ הַגָּבֹהַּ.
לֹא אֲנִי אֲחַבֵּר לָהּ דִּבְרֵי אַהֲבָה,
לֹא מָצָאתִי מִלִּים
גְּדוֹלוֹת כָּמוֹהָ.

. . .

נתן אלתרמן
## [ללא כותרת]

אָז חֶזְרוֹן גָּדוֹל הֵאִיר
אֶת הָרְחוֹבוֹת וְהַשְּׁוָקִים.
עָמַד נָטוּי עַל פְּנֵי הָעִיר
נַחְשׁוֹל שָׁמַיִם יְרֻקִּים.

הַמִּדְרָכוֹת שָׁטְפוּ לְאַט
מְמֻלְמָלוֹת, מְלֵחָשׁוֹת,
שְׁבוּיוֹת בְּרַחַשׁ מְרֻשָּׁת
שֶׁל מַבָּטִים וְשֶׁל פְּגִישׁוֹת.

אַל תְּכַבִּי אֶת הֶעָבָר,
נֵרוֹ יָחִיד כֹּה וְרָפֶה.
אִם לֹא הָיְתָה זוֹ אַהֲבָה,
הָיָה זֶה עֶרֶב סְתָו יָפֶה.

נתן אלתרמן
## שְׂדֵרוֹת בַּגֶּשֶׁם

. . .

נִדְמֶה — גַּם אֲנַחְנוּ הַבֹּקֶר נַגִּיעַ
אֶל בַּיִת אַחֲרוֹן בַּנָּתִיב הָרָחָב
וְשָׁם עוֹד נִצָּב לְבָדַד הָרָקִיעַ
וְיֶלֶד מַשְׁלִיךְ כַּדּוּרוֹ לְרַגְלָיו.

בְּאוֹר וּמָטָר הַשְּׂדֵרָה מְסֹרֶקֶת.
דַּבְּרִי, יְרֻקָּה, רַעֲשִׁי!
רְאֵה, אֱלֹהַי, עִם בִּתִּי הַצּוֹחֶקֶת
אֲנִי מְטַיֵּל בִּרְחוֹבְךָ הָרָאשִׁי.

. . .


נתן אלתרמן
## סֶרֶנָדָה תֵּל־אֲבִיבִית

. . .

אַתְּ — נִסְתַּבַּכְתִּי בָּךְ כְּהֹגֶן
וַאֲחֵרוֹת לִי לֹא הָיוּ...
כָּאֳנִיַּת מִפְרָשׂ אֶל עֹגֶן
נִקְשַׁרְתִּי לָךְ, צוּ דִיר, טוּ יוּ.

. . .

מִלְּטוּפַיִךְ הִתְרַגַּלְתִּי
לָצֵאת בְּעַיִן וּבְשֵׁן...
עַל כָּל אֲשֶׁר מִמֵּךְ קִבַּלְתִּי. —
תּוֹדָה, סְפַּסִיבָּה, דַּנְקֶה־שֶׁן.

לְפִי שְׂפָתֶךָ הַבַּלְלַיְקִית
הָבִינִי אֵת אֲשֶׁר אָבִיא —
כִּרְצוֹי לָךְ, אָז יוּ לַיְק אִיט,
אַלְקֵיְפַק, וִי דוּ וִילְסְט.

. . .

לאה גולדברג
## תֵּל־אָבִיב 1935

הַתְּרָנִים עַל גַּגּוֹת הַבָּתִּים הָיוּ אָז
כְּתָרְנֵי סְפִינָתוֹ שֶׁל קוֹלוּמְבּוּס
וְכָל עוֹרֵב שֶׁעָמַד עַל חֻדָּם
בִּשֵּׂר יַבֶּשֶׁת אַחֶרֶת.

וְהָלְכוּ בָּרְחוֹב צִקְלוֹנֵי הַנּוֹסְעִים
וְשָׂפָה שֶׁל אֶרֶץ זָרָה
הָיְתָה נִנְעֶצֶת בְּיוֹם הַחַמְסִין
כְּלַהַב סַכִּין קָרָה.

אֵיךְ יָכוֹל הָאֲוִיר שֶׁל הָעִיר הַקְּטַנָּה
לָשֵׂאת כָּל כָּךְ הַרְבֵּה
זִכְרוֹנוֹת יַלְדוּת, אֲהָבוֹת שֶׁנָּשְׁרוּ,
חֲדָרִים שֶׁרוֹקְנוּ אֵי־בָּזֶה?

כִּתְמוּנוֹת מַשְׁחִירוֹת בְּתוֹךְ מַצְלֵמָה
הִתְהַפְּכוּ לֵילוֹת חֹרֶף זַכִּים,
לֵילוֹת קַיִץ גְּשׁוּמִים שֶׁמֵּעֵבֶר לַיָּם
וּבְקָרִים אֲפֵלִים שֶׁל בִּירוֹת.

וְקוֹל צַעַד תּוֹפֵף אַחֲרֵי גַּבְּךָ
שִׁירֵי לֶכֶת שֶׁל צָבָא נֵכָר,

וְנִדְמֶה — אַךְ תַּחֲזִיר אֶת רֹאשְׁךָ וּבַיָּם
שָׁטָה כְּנֵסִיַּת עִירְךָ.

. . .


מאיר ויזלטיר
תַּשְׁלִיךְ

הוֹ רְדוּ רְדוּ רְדוּ
רְדוּ יְהוּדִים אֶל שְׂפַת הַיָּם
אֶל שְׂפַת הַיָּם הַיְּרַקְרַק
הֶחָמַצְמַץ, הַמִּתְקַתֵּק
הַמְמַלֵּא אֶת הַמַּחְבַת
אֲשֶׁר הֵלְחִים אֱלֹהֵיכֶם
לְהָכִין בּוֹ חֲבִיתָה,

וְעַל הַחוֹל הַמְצֻנָּן
הַמְשֻׁעֲמָם, הָרַעֲנָן
עַל עֲרוּגַת פִּרְחֵי הַזֶּפֶת
הַקְּטַנִּים

דִּרְכוּ בְּנַעֲלֵי הַזֶּמֶשׁ,
יְרֻשַּׁתְכֶם מֵאֲבוֹתֵיכֶם,
שֶׁהִתְקַשּׁוּ בָּאֲרוֹנוֹת הָאֲפֵלִים
(כִּי נַעֲלַיִם מִתְקַשּׁוֹת כָּאֱגוֹזִים)

כָּאֱגוֹזִים, כַּגַּלְגַּלֹּות מְצֻמָּקוֹת
כְּמוֹ מֹחוֹת מְלֻמְּדֵי הַמְּצוּקוֹת,

וּדְלוּ מִתּוֹךְ כָּל הַכִּיסִים
שֶׁל פְּרִיטֵי מַלְבּוּשֵׁיכֶם
הָעֶלְיוֹנִים הַתַּחְתּוֹנִים הַגְּלוּיִים וְהַסְּמוּיִים

אֶת פֵּרוּרֵי הַחֲוָיָה הַחֲטָאָה וְהַדְּבִיקָה
שֶׁנֶּאֶפְתָה כָּל הַשָּׁנָה בְּחֹם הַגּוּף,
שֶׁמְּעַצְמָהּ לָבֶטַח לֹא תָּסוּף,
אֲשֶׁר כְּנָפַיִם לָהּ וְלֹא תָּעוּף

וּזְרוּ אוֹתָם עַל־פְּנֵי הַגַּל הַצְּהַבְהַב
הַמְלַחֵךְ אֶת הַחוֹלוֹת בְּאֵינְאוֹנִים,
הַמְלַטֵּף אֶת לַהַטָם בְּצוֹנְנִים
וּזְרוּ אוֹתָם עַד הַפֵּרוּר הָאַחֲרוֹן.


אהרן שבתאי
# אַרְצֵנוּ

אֲנִי זוֹכֵר בְּתַשָׁ״ו
זוּגוֹת זוּגוֹת
יָצָאנוּ אֶל הַשָּׂדֶה
בִּגְבוּל פְרִישְׁמָן
לִלְמֹד עַל הַסְּתָו.
לְאוֹר קַרְנַיִם מְלֶכְסָנוֹת
מִבַּעַד לְעַנְנֵי חֶשְׁוָן
פַּלַח פָּתַח תֶּלֶם
בְּמַחְרֵשַׁת עֵץ
וַחֲבֵרוֹ לָבוּשׁ גַּלַבִּיָה,
חֲשׂוּף רַגְלַיִם
הִשְׁתּוֹפֵף עַל תְּלוּלִית.
עוֹד מְעַט נִפְגֵּשׁ
בְּתֵל אָבִיב שֶׁל מַטָּה
עִם וַיְנְשְׁטַיְן הַחַלְבָּן
עִם חַיִּים מוֹבִיל הַקֶּרַח,
עִם סוֹלְגָּנִיק
— וְעוֹבְדֵי הַצַּרְכָנִיָּה

חַנָּה וּפְרִידָה וְצִיטְרוֹן,
עִם הַגֶּדֶם
מֵחֲנוּת הַבְּגָדִים בַּפִּנָּה
לְיַד קָפֶה דִיצָה,
עִם הָרוֹפְאָה לְבוּבָה
וְהָאָחוֹת קַרְסְנוֹבָה,
עִם הָרוֹפֵא הָרַחוּם
ד״ר גוֹטְלִיב.
וְנִפָּגֵשׁ עִם סְטוֹלֶר
וּבְנוֹ בָּרוּךְ מֵהָאַטְלִיז,
עִם הַסַּפָּר מוּזִיקַנְט,
עִם הַסַּפְרָן לָאוּטֶרְבַּךְ,
עִם הַגְּבֶרֶת הַיָּפָה
שְׁחוּמַת הַפָּנִים
מִמִּסְעֶדֶת הָאוֹן,
עִם מְנַקֶּה הָרְחוֹבוֹת
הָאָדוֹן יָרֶצְקִי

גַּם לַפַּלָּחִים הָהֵם,
גַּם לְיַלְדֵי סוּמֵיל
שֶׁרָעוּ עִזִּים
בִּרְחוֹב פְּרוּג,
הַלֵּב יְפַנֶּה מָקוֹם
כְּשֶׁלְּחָן שֶׁדַּפְנוֹתָיו נִפְתָּחוֹת.
כִּי לְגוּף אֶחָד
אָנוּ שַׁיָּכִים
עֲרָבִים וִיהוּדִים.
תֵּל אָבִיב וְטוּל כַּרְם,
חֵיפָה וְרַמַאלְלָה
מֵהֶן אִם לֹא
כְּתֵפַיִם אֲחָיוֹת
שָׁדַיִם תְּאוֹמִים?

. . .

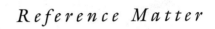

*Reference Matter*

# Notes

## Preface

The epigraphs to the Preface are from Ludwig Lewisohn, "Letter from Abroad: A City Unlike New York," *Menorah Journal* 9, 2 (Apr. 1925): 169–70; and Brian Ladd, *The Ghosts of Berlin: Confronting German History in The Urban Landscape* (Chicago: University of Chicago Press, 1997), 167.

1. The classic arguments are presented in Heinrich Graetz, "The Structure of Jewish History" (1846), translated by Ismar Schorsch in *The Structure of Jewish History and Other Essays* (New York: Jewish Theological Seminary of America, 1975).

2. Michel Foucault, "Of Other Spaces," *Diacritics* 16, 1 (Spring 1986): 22–27.

3. Stuart Hall, "Ethnicity: Identity and Difference," *Radical America* 23, 4 (Oct.–Dec. 1989): 9–20, here 15.

4. Robert Wistrich and David Ohana, "Introduction," in idem, eds., *The Shaping of Israeli Identity: Myth, Memory and Trauma* (London: Frank Cass, 1995), viii.

5. I borrow the term from Rashid I. Khalidi, "Contrasting Narratives of Palestinian Identity," in Patricia Yaeger, ed., *The Geography of Identity* (Ann Arbor: University of Michigan Press, 1995), 187–222.

6. University publications describe the building as "a unique architectural asset remaining from the village of Sheikh Munis." Quoted in Esther Zandberg, "The House Remembers," *Ha-aretz* (16 Nov. 2003).

7. While copyediting this book, I discovered Julie A. Buckler's marvelous *Mapping St. Petersburg: Imperial Text and Cityscape* (Princeton, NJ: Princeton University Press, 2005), whose shape and concerns suggest the interdisciplinary direction the field has taken.

8. Anthony Vidler, *The Architectural Uncanny: Essays in the Modern Unhomely* (Cambridge, MA: MIT Press, 1992).

9. Michel de Certeau, "Walking in the City," in Graham Ward, ed., *The Certeau Reader* (Oxford: Blackwell, 2000), 101–18. Originally published in *L'Invention du quotidien* (1980).

*Chapter 1*

On "Jews in space," see also Sidra Ezrahi, "Lost in Space: S. Y. Abramovitch and the Skeptical Voyage," *Booking Passage: Exile and Homeland in the Modern Jewish Imagination* (Berkeley: University of California Press, 2000), 52–80.

The epigraphs to this chapter are from the Midrash on the Book of Genesis; and Yi-Fu Tuan, *Space and Place: The Perspective of Experience* (Minneapolis: University of Minnesota Press, 1977), 73.

1. Henri Lefebvre, *The Production of Space*, trans. Donald Nicholson-Smith (Oxford: Blackwell, 1991), 15.

2. Ibid., 17.

3. Ibid., 31.

4. Ibid., 48.

5. Lefebvre's distinction between "absolute space" and its modern abstractions is structurally akin to what Pierre Nora has proposed vis-à-vis history. Nora argues that modern "sites of memory" have replaced older forms of "authentic" memory. See the discussion of Nora in Chapter 2.

6. Lefebvre, *The Production of Space*, 38–39.

7. On the common ground between Lefebvre and de Certeau, see James Donald, *Imagining the Modern City* (Minneapolis: University of Minnesota Press, 1999), 13–17.

8. Iain Borden et al., "Things, Flows, Filters, Tactics," in idem, eds., *The Unknown City: Contesting Architecture and Social Space* (Cambridge, MA: MIT Press), 7.

9. Tuan, *Space and Place*, 6.

10. Edward Casey offers an interesting cautionary corrective to the prevailing view of space as preceding place in "How to Get from Space to Place in a Fairly Short Stretch of Time: Phenomenological Prolegomena," in K. Basso and S. Feld, eds., *Senses of Place* (Santa Fe, NM: School of American Research, 1996), 13–52, here 18.

11. Tuan, *Space and Place*, 73.

12. For the various meanings of makom in Hebrew sources, see A. A. Auerbach, "Proximity and Distance: Makom and Heaven" [Hebrew], *Chazal: Pirkey omanut ve-de'ot* (Jerusalem: Magnusm, 1978), 53–68. For a series of meditations on the meaning of makom in contemporary Israeli culture, see Ariel Hirshfeld, *Local Notes* [Hebrew] (Tel Aviv: Am Oved, 2000).

13. Auerbach, "Proximity and Distance," 58–59.

14. Genesis Rabah 68:8.

15. The phrase, originally Heinrich Heine's *aufgeschrieben Vaterland* ("transcribed Fatherland"), has been introduced into contemporary discourse of Jewish cultural studies by George Steiner in his 1985 essay "Our Homeland, The Text," reprinted in idem, *No Passion Spent: 1978–1995* (New Haven, CT: Yale University Press, 1998), 304–27.

16. The importance of the imagination to nationalism is articulated in Benedict Anderson, *Imagined Communities: Reflections on the Origins and Spread of Nationalism* (New York: Verso, 1991 [1983]).

17. Zali Gurevitch, "The Double Site of Israel," in Eyal Ben-Ari and Yoram Bilu, eds., *Grasping Land: Space and Place in Contemporary Israeli Discourse and Experience* (New York: State University of New York Press, 1997), 205; Zali Gurevitch and Gideon Aran, "Al ha-makom," *Alpayim* 4 (1991): 9–44. A number of recent studies have explored this issue in Hebrew literature. See Sidra Ezrahi, *Exile and Homecoming in Modern Jewish Literature* (Berkeley: University of California Press, 2000); and Y. Schwartz, "The Engineering of Man and the Construction of Space in Modern Hebrew Literature" [Hebrew], *Mikan* 1 (May 2000): 9–24.

18. Richard Lehan, *The City in Literature: An Intellectual and Cultural History* (Berkeley: University of California Press, 1998), xv.

19. See Donald, *Imagining the Modernist City*, esp. chap. 2.

20. For essays addressing the variant conditions of Jewish urban life in modern and premodern Europe, see Ezra Mendelsohn, ed., *People of the City: Jews and the Urban Challenge*, Studies in Contemporary Jewry, vol. 15 (New York: Oxford University Press, 1999).

21. See Hillel Kieval, "Anti-Semitism and the City: A Beginner's Guide" in Mendelsohn, ed., *People of the City*, 3–19.

22. Ibid., 5.

23. Ibid., 8.

24. Richard Sennett, *Flesh and Stone: The Body and the City in Western Civilization* (New York: W. W. Norton, 1996 [1994]).

25. Robert Bonfils, "Tropes, Metaphors, Symbols and Historical Rhetoric: The Ghetto and Urban Space in Early Modern Italy," paper delivered at the conference "Urban Diaspora: The City in Jewish History," Princeton University, Princeton, NJ, Apr. 2002.

26. Max Nordau, "Jewry of Muscle," in Paul Mendes-Florh and Jehuda Reinharz, eds., *The Jew in the Modern World: A Documentary History* (New York: Oxford University Press, 1980), 435.

27. Tamar Garb, "Modernity, Textuality, Identity," in Linda Nochlin and Tamar Garb, eds., *The Jew in the Text: Modernity and the Construction of Identity* (London: Thames and Hudson, 1995), 20.

28. Ibid., 21.

29. See Steven Zipperstein, *The Jews of Odessa: A Cultural History, 1794–1881* (Stanford, CA: Stanford University Press, 1985).

30. For a colorful sketch of Bialik's early Odessa years, see Shlomo Shva, *O, Thou Seer, Go, Flee Thee Away* [Hebrew] (Tel Aviv: Dvir, 1990), 67–76. The title comes from Amos 7:12, and immediately precedes Amos's denial that he is a prophet.

31. Zipperstein, *The Jews of Odessa*, 32–33.

32. Ibid., 70.

33. Ibid., 85.

34. Ibid., 131.

35. For a suggestive reading, see Joachim Schlör, "Odessa and Warsaw: Studies in the Pre-history of Tel Aviv," *Jewish Studies in a New Europe* (1998): 703–11.

36. Zipperstein, *The Jews of Odessa*, 2, 3.

37. For a critical survey, see Rachel Elboim-Dror, "Gender and Utopianism: the Zionist Case," *History Workshop Journal* 37 (1994): 99–116. For reprints of lengthy excerpts of a number of utopias, see Elboim-Dror, *The Tomorrow of Yesterday: Zionist Utopia* [Hebrew], vols. 1–2 (Jerusalem: Yitzchak Be-Zvi, 1993).

38. Levinski's novel was originally published in *Pardes* 1 (1892): 128–65. Reprinted in Elboim-Dror, *The Tomorrow of Yesterday*, vol. 2.

39. Elboim-Dror, *The Tomorrow of Yesterday*, vol. 2, 58.

40. Ibid., 62.

41. Ibid., 66.

42. Ibid., vol. 1, 135.

43. For details on the review and Nordau's ferocious counterattack, see Michael Stanislawski, *Zionism and the Fin de Siècle: Cosmopolitanism and Nationalism from Nordau and Jabotinsky* (Berkeley: University of California Press, 2001), 16–18; and Steven J. Zipperstein, *Elusive Prophet: Ahad Ha'am and the Origins of Zionism* (Berkeley: University of California Press, 2001), 194–201.

44. Theodor Herzl, *Old-New Land*, trans. Lotta Levensohn (New York: Bloch, 1960 [1902]), 82.

45. Stanislawski, *Zionism and the Fin de Siècle*, views *Altneuland* as Herzl's most profound attempt to reconcile cosmopolitanism and Zionism.

46. The Hebrew phrase used for "wasteland" is *tel sh'mama*, a citation from Isaiah 17:1. In Elboim-Dror, *The Tomorrow of Yesterday*, vol. 2, 68.

47. David Frischmann, *Ba-aretz* (Warsaw: Akhisefer, 1913), 29.

48. S. Y. Agnon, *Tmol shilshom*, 16th ed. (Jerusalem: Schocken, 1979 [1946]), 93.

49. Ibid., 222.

50. Robert B. Riley, "The Visible, the Visual and the Vicarious: Questions about Vision, Landscape and Experience," in Paul Groth and Todd W. Bressi, eds., *Understanding Ordinary Landscapes* (New Haven, CT: Yale University Press, 1997), 207.

51. Ibid., 203.

52. Frischmann, *Ba-aretz*, 36–37.

53. "Founding Prospectus and Declaration of Intentions Concerning Establishment of Achusat Bayit," 1906. Quoted in Ofer Regev, *A Little Walk in a Big City* [Hebrew] (Tel Aviv: Ministry of Defense, 1999), 105.

54. H. D. Nomberg, *Erets-yisroel: Ayndrukn un bilder* (Warsaw: Jakobson and Goldberg, 1925), 15.

55. In a sense, Jaffa played two antagonistic roles in early conceptions of Tel Aviv: it was seen both as an extension of the *golah* (in terms of its physical and social conditions) and as representative of the local environment.

56. See Nurit Govrin on the tropes associated with Jerusalem and Tel Aviv in Hebrew literature, *Literary Geography: Lands and Landmarks on the Map of Hebrew Literature* [Hebrew] (Jerusalem: Carmel, 1998), 42–64.

57. On the concentration of middle-class wealth in Tel Aviv, see Amir Ben-Porat, *The History of the Israeli Bourgeoisie* [Hebrew] (Jerusalem: Magnes Press, 1999), 77–87.

58. See Erik Cohen, "The City in Zionist Ideology," *Jerusalem Quarterly* 4 (Summer 1977): 126–43. According to Cohen, Tel Aviv was founded during a time when pioneering Zionism had not achieved "the upper hand" (129). Following its establishment, no other cities were created until after the massive immigration of the early State period, when settlement and relocation concerns were paramount. However, despite Zionism's principled, negative view of city life, the vast majority of modern Jewish settlement in Palestine was in urban areas.

59. Dan Miron, *Founding Mothers, Stepsisters* [Hebrew] (Tel Aviv: Ha-kibbutz ha-meuchad, 1992), 198–205.

60. See ibid., 181–245. Miron argues that Alterman's *Kokhavim bachuts* works through the oppositions in Shlonsky's Tel Aviv poems and represents the city as actually embracing the potentially destructive forces of nature as part of its identity.

61. Avraham Shlonsky, "Amal," *Shirim*, vol. 2 (Tel Aviv: Sifriat poalim, 1954 [1927]), 164.

62. All originally published in *Kokhavim bachuts* (Tel Aviv: Yachdav, 1938).

63. Natan Alterman, "Stav atik," *Shirim she-mi-kvar* (Tel Aviv: Ha-kibbutz ha-meuchad, 1972), 38. Originally published in *Kochavim bahuts* (1938).

64. Natan Alterman, *Tel Aviv ha-k'tana* (Tel Aviv: Ha-kibbutz ha-meuchad, 1979), 19.

65. Ibid., 54–55.

66. Lehan, *The City in Literature*, 24.

67. Svetlana Boym, "Estrangement as Lifestyle: Shklovsky and Brodsky," in Susan Rubin Suleiman, ed., *Exile and Creativity: Signposts, Travelers, Outsiders, Backward Glances* (Durham, NC: Duke University Press, 1998), 241.

68. See the discussion of this image in Sidra Ezrahi, "Our Homeland, Our Text . . . Our Text, The Homeland: Exile and Homecoming in the Modern Jewish Imagination," *Michigan Quarterly Review* 31, 4 (1992): 465; and in Michael Gluzman, *The Politics of Canonicity: Lines of Resistance in Modern Hebrew Poetry* (Palo Alto, CA: Stanford University Press, 2003), 58–59.

69. "A—RETZ" evokes someone hawking the daily newspaper *Ha-aretz* (The Land).

70. Shlonsky, *Shirim*, vol. 1, 204–6.

71. Michel Foucault, "Of Other Spaces," *Diacritics* 16, 1 (Spring 1986): 24.

*Chapter 2*

The epigraphs to this chapter are from Marvin Lowenthal, "This Hebrew Renaissance," *Menorah Journal* 11, 4 (Aug. 1925): 321; Benyamin Mintz and Eliezer Steinman, eds., *The Book of Tel Aviv Street Names* [Hebrew] (Tel Aviv: Hama'avir, 1944); Stephen Barber, *Fragments of the European City* (London: Reaktion, 1995), 31; Michel de Certeau, "Practices of Space," in Marshall Blonsky, ed., *On Signs* (Baltimore: Johns Hopkins University Press, 1985), 129; and Roland Barthes, *Camera Lucida: Reflections on Photography*, trans. Richard Howard (London: Flamingo, 1990), 92. An earlier version of Chapter 2 was originally published in *Representations* No. 69 © 2000 by The Regents of the University of California. Reprinted by permission of the University of California Press.

1. Ahad Ha'am ("one of the people") was the pen name of Asher Ginsburg (1856–1927), a Russian Jew whose writings are considered the foundation of cultural Zionism.

2. Gershon Shofman, "Between a Rock and a Hard Place," *Selected Stories* [Hebrew] (Tel Aviv: Am Ha-oved, 1994 [1916]), 75.

3. For a discussion of Hebrew literature in relation to modernism's valorization of exile, see Michael Gluzman, "Modernism and Exile: A View from the Margins," in David Biale et al., eds., *Insider/Outsider: American Jews and Multiculturalism* (Berkeley: University of California Press, 1998), 231–53.

4. S. Ilan Troen, "Establishing a Zionist Metropolis: Alternative Approaches to Building Tel-Aviv," *Journal of Urban History* 18, 1 (Nov. 1991): 10–36.

5. Sigmund Freud, "The 'Uncanny,'" *Writings on Art and Literature* (Stanford, CA: Stanford University Press, 1997), 195, 217. Subsequent citations of this work appear in the text.

6. See Linda Nochlin and Tamar Garb, eds., *The Jew in the Text: Modernity and the Construction of Identity* (London: Thames and Hudson, 1995). For a discussion of the figure of a "Jewish uncanny" in European thought, see Susan E. Shapiro, "The Uncanny Jew: A Brief History of an Image," *Judaism* 46, 1 (1997): 63–78.

7. In Nurit Govrin, ed., *The Second Half* [Hebrew] (Jerusalem: Mosad Bialik, 1988 [1920–21]), 632.

8. Ibid., 634–35.

9. According to one of the dictionaries Freud refers to, a cemetery may be "quiet, lovely and *heimlich*, no place more fitted for [her] rest." From Daniel Sanders's 1860 *Wortbuch*, cited in Anthony Vidler, *The Architectural Uncanny: Essays in the Modern Unhomely* (Cambridge, MA: MIT Press, 1992), 26.

10. In this Baron resembles Shofman and other fin-de-siècle Hebrew writers. According to a recent study, "the meeting of decadent pessimism with the optimistic belief in the revival of the Jewish people was an important source of tension and complexity" in the work of Bialik, Y. H. Brenner, and M. J. Berdischevski. Hamutal Bar-Yosef, *Decadent Trends in Hebrew Literature: Bialik, Berdischevski,*

*Brenner* [Hebrew] (Jerusalem: Mosad Bialik, 1997), 374. Of special relevance is a nearly contemporaneous story by Brenner, "Ha-motsa" (The Exit), which also contains elements of disease and death in an Eretzyisraeli setting.

11. The ability of a single death to stand in for collective, national sacrifice is characteristic of military cemeteries in contemporary Israel, where each grave is "a microcosm of the entire nationalist landscape of self-sacrifice." Don Handelman and Lea Shamgar-Handelman, "The Presence of Absence: The Memorialization of National Death in Israel," in Eyal Ben-Ari and Yoram Bilu, eds., *Grasping Land: Space and Place in Contemporary Israeli Discourse and Experience* (Albany: State University of New York Press, 1997), 90.

12. A. Remba, *Israel Rokach: The Mayor of Tel Aviv* [Hebrew] (Tel Aviv: Masada, 1969), 27–28.

13. See Shlomo Shva, *Ho Ir, Ho Em: The Romance of Tel Aviv–Jaffa* [Hebrew] (Tel Aviv: American Israel Fund and Tel Aviv Fund for Art and Literature, 1977), 222–24. A newspaper report from *Ha-chavatzelet* in 1903 cited in *The Book of the Old Cemetery* also contains details about the music of the weddings and the burial of holy scrolls. Zvi Kroll and Zadok Leinman, eds., *The Book of the Old Cemetery* [Hebrew] (Tel Aviv: Private publication, 1939).

14. Kroll and Leinman, *The Book of the Old Cemetery*, vii. Subsequent citations appear in the text.

15. Dov Sadan, "Tel Aviv Scenes (*Al Zvi Kroll*)" [Hebrew], *Gazit* 50 (Apr. 1984): 221.

16. Vidler, *The Architectural Uncanny*.

17. TAMA (Tel Aviv Municipality Archives), Burial Society file 4-1355/3807.

18. Letter and membership subscription form, from Burial Society file 4-1355/3807; letter from the city engineer to the Department of Education and Culture at the Tel Aviv Municipality, TAMA (Tel Aviv Municipal Archives) 4-1355/3807.

19. Protocol of the Association for the Improvement of the Old Cemetery, meeting dated 21 May 1937, TAMA 4-1355/3807.

20. Roland Barthes, "Semiology and Urbanism," *The Semiotic Challenge*, trans. Richard Howard (Berkeley: University of California Press, 1988 [1967]), 197–98.

21. Y. H. Brenner (1878–1921) was a writer, journalist, and influential ideologue in Russian Zionist circles. He lived in Palestine from 1909 until his violent death in 1921, during the Jaffa riots of that year. See Nurit Govrin, *Brenner: Guide and Non-plussed* [Hebrew] (Jerusalem: Ministry of Defense, 1991) for a full account of the impact of his death.

22. *Ha-aretz* (5 May 1921), cited in Govrin, *Brenner*, 171.

23. *Ha-poel ha-tsa'ir* (6 May 1921), ibid.

24. Some of the earliest records were lost in a fire in the 1920s, but the Burial Society in Tel Aviv contains a computerized list of the names on every gravestone in the cemetery.

25. See, for example, Yoram Kaniuk's reminiscence in which he reviews the national pantheon and concludes, "And I, when I come [to the cemetery], connect to the city by way of the modest tombstone of the first Yemenite pioneer." Yoram Kaniuk, "Arlozorov, Shenkin, Ahad Ha'am—Everyone Is Here" [Hebrew], *A Matter of Life and Death* [playbill], *Ha-bima* (Tel Aviv: National Theater, 1997).

26. Pierre Nora, "Between Memory and History: *Les Lieux de Mémoire*," *Representations* 26 (1989): 7.

27. According to the story of Simonides's invention of the art of memory, people "must select places and form mental images of the things they wish to remember and store those images in the palaces, so that the order of the places will preserve the order of the things." Cited in Frances A. Yates, *The Art of Memory* (Chicago: University of Chicago Press, 1966), 2. See also M. Christine Boyer, *The City of Collective Memory: Its Historical Imagery and Architectural Entertainments* (Princeton, NJ: Princeton University Press, 1994), 129–202.

28. The cemetery on the Mount of Olives in Jerusalem most approximates the sprawling city-like feel of Père Lachaise. See Meron Benvenisti's study of Jerusalem's cemeteries, *City of the Dead* [Hebrew] (Jerusalem: Keter, 1990), 56–85.

29. For a short history, see *Plan et Histoire du Père-Lachaise* (Paris: Éditions Vermet, 1996).

30. See Ctibor Rybár, *Jewish Prague: Notes on History and Culture—A Guidebook*, trans. Joy Turner-Kadecková and Slavos Kadecka (Prague: Akropolis, 1991), 279–93. See also Rachel L. Greenblatt, "The Shapes of Memory: Evidence in Stone from the Old Jewish Cemetery in Prague," *Leo Baeck Institute Yearbook* 44 (London: Martin Secker and Warburg, 1999): 43–67.

31. The Society for the Protection of Nature runs occasional tours. Indeed, inasmuch as the cemetery has a "history," it is contained within the factual information and anecdotes shared among the small group of guides who frequent the place. See also Shlomo Shva's survey of the cemetery's pantheon, "Where Are the Living in Tel Aviv?" [Hebrew], *Dvar ha-shavua* (25 July 1986): 18–19; and his *Rising from the Sands, Tel Aviv: The Early Years* [Hebrew] (Tel Aviv: Zmora Bitan, 1989), 41.

32. See Maoz Azaryahu, "Mount Herzl: The Creation of Israel's National Cemetery," *Israel Studies* 1, 2 (Fall 1996): 46–74.

33. See also Yehudit Hendel, *The Mountain of Losses* [Hebrew] (Tel Aviv: Hakibbutz ha-meuchad, 1991); and Hannah Naveh, *Captives of Mourning: Mourning in Modern Hebrew Literature* [Hebrew] (Tel Aviv: Ha-kibbutz ha-meuchad, 1993).

34. Meir Shalev, *Roman rusi* (Tel Aviv: Am Oved, 1988), 196. This novel has appeared in English as *The Blue Mountain* (1991).

35. Batia Gur, *A Stone for a Stone* [Hebrew] (Jerusalem: Keter, 1998), 31.

36. Eldad Ziv's *A Matter of Life and Death*, which ran recently at the National Theater (Habima) in Tel Aviv, is an interesting exception to the general lack of public or literary discourse. See discussion below.

37. See Guy Raz, ed., *Soskin: Retrospective, Photographs 1905–1945* [Hebrew] (Tel Aviv: Tel Aviv Museum of Art / Tel Hai Museum of Photography, 2003); Batia Carmiel, ed., *Korbman: A Different Tel Aviv Photographer, 1909–1936* [Hebrew] (Tel Aviv/Jerusalem: Eretzyisrael Museum / Yad Yitzhak Ben Tzvi, 2004).

38. For a related discussion, see Richard Shusterman, "The Urban Aesthetics of Absence: Pragmatist Reflections in Berlin," *New Literary History* 28 (1997): 739–55.

39. *Tel Aviv Municipal Bulletin* [Hebrew], vol. 4 (July 1922): 25–26.

40. For a discussion of the cemetery as a reflection of societal values, see Randall H. McGuire, "Dialogues with the Dead: Ideology and the Cemetery," in Mark P. Leone and Parker B. Potter, Jr., eds., *The Recovery of Meaning: Historical Archaeology in the Eastern United States* (Washington, D.C.: Smithsonian Institution Press, 1988), 435–80.

41. Even though Jewish cemeteries are under the religious jurisdiction of the Burial Society, they seem to be the site of a relatively liberal degree of visual expression.

42. Plans for the design of Theodor Herzl's tomb in 1952 were characterized by a similar tension: the desire for a more populist simplicity won out over monumentality. See Azaryahu, "Mount Herzl," 51.

43. Tel Aviv's uniqueness in this regard is noted in a response to the publication of *The Book of the Old Cemetery*: "It is to Tel Aviv's credit, beyond that of many communities, that already in its earliest days there are those who show concern for her cemetery, and bequeath it eternal life" (Z. David, *Davar*, 21 Kislev 1940).

44. David Magid, *The City of Vilna* [Hebrew] (Vilna: Ha-almana ve-ha-achim, 1900), ix–x.

45. See David Roskies, "A Revolution Set in Stone; or The Art of Burial," *Pakn-Trager* 28 (Spring 1998): 36–47.

46. Letter from S. Ostblum, dated 15 Apr. 1928, TAMA 4-1355/3807.

47. The book is Leon Przysuskier, *Cmentarze żydowskie w Warszawie* (Warsaw: Weicznosc, 1936).

48. See Arnold Schwartzman, *Graven Images: Graphic Motifs of the Jewish Gravestone* (New York: H. N. Abrams, 1993) for beautifully photographed examples.

49. Following the custom of reinterring bones from the Diaspora in Israel, the first ashes from the death camps were brought as early as 1947. Handelman and Handelman, "The Presence of Absence," 122.

50. See James Young, *The Texture of Memory: Holocaust Memorials and Meaning* (New Haven, CT: Yale University Press, 1993), 209–81.

51. Handelman and Handelman, "The Presence of Absence," 109.

52. The major shoah memorial in Tel Aviv, Yigal Tumarkin's monumental, inverted steel triangle *Shoah and Redemption* (1975), is located in Rabin Square, in front of the City Hall.

53. The grave of Dov Sterngelz, a member of the Etzel (pre-State right-wing underground group) who died in 1946, is a rare exception; it bears the conventional military marker and inscription.

54. "For the Living—To the Dead" [Hebrew], *Moznayim* 10 (1940): 325.

55. One of the editors, Zvi Kroll, is himself buried in the cemetery.

56. Rybár, *Jewish Prague*, 289.

57. Michel Foucault, *The Archaeology of Knowledge*, trans. A. M. Sheridan Smith (New York: Pantheon, 1972 [1969]), 130.

58. From Yitzchak Bezalel, *Everything Is Writing in the Book: Interviews with Contemporary Israeli Writers* [Hebrew] (Tel Aviv: Ha-kibbutz ha-meuchad, 1969), 39. Cited as the epigraph to Michael Gluzman, "Passover on Caves," in Adi Ophir, ed., *Fifty for '48* [Hebrew] (Jerusalem: Van Leer Institute, 1998), 113–23.

59. The phrase "father bought," in Aramaic in Yeshurun's original, is the opening line of *Had Gadya*, a folk song traditionally sung at the Passover meal, relating a widening cycle of violence and destruction, wherein the kid goat "father bought" at market is devoured.

60. Avot Yeshurun, *Kol shirav*, vol. 2 (Tel Aviv: Ha-kibbutz ha-meuchad, 1997), 37–38. Originally published in *Ha-shever ha-suri afrikani* (1974). Translation by Harold Schimmel from *The Syrian-African Rift and Other Poems* (Philadelphia: JPS, 1980), 53–55.

61. This remained the relation between the two sites in Avot Yeshurun's poetics. In his final volume, the poem-series *House* details the destruction of a building on Berdischevski Street in the poet's neighborhood in Tel Aviv. A short lyric bears the title "Krasnistav House" (Krasnistav was the poet's birthplace): "In Tel Aviv/I loved houses/until they were destroyed/and rebuilt./I was sorry they were destroyed/the old I forgot./If only I had forgotten/Krasnistav house." Avot Yeshurun, *I Have Not Now* [Hebrew] (Tel Aviv: Ha-kibbutz ha-meuchad/Siman Kri'a, 1992), 27.

62. Leah Goldberg, "Tel Aviv, 1935," *Writings* [Hebrew], vol. 3 (Tel Aviv: Sifriat ha-poalim, 1986), 14.

63. The enormous impact of Bialik's death in 1934 was heightened by the fact that he died abroad, in Vienna. During the nearly two weeks it took his coffin to reach Palestine, Hebrew newspapers were filled with reports tracking the coffin's progress and how it was received by Jewish delegations along the way, articles relating to the poet's life, remembrances by friends and colleagues, and descriptions of commemorative ceremonies in Jewish communities all over the world. Banner headlines ran in papers on both the day of his death and that of his funeral, which was attended by more than 100,000 people. Editions of *Davar* and *Ha-aretz* from 17 July 1934 contain examples of the extensive coverage and attention his funeral commanded.

64. "For the Living—To the Dead," 324.

65. Avot Yeshurun, *Collected Poems* [Hebrew], vol. 2 (Tel Aviv: Ha-kibbutz ha-meuchad, 1997), 121.

66. For a sensitive reading of the role of Yiddish in Yeshurun's work, see Michael Gluzman, "The Return of the Politically Repressed: Avot Yeshurun's 'Passover on Caves,'" *The Politics of Canonicity: Lines of Resistance in Modernist Hebrew Poetry* (Stanford, CA: Stanford University Press, 2003), 141–72.

67. The property on which Dizengoff Center was built originally belonged to an Arab family from Jaffa who left in 1948. See Tamar Berger, *Dionysus at Dizengoff Center* [Hebrew] (Tel Aviv: Ha-kibbutz ha-meuchad, 1998), 143–49.

68. On street names, see Maoz Azaryahu, "The Power of Commemorative Street Names," *Environment and Planning D: Society and Space* 14 (1996): 314–30; and Yoram Bar-Gal, "Tel Aviv Street Names" [Hebrew], *Katedra* 47 (1987): 118–31.

69. Dalia Rabikovitch, "Tikvat ha-meshorer," *The Complete Poems So Far* [Hebrew] (Tel Aviv: Ha-kibbutz ha-meuchad, 1995), 318–19.

70. The scene described in the second stanza is strongly reminiscent of Bialik's 1917 ars poetical essay, "The Rule of the March," *Collected Writings* [Hebrew] (Tel Aviv: Dvir, 1956), 181–82. I am grateful to Vered Shem-Tov for bringing this reference to my attention, and for her help in reading Rabikovitch's reading of Bialik.

71. 1 Kings 1:50.

72. Job 40:30.

73. Rabikovitch, *The Complete Poems So Far*, 219–21, 287–88.

74. This metaphorical usage should not be confused with the narrative, psychoanalytic function of fictional Arab characters described in Mordechai Shalev's influential critique of A. B. Yehoshua's "Facing the Forests." According to Shalev, the novella's Arab character is conceived of as part of the native Israeli's identity complex, and not as a character in his own right. See Mordechai Shalev, "The Arab as a Literary Solution," *Ha-aretz* (30 Sept. 1970): 50–51.

75. A review of the book by the poet Meir Wieseltier, who may have some personal interest in the issue, ironically raised the objection that the poem was overly optimistic in this regard; practically speaking, no amount of effort could now get any poet buried in the Trumpeldor Cemetery. See Meir Wieseltier, "True Love Is Not What It Seems," *Sefarim* (6 Sept. 1995): 1.

76. 1 Kings 6:2; Ezekiel 40:14.

77. Minister of Tourism Visit in Tel Aviv (20 Jan. 1998), 7. Report issued by Tel Aviv–Jaffa Municipality.

78. Ziv, *A Matter of Life and Death*. This quote is from my memory of a performance of the play in July 1998. To the best of my knowledge, there is no published version of the script.

79. Geddes Plan files, TAMA 3-110A–B.

80. According to a report prepared by the Tel Aviv Municipality, dated 14 Apr. 1939, TAMA 4-2790.

81. See Meron Benvenisti, *Sacred Landscape: The Buried History of the Holy Land since 1948* (Berkeley: University of California Press, 2000).

82. See Yigal Zalmona, ed., *Kadima: The East in Israeli Art* [Hebrew] (Jerusalem: Israel Museum, 1998).

83. For "outsider" appreciations, see "Hilton Hotel, Tel Aviv," *Architectural Review* 140 (Sept. 1966): 206–10; and "Hilton-Hotel, Tel Aviv," *Baumeister* 63 (Mar. 1966): 229–35.

84. See Ariel Hirshfeld, "Independence Park" [Hebrew], *Local Notes* (Tel Aviv: Am Oved, 2000), 21–25, for an evocative examination of the park.

85. Letter dated Aug. 1925, TAMA 3-139G.

86. Letter dated 26 July 1934, TAMA 4-2970.

87. Letter from Pinchas Yentis, dated 28 June 1943, TAMA 4-3643.

88. Letter from Bella Heyman, dated 16 Apr. 1939, TAMA 4-2970.

89. Letter from David Zilman, dated 9 July 1945, TAMA 4-2970.

90. See Benny Morris, *The Birth of the Palestinian Refugee Problem, 1947–1949* (New York: Cambridge University Press, 1987).

91. See Benvenisti, "The Hebrew Map," *Sacred Landscape*.

92. J. B. Jackson, *The Necessity for Ruins and Other Topics* (Amherst: University of Massachusetts Press, 1980), 102.

93. Dani Karavan, "Save the Archaeological Site" [Hebrew], *Ha-ir* (21 Aug. 1998): 29.

94. For a discussion of the treatment of cemeteries and other Moslem holy sites in Israel since 1948, see Benvenisti, *Sacred Landscape*, 288–99.

95. This is a paraphrase of the title of Susan Slymovics's study of Ein Hod, an Israeli artists' village, and Ein Houd, the Palestinian village on whose site it was built. See *The Object of Memory: Arab and Jew Narrate the Palestinian Village* (Philadelphia: University of Pennsylvania Press, 1998).

*Chapter 3*

The epigraphs to this chapter are from Sh. Tchernovitz, "Tel Aviv Will Be Built Quickly in Our Time" [Hebrew], in Aharon Vardi, ed., *City of Miracles* (Tel Aviv: Le-ma'an ha-sefer, 1928), 64; M. Christine Boyer, *The City of Collective Memory: Its Historical Imagery and Architectural Entertainment* (Cambridge, MA: MIT Press, 1994), 322; Nachum Sokolov, "The Spirit of Tel Aviv" [Hebrew], *Tel Aviv: A Historical-Literary Anthology, 1909–1959* (Tel Aviv: Tel Aviv–Jaffa Municipality, 1959 [1934]), 290–91; and Alter Druyanov, ed., *Sefer Tel Aviv*, vol. 1 (Tel Aviv: Va'adat sefer Tel Aviv, 1936), 106. An earlier version of Chapter 3 was originally published in *Jewish Social Studies* No. 7: 2 as "Tel Aviv's Rothschild: When a Boulevard Becomes a Monument" by Barbara Mann. Reprinted by permission of the Indiana University Press.

1. See Michel de Certeau, *The Practice of Everyday Life*, trans. Steven Randall (Berkeley: University of California Press, 1984), 91–130.

2. Roland Barthes, "The Blue Guide," *Mythologies*, trans. Annette Lavers (London: Vintage, 1993 [1957]), 76.

3. The quotation about nostalgia that forms the heading for this section is from Yoram Kaniuk, *Wooden Horse* [Hebrew] (Tel Aviv: Sifriat poalim, 1973), 192. Dolores Hayden, *The Power of Place: Urban Landscapes as Public History* (Cambridge, MA: MIT Press, 1997), 20.

4. See Mark LeVine, "A Nation from the Sands," *National Identities* 1, 1 (1999): 15–37.

5. Anecdotal details may be found in Shlomo Shva, *Ho Ir, Ho Em: The Romance of Tel Aviv–Jaffa* [Hebrew] (Tel Aviv: American Israel Fund and Tel Aviv Fund for Art and Literature, 1977). The altered photo appears in Dr. E. Mechner, ed., *The New Palestine in Pictures: Tel Aviv* (Tel Aviv: Maon Press, 1937), 2.

6. Avraham Soskin, *Tel Aviv Views* (Berlin: n.p., 1926).

7. The depiction of wonder and nostalgia through dichotomous photographic images from two points in time may be seen in several recent Israeli coffee-table editions. For a critical discussion, see Dan Rabinowitz, "The Visualization of a National Narrative of Space," *Visual Anthropology* 6 (1994): 381–93.

8. See Vivienne Silver-Brody, *Documenters of the Dream: Pioneer Jewish Photographers in the Land of Israel, 1890–1933* [Hebrew] (Jerusalem: Magnes Press/Hebrew University, 1998); and Guy Raz, *Eyes That Have Seen Soskin, 1909–1933* (exhibition catalog) [Hebrew] (Tel Aviv: Artists House, 1999).

9. See the essays in W. J. T. Mitchell, ed., *Landscape and Power* (Chicago: University of Chicago Press, 1994).

10. See Ruth Oren, "Constructing Place: Propaganda and Utopian Space in Zionist Landscape Photography, 1898–1948" [Hebrew], *Dvarim achadim* 2 (Fall 1997): 13–30.

11. The painter is referred to primarily by his first name, Reuven.

12. See *The 1920s in Israeli Art* [Hebrew] (Tel Aviv: Tel Aviv Museum, 1982); and A. Yoffe, ed., *The First Twenty Years: Literature and Arts in Tel Aviv, 1909–1929* [Hebrew] (Tel Aviv: Ha-kibbutz ha-meuchad, 1980).

13. For example, Yitzhak Katz, "New Trends in Hebrew Art in the Land" [Hebrew], *Te'atron ve-omanut* 1 (17 June 1925): 10–13; Yosef Zaritzki, "Exhibit of Artists' Guild in Jerusalem" [Hebrew], *Te'atron ve-omanut* 9 (1926): 10.

14. Yael Zerubavel uses the term "master commemorative narratives" regarding founding myths of Israeli national consciousness in her *Recovered Roots: Collective Memory and the Making of Israeli National Tradition* (Chicago: University of Chicago Press, 1995).

15. For a survey of literary texts about Tel Aviv, see Ehud Ben-Ezer, "The Beginnings of Tel Aviv as Reflected in Literature" [Hebrew], in Mordechai

Na'or, ed., *The Beginnings of Tel Aviv, 1909–1934* (Jerusalem: Yad Ben Zvi, 1984), 122–42.

16. Y. H. Brenner, "The Eretzyisraeli Genre and Its Parts" [Hebrew], *Ktavim*, vol. 3 (Tel Aviv: Ha-kibbutz ha-meuchad / Sifriat ha-poalim, 1985), 569–78; originally appeared in *Ha-poel ha-tsa'ir* in 1911.

17. Yoram Kaniuk, *The Story of the Great Aunt Shlomtsion* [Hebrew] (Tel Aviv: Ha-kibbutz ha-meuchad, 1975), 89.

18. Nachum Gutman, "A Colorful Adventure in the East" [Hebrew], *Ha-aretz* (8 Oct. 1965).

19. Batia Carmiel, "The Beginnings of Tel Aviv in Nachum Gutman's Depiction" [Hebrew], *Gutman's Tel Aviv, Tel Aviv's Gutman* (Tel Aviv: Gutman Museum, 1999), 19.

20. Alter Druyanov, ed., *Sefer Tel Aviv*, vol. 1 (Tel Aviv: Va'adat sefer Tel Aviv, 1936), xi. Though a projected two-volume set, volume two never appeared.

21. Ibid., 130. Illustration on p. 131.

22. Ibid., 149.

23. Shlomo Shva, "Tel Aviv in Painting," in Na'or, ed., *The Beginnings of Tel Aviv, 1909–1934*, 109.

24. Druyanov, *Sefer Tel Aviv*, 252.

25. Nurit Govrin, *Literary Geography: Lands and Landmarks in the Map of Hebrew Literature* [Hebrew] (Jerusalem: Carmel, 1998), 59.

26. Untitled article by Ya'akov Fichman, in Aharon Vardi, ed., *City of Miracles* [Hebrew] (Tel Aviv: Le-ma'an ha-sefer, 1928), 33.

27. Statistics are drawn from Ze'ev Vilnai, *Madrich Eretzyisrael: Tel Aviv, ha-sharon ve-hashfeyla* (Tel Aviv: Tor, 1941), 11; and Ya'akov Shavit and Gideon Birger, *The History of Tel Aviv*, vol. 1, *The Birth of a Town (1909–1936)* [Hebrew] (Tel Aviv: Ramot, 2001), 94.

28. Asher Barash, *Like a Besieged City* [Hebrew] (Tel Aviv: Masada, 1969 [1945]), 1.

29. Nachum Gutman, "On Illustration" [Hebrew], *Ktuvim* (28 May 1928): 2.

30. Nachum Gutman, *A Little Town and Few People in It* [Hebrew] (Tel Aviv: Dvir, 1999 [1959]), 203–4.

31. Ibid., 201.

32. A recent reference to this drawing may be seen in an installation in the form of an "open letter" to Gutman at the Mumche Gallery in Neve Tsedek, protesting the demolition of the gallery and the construction of an apartment building on Shabazi Street.

33. Gutman, *A Little Town and Few People in It*, 202.

34. Historical tours of Tel Aviv often culminate with a visit to Gutman's mosaics in the Shalom Tower, itself an odd kind of monument, marking the spot where the Herzliya Gymnasium stood before it was destroyed in the 1960s to ease the flow of traffic in the area. See, for example, Ayal Peled, *Tel Aviv Walks* [Hebrew] (Tel Aviv:

Society for the Protection of Nature, 1984). The gymnasium was a major point of architectural pride for Tel Aviv. It represented the founders' hopes for the city as a center of a new kind of society and culture. Abba Kovner, "The Shalom Tower Rises," eulogizes the gymnasium and ideals of the period it symbolized. See *Poems of Tel Aviv* [Hebrew], vol. 2 (Tel Aviv: Ha-kibbutz ha-meuchad, 1982), 17–19.

35. Boyer, *The City of Collective Memory*, 322.

36. Matetyahu Kalir, *Tel Aviv–Jaffa* [Hebrew] (Tel Aviv: Hotsa'ah Yisraelit, 1965), 7–8.

37. Boyer, *The City of Collective Memory*, 14–15.

38. On the importance of hiking, leaders, and guidebooks, see Shaul Katz, "The Israeli Teacher Guide: The Emergence and Perpetuation of a Role," *Annals of Tourism Research* 12 (1985): 49–72.

39. *Tel Aviv* (Jerusalem: Keren ha-yesod, 1926); appeared in English in 1929.

40. A. Z. Ben-Yishai, *Tel Aviv: Ir va-em ba-yisrael* (Jerusalem: Keren ha-yesod, 1935).

41. Benjamin Mintz and Eliezer Steinman, eds., *The Book of Tel Aviv Street Names* [Hebrew] (Tel Aviv: Ha-ma'avir, 1944), 8.

42. *Tel Aviv and Its Buildings* [Hebrew] (Tel Aviv: Ha-poel ha-tsa'ir, Apr. 1925). The names were mainly chosen by the Town Committee (an unelected body, predecessor to the Town Council), but there is also some evidence of a more grass-roots approach: the Tel Aviv–Jaffa Municipal archives contain a number of examples of letters written by residents asking that their street be given a particular name.

43. Documentary and propaganda films about Tel Aviv from the 1930s repeatedly feature the city's more ostensibly European aspects—its outdoor cafés, promenades, and banks—in their bid to make the Middle Eastern city appear to be a secure and familiar haven for European Jews.

44. Mintz and Steinman, *The Book of Tel Aviv Street Names*, 167.

45. Yitzhak Anavi, *Know Your City: Metropolitan Tel Aviv* [Hebrew] (Tel Aviv: Uri, n.d. [1967?]).

46. A glance at English-language maps of Tel Aviv published in Israel reveals a plethora of misspelled street names, despite the fact that many of these names originated in Latinate languages. Thus the original Polish or German spelling has been superseded by a disfigured phonetic rendering of the Hebraized versions.

47. This is also the view of Dan Miron in his comprehensive treatment of early Tel Aviv poetry culminating in Alterman's work of the 1930s. See his *Founding Mothers, Stepsisters* [Hebrew] (Tel Aviv: Ha-kibbutz ha-meuchad, 1991), 228–45.

48. Natan Alterman, *Tel Aviv ha-k'tana* (Tel Aviv: Ha-kibbutz ha-meuchad, 1979), 20.

49. Ibid., 30, 39.

50. Ibid., 33.

51. Natan Alterman, *Rega'im*, vol. 1 (Tel Aviv: Ha-kibbutz ha-meuchad, 1974 [1934]), 25. "Rega'im" (Moments) was the name of Alterman's column in the daily *Ha-aretz*, a precursor to his later, immensely popular "Seventh Column."

52. Ibid., 27.

53. Alterman, *Tel Aviv ha-k'tana*, 17.

54. Ibid., 60.

55. Ibid., 64.

56. Sh. Tchernovitz, "Tel Aviv tuviva," in Vardi, ed., *City of Miracles*, 64.

57. Alterman, *Tel Aviv ha-k'tana*, 72.

58. On the affinity of Alterman's work for the Parisian work of Charles Baudelaire, see Dror Eydar, *Alterman-Baudelaire, Paris–Tel Aviv: Urbanism and Myth in the Poetry of Natan Alterman and Charles Baudelaire* [Hebrew] (Jerusalem: Carmel, 2003).

59. Alterman, *Tel Aviv ha-k'tana*, 53.

60. Alterman, "Layl sharav," *Kokhavim bachuts*, in *Shirim she-mi-kvar* (Tel Aviv: Ha-kibbutz ha-meuchad, 1972), 96.

61. Alterman, "Yom ha-shuk," *Kokhavim bachuts*, 87.

62. Alterman, "Huledet ha-rechov," *Kokhavim bachuts*, 109.

63. Alterman, "Sdeyrot be-geshem," *Kokhavim bachuts*, 49–50.

64. See Yoram Bar-Gal, "Tel Aviv Street Names: A Chapter of Cultural Urban History (1909–1933)" [Hebrew], *Katedra* 47 (Mar. 1988): 118–31, here 119. On the baron's 1914 visit to Tel Aviv, see Yehoash, *From New York to Rechovot and Back* [Yiddish], vol. 1 (New York: Hebrew Publishing Company, 1917), 143–50.

65. Nitza Smok, *Houses from the Sand: International Style Architecture in Tel Aviv* [Hebrew] (Jerusalem: Ministry of the Defense, 1993).

66. Abu Yosef, "Tel Aviv," *Do'ar ha-yom* (17 July 1922): 5.

67. Marvin Lowenthal, "This Hebrew Renaissance," *Menorah Journal* 11, 4 (Aug. 1925): 321–31, here 327–29.

68. Jessie E. Sampter, "The 'Soap-Bubble' City," *Menorah Journal* 11, 3 (Aug. 1923): 238–40, here 238.

69. Druyanov, *Sefer Tel Aviv*, 151.

70. S. Yizhar, *Mikdamot* (Tel Aviv: Zmora Beitan, 1992), 107–8.

71. The trees have been repeatedly threatened with uprooting and remain the subject of battles between local residents and the Municipality. "The Sycamores of Rothschild Boulevard" [Hebrew], in Gideon Birger and Eli Shiller, eds., *Ariel* 48–49 (Tel Aviv: Ariel, 1987), 151.

72. Marshall Berman, "Petersburg: The Modernism of Underdevelopment," *All That Is Solid Melts into Air: The Experience of Modernity* (New York: Penguin, 1988), 196.

73. Natan Alterman, "Around the Tree of Knowledge" [Hebrew], *Tel Aviv ha-k'tana*, 21.

74. For a selection of paintings of the boulevard, see *Tel Aviv at Eighty* [Hebrew] (Tel Aviv: Reuben House Museum, 1989). For a good survey of painters in the city's early years, see Shva, "Tel Aviv in Painting," 107–21.

75. Kaniuk, *The Great Aunt Shlomtsion*, 79.

76. Natan Alterman, *Kinneret, Kinneret*. The play was first performed in 1962. These excerpts are from "What Does Alterman Have To Do with the History of Local Photography?" [Hebrew] *Studio* 113 (May 2000): 86–89.

77. Central Zionist Archives, Jerusalem, Keren Ha-yesod Collection, Tel Aviv photographs #202: 7049.

78. Boyer, *The City of Collective Memory*, 187.

79. Gilead Duvshani, *I. Megidovitch, Architect* [Hebrew] (Jerusalem: Ministry of Defense, 1993).

80. Ibid., 84–85.

81. Ibid., 88.

82. I am grateful to Tsila Streichman for making this painting available to me.

83. See Naomi Schor, "*Cartes Postales*: Representing Paris 1900," *Critical Inquiry* (Winter 1992): 188–241.

84. Twelve of Soskin's photographs from 1912 were reproduced on 30,000 (!) postcards. After the war, many were printed over with English captions in Egypt, and became a favorite of British troops. See *Postcards of Palestine*, July 1990, no. 31, special issue, "Tel Aviv, 1912"; and Batia Carmiel, ed., *Tel Aviv in Photographs: The First Decade, 1909–1918* [Hebrew] (Tel Aviv: Ha-aretz Museum, 1990), 11.

85. Postcard from collection at Central Zionist Archives, Tel Aviv photographs #070568.

86. Advertisement in *Ha-aretz* (20 June 1922): 1.

87. Adina Meir-Meril, "The Great Synagogue in Tel Aviv and Alex Bervald's Contribution to Its Establishment" [Hebrew], *Katedra* 57 (Sept. 1990): 105–19, here 116.

88. *A City in Advertisements: Tel Aviv–Jaffa, 1900–1935* [Hebrew], vol. 3 (Tel Aviv: Eretzyisrael Museum, 1988), 446.

89. Shach, "Art in Tel Aviv" [Hebrew], *Do'ar ha-yom* (19 July 1922).

90. See *Ha-aretz* (16 July 1922). For the opinion of the *Va'ad ha-poel*, see Tel Aviv–Jaffa Municipal Archives, Protocols of *Va'ad ha-poel*, file 19-01-003, meeting 18, 12 July 1922.

91. Ilan Shchori, *The Dream That Became a Metropolis: The Birth and Growth of Tel Aviv, the First Hebrew City* [Hebrew] (Tel Aviv: Avivim, 1990), 54.

92. Ofer Regev and Shula Vidrich, eds., *Boulevard: Rothschild Boulevard in Tel Aviv* [Hebrew] (Tel Aviv: Ramot / Tel Aviv University, 1999), 79.

93. For details on the influence of the so-called Grabski wave of immigration on Tel Aviv, see Amir Ben-Porat, *The History of the Israeli Bourgeoisie* [Hebrew] (Jerusalem: Magnes Press, 1999), 77–87.

94. Batia Carmiel, *Tel Aviv Ceramics* [Hebrew] (Tel Aviv: 1996), 63.

95. Ilan Shchori, "The Son Designed the Crest and the Father Chose the Slogan" [Hebrew], *Etmol* (Oct. 1990): 12–13.

96. Gordon himself was not seen as a major sculptor. He went on to design a statue of Trumpeldor for Tel Chai, which he later destroyed after he could not find a purchaser for it. In Tel Aviv, his work can still be seen in the lion at the end of Simta Plonit Street. See Natan Harpaz, "From 'Dream Houses' to 'Boxes': The Architectural Revolution in Tel Aviv in the 1930s" [Hebrew], in Na'or, ed., *The Beginnings of Tel Aviv, 1909–1934*, 101–2.

97. See Carmiel, *Tel Aviv Ceramics*.

98. M. H. A. Petki, "Tel Aviv–Jaffa" [Hebrew], *Ha-binyan* 2 (Feb. 1935), 5. See Chapter 4 for a fuller discussion of this aspect of architecture in the public sphere.

99. *Yediot Tel Aviv–Yafo*, 1–2, 21 (Sept. 1950): 23.

100. From Levinsky's *A Voyage to the Land of Israel in 2040*, in Rachel Elboim-Dror, *The Tomorrow of Today: Zionist Utopia* [Hebrew], vol. 2 (Jerusalem: Yitzchak Be-Zvi, 1993), 62.

101. Boyer, *The City of Collective Memory*, 187.

102. "A Hole Which Is a Statue" [Hebrew], interview with Micha Ulman, *Mishkafayim* 31 (1997): 40.

103. Dalia Karpel, "An Artistic Mole" [Hebrew], *Musaf ha-aretz* (22 Mar. 1996): 80.

104. "A Hole Which Is a Statue," 39.

105. An option suggested by the artist, according to Udi Rosenwein, "Outdoor Sculpture on Rothschild Boulevard" [Hebrew], in Regev and Vidrich, eds., *Boulevard*, 136.

106. Tamar Berger also links Ulman's work with Shabtai's novel in her study *Dionysus at Dizengoff Center* [Hebrew] (Tel Aviv: Ha-kibbutz ha-meuchad, 1998), 89–99.

107. Hanan Hever, *Literature Written from Here: A Brief History of Israeli Literature* [Hebrew] (Tel-Aviv: Yediot aharonot, 1999), 94–115.

108. Eyal Ben-Ari and Yoram Bilu, eds., *Grasping Land: Space and Place in Contemporary Israeli Discourse and Experience* (Albany: State University of New York Press, 1997), 232–33.

109. Ya'akov Shabtai, *Zikhron devarim* (Tel Aviv: Siman Kria / Ha-kibbutz ha-meuchad, 1977), 195–96. Translation from Ya'akov Shabtai, *Past Continuous*, trans. Dalya Bilu (New York: Schocken, 1985), 267–68. Subsequently referred to by page number within the text.

110. For two different readings of the role of Tel Aviv in Shabtai's work, see Edna Shabtai, "Tel Aviv in Ya'akov Shabtai's Prose" [Hebrew], *Moznayim* 65 (Sept. 1988): 54–78; and Chana Soker-Shvayger, "The Bible Is No Parcellation Plan for the Land of Israel: The Social and the Political in *Zikhron devarim*" [Hebrew], *Teoria u-vikoret* 8 (Summer 1996): 181–97.

111. Ya'akov Shabtai, "Interview with Ilana Zuckerman" [Hebrew], *Yediot aharonot* (2 Aug. 1991), originally broadcast in the summer of 1981, shortly before the writer's death. For an extended reading of the role of walking and flânerie in Shabtai's work, see Chana Soker-Shvayger, "This is the Place: On Space in the Work of Ya'akov Shabtai" [Hebrew], *Mikan* 2 (July 2001): 33–64.

112. Dan Miron, "Memory as Idea" [Hebrew], *Yediot aharonot* (27 Apr. 1978).

113. Photographs are more generally represented in the novel via Cesar's studio work as cheap, transient, manipulative, and exploitative.

114. Berger, *Dionysus at Dizengoff Center*, 96.

*Chapter 4*

The epigraphs to this chapter are from Henri Lefebvre, *The Production of Space*, trans. Donald Nicholson-Smith (Oxford: Blackwell, 1991), 153; Ludwig Lewisohn, "Letter from Abroad: A City Unlike New York," *Menorah Journal* 9, 2 (Apr. 1925): 168; Griselda Pollock, "Modernity and the Spaces of Femininity," *Vision and Difference: Feminism, Femininity and Histories of Art* (New York: Routledge, 1988), 66; Marvin Lowenthal, "This Hebrew Renaissance," *Menorah Journal* 11, 4 (Aug. 1925): 331; Walter Benjamin, "The Flâneur," *Charles Baudelaire: A Lyric Poet in the Era of High Capitalism*, trans. Harry Zohn (London: Verso, 1997 [1969]), 37; and Michel de Certeau, "Walking in the City," in Graham Ward, ed., *The Certeau Reader* (Oxford: Blackwell, 2000), 110. A portion of Chapter 4 was originally published in *Prooftexts* No. 21:3 as "The Vicarious Landscape of Memory in Tel Aviv Poetry" by Barbara Mann. Reprinted by permission of the Indiana University Press.

1. See Vivian Silver-Brody, *Documenters of the Dream: Pioneer Jewish Photographers in the Land of Israel, 1890–1933* (Jerusalem: Magnes Press/Hebrew University, 1998); and Rona Sela, *Photography in Palestine/Eretzyisrael in the 1930s and 1940s* [Hebrew] (Tel Aviv: Ha-kibbutz ha-meuchad/Herzliya Museum of Art, 2001).

2. "Living Room of Tel Aviv Home, 1910s," in Batia Carmiel, ed., *Tel Aviv in Photographs: The First Decade, 1909–1918* [Hebrew] (Tel Aviv: Ha-aretz Museum, 1990), 75.

3. See A. Arlik, "The Beginnings of Architecture in Tel Aviv" [Hebrew], *The First Twenty Years: Literature and Art in Little Tel Aviv 1909–1929* (Tel Aviv: Ha-kibbutz ha-meuchad, 1980), 214–34.

4. Even later immigrants who moved into smaller, simpler quarters often stuffed their new homes with the ornate furnishings they had brought with them. See Ya'akov Shavit and Gideon Birger, *The History of Tel Aviv*, vol. 1, *The Birth of a Town (1909–1936)* [Hebrew] (Tel Aviv: Ramot, 2001), 289–90.

5. Soskin produced approximately 22,500 photographs during his twenty-three most active years as a photographer (he kept copious records, noting negative

number 1 in 1909 with the name of Rosenfeld, up until number 22,500, on 7 January 1933, with the name of G. Horowitz). He apparently was familiar with Sander's work. For details concerning the negatives, Soskin's technical apparatus, and possible influences, see Guy Raz, *Eyes That Have Seen Soskin* [Hebrew] (exhibition catalog) (Artists House, Tel Aviv, 1999).

6. Graham Clarke, "Public Faces, Private Lives: August Sander and the Social Typology of the Portrait Photograph," in idem, ed., *The Portrait in Photography* (London: Reaktion, 1992), 71.

7. Raz, *Eyes That Have Seen Soskin*, 10.

8. Raz identifies seven different backgrounds in Soskin's studio portraits, ranging from a bare wall to a furnished salon to a European landscape. Ibid., 8.

9. Clarke, "Introduction," *The Portrait in Photography*, 4.

10. Roland Barthes, *Camera Lucida: Reflections on Photography*, trans. Richard Howard (London: Flamingo, 1990), 40, 27.

11. The quotation is from Pollock, "Modernity and the Spaces of Femininity," 68.

12. See Carmela Rubin, "Rubin: A Self-Portrait," in *Reuven: Self-Portrait—An Exhibition Marking Reuven's Centenary, 1893–1993* [Hebrew] (Tel Aviv: Rubin House, 1993).

13. See for example Milly Heyd, "The Uses of Primitivism: Reuven Rubin in Palestine," *Studies in Contemporary Jewry* 6 (1990): 43–70. An early review of the painter by George S. Hellman is called "Palestine's Gauguin," *New Palestine* 15 (1928): 467–69.

14. James Herbert, "Painters and Tourists in the Classical Landscape," *Fauve Painting: The Making of Cultural Politics* (New Haven, CT: Yale University Press, 1992), 82–111.

15. According to a contemporary, "the savage, the peasant prefer[s] vivid colors . . . because [his] optic is not sufficiently refined." In Herbert, "Painters and Tourists," 90.

16. See Rubin, *Reuven: Self-Portrait*, 21–23.

17. Homi K. Bhabha, "Of Mimicry and Man: The Ambivalence of Colonial Discourse," *The Location of Culture* (London: Routledge, 1994), 86. Emphasis in the original.

18. Ibid., 88. Emphasis in the original.

19. Ibid.

20. See Yigal Zalmona, "The East in Eretzyisraeli Art in the 1920s" [Hebrew], in Marc Scheps et al., eds., *The 1920s in Eretzyisraeli Art* (Tel Aviv: Tel Aviv Museum of Art, 1982), 25–33.

21. Quoted in Benjamin Tammuz, *The Story of Art in Israel* [Hebrew] (Jerusalem: Masada, 1980), 39. The attitudes of many artists toward oriental themes changed in the wake of the Jewish-Arab riots of 1929.

22. See Gideon Ofrat, "Windows on Reuven's Work," *On the Ground* [Hebrew], vol. 2 (Jerusalem: Omanut Yisrael, 1993), 597–630.

23. Ibid., 608.

24. Herbert, "Painters and Tourists," 83.

25. When compared to Ze'ev Raban's art nouveau illustrations of *The Song of Songs* published by Bezalel in 1923 (a year before *View from the Balcony*), the challenge becomes more explicit.

26. See Yossi Katz, "Ideology and Urban Development: Zionism and the Origins of Tel Aviv, 1906–1914," *Journal of Historical Geography* 12, 4 (1986): 402–24.

27. M. Charizman, "Jerusalem and Tel Aviv" [Hebrew], *Gazit* (Feb. 1932): 16.

28. A. S. Yuris, "Tel Aviv in Silence" [Hebrew], *Ha-poel ha-tsa'ir* 27, 5 (3 Nov. 1933): 3–4.

29. Marvin Lowenthal, "Marrying the Land," *Menorah Journal* 11, 6 (Dec. 1925): 560–69, here 560; Ludwig Lewisohn, "Letter from Abroad: A City Unlike New York," *Menorah Journal* 9, 2 (Apr. 1925): 169.

30. Gedalia Bublik, *My Journey to Erets-yisroel* [Yiddish] (New York: Togblatt, 1921), 71.

31. Ibid., 68

32. David Frischmann, *In the Land* (Ba-aretz) (Warsaw: Akhisefer, 1913), 8–9.

33. Saul Tchernichovksy, "There Is Another Tel Aviv" [Hebrew], in Yosef Arikha, ed., *Tel Aviv: A Historical-Literary Sourcebook* (Tel Aviv: Tel Aviv Municipality, 1959 [1942]), 293–94.

34. See Anat Helman, " 'Even the Dogs in the Street Bark in Hebrew': National Ideology and Everyday Culture in Tel Aviv," *Jewish Quarterly Review* 92, 3–4 (Jan.–Apr. 2002): 359–82.

35. From an untitled article by Dr. Y. Klausner, excerpted in Aharon Vardi, ed., *City of Miracles* (Tel Aviv: Le-ma'an ha-sefer, 1928), 22.

36. Alter Druyanov, ed., *Sefer Tel Aviv*, vol. 1 (Tel Aviv: Va'adat sefer Tel Aviv, 1936), 126.

37. Lewisohn, "Letter from Abroad," 167–72.

38. Lowenthal, "Marrying the Land," 561.

39. Shavit and Birger, *The History of Tel Aviv*, 316. See also Tom Segev, *One Palestine, Complete: Jews and Arabs under the British Mandate*, trans. Haim Watzman (New York: Henry Holt, 2000), 263–69.

40. D. Afer, "Polyglot in the Streets of Tel Aviv" [Hebrew], *Turim* (22 Mar. 1939): 5.

41. Ibid.

42. Natan Alterman, *Rega'im*, vol. 1 (Tel Aviv: Ha-kibbutz ha-meuchad, 1974 [1934]), 109–110.

43. Shavit and Birger, *The History of Tel Aviv*, 317.

44. Letter dated 7 Nov. 1924, TAMA (Tel Aviv Municipal Archives) 3-138A.

45. Der Tunkeler, *Fort a yid keyn Erets-yisroel* (Warsaw: M. Nomberg, 1932), 56. This same observer remarks that in official settings, where Yiddish is not appropriate, Russian is spoken.

46. Ibid., 56.

47. Ibid., 48. "Shabbes-goy" is a colloquial term in Yiddish, referring to a non-Jewish person employed by a Jewish family or community to perform those activities prohibited on the Sabbath, such as turning on and off lights, or lighting a stove.

48. Shavit and Birger, *The History of Tel Aviv*, 163.

49. TAMA 3-138A.

50. TAMA 2-63B.

51. Ilan Shchori, *The Dream That Became a Metropolis: The Birth and Growth of Tel Aviv, the First Hebrew City* [Hebrew] (Tel Aviv: Avivim, 1990), 54.

52. Shalom Asch in Vardi, *City of Miracles*, 65.

53. The term *adloyada* is a fusion of three words meaning, literally, "until one doesn't know," from the Talmudic edict regarding Purim that one should drink until one does not know the difference between blessed and cursed.

54. A reminiscence of Y. Harari, cited in Shavit and Birger, *The History of Tel Aviv*, 318.

55. See Batia Carmiel, *Purim Celebrations in Tel Aviv, 1912–1935* [Hebrew] (Tel Aviv: Eretzyisrael Museum, 1999), 59–83.

56. Ibid.

57. See Peter Stallybrass and Alon White, *The Poetics and Politics of Transgression* (Ithaca, NY: Cornell University Press, 1986). A chapter entitled "The Fair, The Pig, Authorship" describes how the Jew and the pig were elided during carnivals.

58. See Chapter 1.

59. Elliot Horowitz, "The Rite to Be Reckless: On the Perpetration and Interpretation of Purim Violence," *Poetics Today* 15, 1 (1994): 9–54, here 11.

60. Ibid., 34.

61. Harold Fisch, "Reading and Carnival: On the Semiotics of Purim," *Poetics Today* 15, 1 (1994): 68.

62. See Carmiel, *Purim Celebrations in Tel Aviv*, 48–54.

63. From accounts in *Davar* and *Ha-aretz* in the 1920s, cited in Carmiel, *Purim Celebrations in Tel Aviv*, 48.

64. Saul Raskin, *Erets-yisroel in Word and Picture: Impressions from Two Journeys, 1921–1924* [Yiddish] (New York: Reznik, Menshel, n.d.), 49.

65. H. D. Nomberg, *Erets-yisroel: Impressions and Pictures* [Yiddish] (Warsaw: Jakobson and Goldberg, 1925), 21.

66. A similar argument about Yiddish literature generally is the subject of Yael Chaver, *What Must Be Forgotten: The Survival of Yiddish in Zionist Palestine* (Syracuse, NY: Syracuse University Press, 2004).

67. From an article in *Ha-poel ha-tsa'ir* 1 (1913), cited in Druyanov, *Sefer Tel Aviv*, 188.

68. Horowitz, "The Rite to be Reckless," 36.

69. For more on the perceived differences between Tel Aviv and Jaffa, see Chapter 5.

70. James Donald, *Imagining the Modernist City* (Minneapolis: University of Minnesota Press, 1999), 22. Emphasis in the original.

71. See for example the colonial development of the *ville nouvelle* established alongside Rabat, Morocco described in Gwendolyn Wright, "Rabat: Boulevard Muhammed V," in Zeynep Celik, Diane Favro, and Richard Ingersoll, eds., *Streets: Critical Perspectives on Public Space* (Berkeley: University of California Press, 1994), 225–34.

72. Another important distinguishing factor was that Tel Aviv was not sponsored by a European government, but began as a private endeavor that was subsequently funded by the Zionist movement. See Katz, "Ideology and Urban Development," 402–6.

73. TAMA 2-62A.

74. Shavit and Birger, *The History of Tel Aviv*, 215–17.

75. A letter in English from Dizengoff to the district governor dated 24 Aug. 1922, regarding sanitary conditions in Tel Aviv, requested that the following quarters be incorporated into Tel Aviv: Neve Shalom, Neve Tsedek, Mahane Yehuda, Ohel Moshe, Machaneh Yosef, Mahane Israel, Merkaz Baale Hamalacha, Badrani, Kassab, Geula, Zarifa, Mea Shaarim, Neve Sha'anan, Mehussarei Dirot, Hamanhil, and Brenner (TAMA 2-63A).

76. Dr. Abdel Al, MOH Jaffa [M. O. Hospital] report to PMO Jaffa, 6 Mar. 1923, TAMA 2-63A.

77. TAMA 3-139B.

78. Yuris, "Tel Aviv in Silence."

79. Druyanov, *Sefer Tel Aviv*, 170.

80. TAMA City Police Files, Hativa 2 (7 June 1921–20 Sept. 1922), internal report from 3 July 1921.

81. Lewisohn, "Letter from Abroad," 167–72, here 168.

82. Alan Wald, "The Menorah Group Moves Left," *Jewish Social Studies* (Summer–Fall 1976), 290.

83. The journal took a more critical stance toward Zionism in later years. See ibid.

84. Lowenthal, "This Hebrew Renaissance," 321–31, here 327.

85. Ibid., 328–29. Emphasis in the original.

86. Lewisohn, "Letter from Abroad," 168.

87. *Yediot iriyat Tel Aviv* 1 (Oct. 1932): 17–18.

88. The kibbutz is probably the most extreme example of this belief in space as a tool of social engineering. See also Oz Almog, *The Sabra: The Creation of the New*

*Jew*, trans. Haim Watzman (Berkeley: University of California, 2000).

89. For a lavishly illustrated history of the period, see Nitza Smok, *Houses from the Sand: International Style Architecture in Tel Aviv* [Hebrew] (Jerusalem: Ministry of the Defense, 1993). The city's ugliness, however, continued to be a motif. See Abba Elchanani, "Is Tel Aviv Ugly?" *Gazit* 50 (1984); and Ya'akov Rechter, "Nostalgya urbanit," *Studio* 122 (Mar.–Apr. 2001): 61–62 for retrospective reflections on the city's uninspiring aesthetic reputation by two of Tel Aviv's leading architects.

90. Rachel Kallus, "Patrick Geddes and the Evolution of a Housing Type in Tel Aviv," *Planning Perspectives* 12 (1997), 281–20, here 303.

91. The quotation is from M. Christine Boyer, *The City of Collective Memory: Its Historical Imagery and Architectural Entertainments* (Princeton, NJ: Princeton University Press, 1994), 19. See also, Natan Harpaz, "From Dream Houses to Box Houses: The Architectural Revolution of the 1930s in Tel Aviv" [Hebrew], in Mordechai Na'or, ed., *Tel Aviv ba-reyshita, 1909–1934* (Jerusalem: Yad Ben Zvi, 1984), 91–106.

92. See Segev, *One Palestine, Complete.*

93. Alona Nitzan-Shiftan, "Contested Zionism–Alternative Modernism: Erich Mendelsohn and the Tel Aviv Chug in Mandate Palestine," *Architectural History* 39 (1996): 147–80, here 158.

94. A valuable English account of Geddes and Tel Aviv is Neil I. Payton's "Patrick Geddes (1854–1932) and the Plan of Tel Aviv: Modern Architecture and Traditional Urbanism," *New City* 3 (Fall 1996): 4–25.

95. Kallus, "Patrick Geddes and the Evolution of a Housing Type," 297.

96. For sociological details of this group, see Yoav Gelber, *New Homeland: Immigration and Absorption of Central European Jews, 1933–1948* [Hebrew] (Jerusalem: Leo Baeck Institute, 1990), 423–25.

97. *Ha-binyan ba-mizrakh ha-karov* 1 (Dec. 1934).

98. Nitzan-Shiftan, "Contested Zionism," 153.

99. Dov Carmi, "The Orientation of the Tel Aviv Apartment" [Hebrew], *Ha-binyan* 9–10 (Nov. 1936): 5; and Oygen Shtulzer, "Garden, Tree, and Construction in the City" [Hebrew], *Ha-binyan ba-mizrakh ha-karov* 1 (Dec. 1934): 10.

100. *Ha-binyan* 5–6 (Dec. 1935): 13.

101. A. Patki, "Yafo–Tel Aviv" [Hebrew], *Ha-binyan* 2 (Feb. 1935): 5–8.

102. See Katz, "Ideology and Urban Development," 417–18; and Mark Levine, "A Nation from the Sands," *National Identities* 1, 1 (1999): 15–38, esp. 26–30.

103. Miriam Tovia and Michael Boneh, *Binyan Ha-aretz: Public Housing in the 1950s* [Hebrew] (Tel Aviv: Ha-kibbutz ha-meuchad, 1999), 79–82. For original plans, see Arieh Sharon, "Planning of Cooperative Housing" [Hebrew], *Ha-binyan* (Aug. 1937): 1–3.

104. Sharon, "Planning of Cooperative Housing," 3.

105. See my discussion of Meir Wieseltier's work in "The Vicarious Landscape of Memory in Tel Aviv Poetry," *Prooftexts: A Journal of Jewish Literary History* 21, 3 (Winter 2002): 350–78.

106. For a suggestive reading of the ongoing "fusion of private and public spheres" in Israel, see Rina Shapira and David Navon, "Alone Together: Public and Private Dimensions of a Tel-Aviv Cafe," *Qualitative Sociology* 14, 2 (1991): 107–25.

107. Kallus, "Patrick Geddes and the Evolution of a Housing Type," 312.

108. Bracha Kunda, *The International Style* [Hebrew] (Tel Aviv: n.p., 1994), 22.

109. Amos Keynan, "Mirpasot—chol—dinamit," *Tvai* (Apr. 1966): 32.

110. Benjamin, "The Flâneur," 49.

111. It was Menachem Shenkin who most vigorously opposed the opening of stores in Achusat Bayit; he painted a scenario in which the raucous commercial environment would lead to public Arab drinking and Jewish storekeepers, operating under a "pogrom mentality," closing up shop and crying "they're beating the Jews!" (public lecture from 1909, cited in Druyanov, *Sefer Tel Aviv*, 121–22). Ironically, one of the city's most lively commercial thoroughfares bears Shenken's name.

112. See Hillel Tryster, "'The Land of Promise' (1935): A Case Study in Zionist Film Propaganda," *Historical Journal of Film, Radio and Television* 15, 2 (1995): 187–217.

113. Natan Alterman, *Tel Aviv ha-k'tana* (Tel Aviv: Ha-kibbutz ha-meuchad, 1979), 18.

114. *Yediot iriyat Tel Aviv* 1 (Oct. 1932): 17–18.

115. Yisrael Cohen, "Tel Aviv," *Ha-poel ha-tsa'ir* (16 Feb. 1940): 9.

116. Central Zionist Archives, Jerusalem, Keren Ha-yesod Collection, Tel Aviv photographs #199: 2042 (1939?).

117. Ibid., Tel Aviv photographs, "In Allenby Street," #199: 2043 (no date).

118. Ibid., Tel Aviv photographs #207: 2074 (Feb. 1934).

119. Sela, *Photography in Palestine/Eretzyisrael*, 40.

120. Ibid., 163–64.

121. Oded Yeda'ayah, "Zultan Kluger's Photographs" [Hebrew], *Kav: ketav 'et le-omanut* 10 (July 1990): 12–21.

122. Ibid., 16.

123. The literature on this topic is voluminous. For a good introduction, see Janet Wolff, "The Invisible *Flâneuse*: Women and the Literature of Modernity," *Feminine Sentences: Essays on Women and Culture* (Berkeley: University of California Press, 1990), 34–50.

124. Leah Goldberg, "Hamasah hakatsar beyoter," in *Im halayla hazeh* (Tel Aviv: Sifriat poalim, 1964 [1961]), 13.

125. Ibid., 8. Translation from T. Carmi, *Penguin Book of Hebrew Verse* (New York: Penguin, 1981), 553–54.

126. Leah Goldberg, "Ha-ir hazot," *Turim* (15 Feb. 1939). Unless otherwise indicated, all quotations in this section are from this article.

127. Peter Fritzsche, *Reading Berlin 1900* (Cambridge, MA: Harvard University Press, 1996), 148–49.

128. Goldberg also composed a book of children's rhymes describing a children's "campaign" to keep their city clean, with particular attention to the streets. The concluding lines: "So the peoples of the world will say: what a beautiful and flowering land is Israel, its people are clean and the first Hebrew city is polished clean!" See Leah Goldberg, *Dav and Dina Stroll Around Tel Aviv* [Hebrew] (Tel Aviv: n.p., 1940s).

129. The comparative structure of "This City" bears some resemblance to a series of poems published by Yokheved Bat-Miriam in *Davar* from 1936 to 1938 and included later in her *Collected Poems* under the title "Five Cities." See the discussion in Dan Miron, *Emahot meyasdot, ahayot horgot* (Tel Aviv: Ha-kibbutz hameuchad, 1992), 220–28.

130. Benedict Anderson, *Imagined Communities: Reflections on the Origins and Spread of Nationalism* (New York: Verso, 1991 [1983]).

131. See Michael Gluzman, *The Politics of Canonicity: Lines of Resistance in Modernist Hebrew Poetry* (Stanford, CA: Stanford University Press, 2003).

132. See the discussion of this topos, especially the important analysis of Avraham Shlonsky's "Harey at," in Chana Kronfeld, *On the Margins of Modernism: Decentering Literary Dynamics* (Berkeley: University of California Press, 1996), 103–9.

133. Alterman, *Tel Aviv ha-k'tana*, 23.

134. See Barbara Mann, "Framing the Native: Esther Raab's Visual Poetics," *Israel Studies* 4, 1 (1999): 234–57; and Chana Kronfeld, "Subverting Gender: The Poetry of Esther Raab" (unpublished paper).

*Chapter 5*

The epigraphs to this chapter are from Doron Rosenblum, "The Arena" [Hebrew], *Israeli Blues* (Tel Aviv: Am Oved, 1996), 93; Ronit Matalon, *Sarah, Sarah* [Hebrew] (Tel Aviv: Am Oved, 2000), 182; Richard Sennett, *The Conscience of the Eye: The Design and Social Life of Cities* (New York: W. W. Norton, 1996); S. Y. Agnon, *Tmol shilshom*, 16th ed. (Jerusalem: Schocken, 1979 [1946]), 98, as translated in idem, *Only Yesterday*, trans. Barbara Harshav (Berkeley: University of California, 2000), 99; Ari Shavit, "Now It's Your Turn," interview with Haim Gouri [Hebrew] *Ha-aretz Magazine* (3 Mar. 2000): 16–22, here 18; and Tel Aviv Municipal Archives 4-3642.

1. S. Y. Agnon, "Tishrey," *Ha-poel ha-tsa'ir* 5 (1911): 1–5.

2. See Nurit Govrin, *Literary Geography: Lands and Landmarks on the Map of Hebrew Literature* [Hebrew] (Jerusalem: Carmel, 1998), 65–81.

3. Agnon's years in Neve Tsedek are described in Haim Be'er, *Their Love and Their Hate: Agnon, Bialik, Brenner—Relations* [Hebrew] (Tel Aviv Am Oved, 1992).

4. "Giv'at ha-chol" was published in Berlin in two versions, in 1919 and in 1931. On the dating of the story and its various versions, see Hillel Barzel, "Green Before Its Time: The Case of 'Giv'at ha-chol,'" *Gazit* 393–408 (1980–82) special issue on Tel Aviv: 73–86.

5. S. Y. Agnon, "Giv'at ha-chol," *Kol sipurav shel Shmuel Yosef Agnon*, vol. 4 (Berlin: Schocken, 1931), 225.

6. Agnon, *Tmol shilshom*, 107, translation from idem, *Only Yesterday*, 108–9.

7. Agnon, "Giv'at ha-chol," 179.

8. Hemdat's house is depicted by Nachum Gutman in his memoirs of growing up in Neve Tsedek. Nachum Gutman, *A Little Town and Few People in It* [Hebrew] (Tel Aviv: Dvir, 1999 [1959]).

9. Agnon, "Giv'at ha-chol," 221.

10. Spiro Kostof, "The City Edge," *The City Assembled: The Elements of Urban Form through History* (London: Thames & Hudson, 1992), 12.

11. Dolores Hayden, "Urban Landscape History: The Sense of Place and the Politics of Space," in Paul Groth and Todd W. Bressi, eds., *Understanding Ordinary Landscapes* (New Haven, CT: Yale University Press), 111–33, here 111.

12. Adriana Kemp, "The Border as a Productive Workshop of Culture and Politics," *Teoria u-vikoret* 18 (Spring 2001): 201.

13. Oren Yiftachel, "Ashkenazi Domination in the Israeli 'Ethnocracy,'" *Nationalism and Ethnic Politics* 4 (1998): 36–37.

14. Ya'akov Shavit and Gideon Birger, *The History of Tel Aviv*, vol. 1, *The Birth of a Town (1909–1936)* [Hebrew] (Tel Aviv: Ramot, 2001), 161–62.

15. Yossi Katz, "Ideology and Urban Development: Zionism and the Origins of Tel Aviv, 1906–1914," *Journal of Historical Geography* 12, 4 (1986): 414.

16. See Mark Levine, "Conquest through Town Planning: The Case of Tel Aviv, 1921–1948," *Journal of Palestine Studies* 27, 4 (Summer 1998): 36–52.

17. Shavit and Biger, *The History of Tel Aviv*, 197.

18. Stephen Barber, *Fragments of the European City* (London: Reaktion, 1995), 11.

19. Ruth Kark, *Jaffa: A City in Evolution* [Hebrew] (Jerusalem: Yad Yitzhak Ben-Zvi, 1990), 8.

20. Ibid., 193.

21. On Jaffa's social and ethnic composition in the years preceding and during Tel Aviv's establishment, see ibid., 156–99.

22. Ibid., 189.

23. Sh. L. Gordon, "Jaffa" [Hebrew], in Yosef Arikha, ed., *Jaffa: A Historical-Literary Sourcebook* (Tel Aviv–Jaffa Municipality, 1968), 89.

24. Yisrael Zarchi, "Facing the Desired Shore" [Hebrew], in Arikha, *Jaffa: A Historical-Literary Sourcebook*, 107.

25. Moshe Smilanksi, "At Jaffa's Shore" [Hebrew], in Arikha, *Jaffa: A Historical-Literary Sourcebook*, 119.

26. Gedalia Bublik, *My Journey in Erets-yisroel* [Yiddish] (New York: Togblatt, 1921), 73.

27. El Sayyid Nosair, "On the Shore in Jaffa" [Hebrew], *Shirey Tel Aviv* (Tel Aviv: Ha-kibbutz ha-meuchad, 1980), 9–10.

28. Govrin, *Literary Geography*, 60–61.

29. Saul Tchernichovski, "By the Sea in Jaffa" [Hebrew], *Shirim ve-baladot*, vol. 1 (Tel Aviv: Dvir, 1966), 343.

30. Ya'akov Fichman, "Afternoon in Jaffa" [Hebrew], *Kitvey Ya'akov Fichman* (Tel Aviv: Dvir, 1959), 66.

31. Eliezer Steinman, "Dread" [Hebrew], in Aharon Vardi, ed., *City of Miracles* (Tel Aviv: Le-ma'an ha-sefer, 1928), 53.

32. Y. H. Brenner, "From the Notebook," *Kol kitvey Y. H. Brenner*, vol. 4 (Tel Aviv: Ha-kibbutz ha-meuchad, 1978), 1833.

33. Ibid., 1834.

34. Michel de Certeau, "Walking in the City," in Graham Ward, ed., *The Certeau Reader* (Oxford, Blackwell, 2000), 115. Emphasis in the original.

35. For a sampling, see the section entitled "Jaffa's Groves" [Hebrew], in Arikha, *Jaffa: A Historical-Literary Sourcebook*, 173–98.

36. Gideon Ofrat, *Back Turned to the Sea* [Hebrew] (Tel Aviv: Omanut Yisrael, 1990), 62.

37. Benjamin Tammuz, "Tacharut ha-schiya," *Mivhar sipurim* (Tel Aviv: Ha-kibbutz ha-meuchad, 1973), 190–91.

38. Ibid., 196.

39. Ibid., 201.

40. Haim Gouri, *Ha-sefer ha-meshuga* (Tel Aviv: Am Oved, 1972), 97–98.

41. Ibid., 98.

42. Ibid., 97–100.

43. Haim Gouri, "Ha-keta ha-nosaf," *Alpayim* 9 (1994).

44. See Baruch Kimmerling and Joel Migdal, "The City: Between Nablus and Jaffa," *Palestinians: The Making of a People* (New York: Free Press, 1993), 36–63.

45. S. Yizhar, *Mikdamot* (Tel Aviv: Zmora Bitan, 1992), 7.

46. Ibid., 67–68.

47. Ibid., 75.

48. Gershon Shaked, *Modern Hebrew Fiction* (Bloomington: Indiana University Press, 2000), 147.

49. Certeau, "Walking in the City," 116.

50. Shavit, "Now It's Your Turn," 20.

51. Specifically for Eastern European Jewish immigrants. On the absence of the sea as a motif in *Mizrahi* immigration narratives, see Hanan Hever, "We Have Not Arrived from the Sea: Toward a Mizrahi Literary Geography" [Hebrew], *Teoria u-vikoret* 16 (Spring 2000): 181–96.

52. Henri Lefebvre, "Rhythmanalysis of Mediterranean Cities," *Writings on*

*Cities*, ed., trans., and introduced by Eleonore Kofman and Elizabeth Lebas (Cambridge, MA: Blackwell, 1996), 228–40.

53. Ofrat, *Back Turned to the Sea*, 123–50.

54. Ibid., 134.

55. See Hanan Hever, "The Zionist Sea: Symbolism and Nationalism in Modernist Hebrew Poetry" [Hebrew], in Zvia Ben-Porat, ed., *An Overcoat for Benjamin* (Tel Aviv: Porter Institute for Poetics, 2001), 13–35.

56. Moshe Shamir, *With His Own Hands*, trans. Joseph Schachter (Jerusalem: Institute for the Translation of Hebrew Literature, 1970 [1951]), 1.

57. Yisrael Cohen, "Tel Aviv," *Ha-poel ha-tsa'ir* (16 Feb. 1940): 8–9.

58. Letter dated 3 Sept. 1925, TAMA (Tel Aviv Municipal Archives), 4-2970.

59. A thorough evaluation of the medicinal qualities of Tel Aviv's climate, as compared to that of other European and Middle Eastern cities on the Mediterranean, can be found in a proposal by Dr. A. Benyamini, *Tel Aviv–Riviera* (Tel Aviv: n.p., 1929).

60. Gilead Duvshani, *I. Megidovitch—Architect* (Jerusalem: Ministry of Defense, 1993), 50.

61. It appears that Dizengoff long had designs on the sea. Druyanov describes Dizengoff's suggestion from 1911 to buy the land of Mahloul as evidence of a "natural aspiration" to "conquer the seashore." Alter Druyanov, ed., *Sefer Tel Aviv*, vol. 1 (Tel Aviv: Va'adat sefer Tel Aviv, 1936), 180.

62. Jabotinsky's remarks were made during a speech at the 1929 fair, and are cited in Joachim Schlör, *Tel Aviv: From Dream to City* (London: Reaktion, 1999), 198.

63. See Barbara Mann, "The Vicarious Landscape of Memory in Tel Aviv Poetry," *Prooftexts: A Journal of Jewish Literary History* 21, 3 (Winter 2002): 350–78.

64. Meir Wieseltier, *Davar optimi asiyat shirim* (Tel Aviv: Zmora Bitan, 1976), 89.

65. For a translation of "Sealed in a Bottle," see Meir Wieseltier, *The Flower of Ararchy*, trans. by Shirley Kaufman with the author (Berkeley: University of California Press, 2003), 54.

66. TAMA 4-3643, dated 27 Dec. 1939; TAMA 8-1111, no date (1930s?); TAMA 4-3642, dated 13 Feb. 1938.

67. TAMA 3-92A.

68. TAMA 4-2209C.

69. TAMA 4-3642. The letter in the file has a Hebrew translation attached to the original Arabic.

70. Letter dated 6 Oct. 1937, TAMA 4-3642.

71. Walid Khalidi, ed., *All That Remains: The Palestinian Villages Occupied and Depopulated by Israel in 1948* (Washington, D.C.: Institute of Palestine Studies, 1992), 230–62.

72. Visotski in Vardi, *City of Miracles*, 42.

73. Ya'akov Fichman in Vardi, *City of Miracles*, 33.

74. Eitan Eilon, Ofer Regev, Avi Moshe, and Tamar Tokhler, eds., *Sharona-ha-kirya* (Tel Aviv: Council for Building and Site Preservation, 1998).

75. Avraham Hus, "Tel Aviv's Micro-climate of My Youth" [Hebrew], *Gazit* 50 (Apr. 1984): 203.

76. Shavit and Biger, *The History of Tel Aviv*, 178.

77. Ibid., unattributed quotations, 61.

78. Ibid., 163.

79. Details culled from Shlomo Shva, *To Paint the Homeland: The First Painters of Modern Israel* [Hebrew] (Jerusalem: Ministry of Defense, 1992), 36–43.

80. In A. Koleb's retrospective description: "The light of our land is monumental, graphic, very sharp, and lacking in those delicate passages and changes of hue in Europe." "On Israeli Art" [Hebrew], *Masa* (21 Aug. 1952).

81. Benjamin Tammuz, "Cholot zahav," *Mivchar sipurim* (Tel Aviv: Hakibbutz ha-meuchad, 1973).

82. Ibid., 14.

83. Ibid., 14–15.

84. Ibid., 16.

85. The large red house that he seeks was actually located in the groves of Abu-Kabir, the site of violence during the Jewish-Arab disturbances of 1921; the red house was a nickname for Beyt Yatzker, where Brenner was killed.

86. Devora Baron, "Ba-lev ha-krakh," *Parshiyot* (Jerusalem: Mosad Bialik, 1951), 563–66.

87. Christine Sizemore, "Doris Lessing's *Four-Gated City*," in Susan Merrill Squier, ed., *Women Writers and the City: Essays in Feminist Literary Criticism* (Knoxville: University of Tennessee Press, 1984), 178.

88. See Amia Lieblich, *Conversations with Dvora: An Experimental Biography of the First Modern Hebrew Woman Writer/Amia Lieblich*, trans. by Naomi Seidman, ed. by Chana Kronfeld and Naomi Seidman (Berkeley: University of California, Press, 1997).

89. Orly Lubin, "Alternative Nationalism in Devora Baron's *The Exiles*" [Hebrew], *Teoria u-vikoret* 7 (Winter 1995): 159–76.

90. Ibid., 161. *Ha-golim*, which appeared in 1970, consists of two separate stories, originally published in 1943 and 1955 respectively.

91. Yiftachel, "Ashkenazi Domination in the Israeli 'Ethnocracy,'" 37.

92. Adriana Kemp, "The Border as a Productive Workshop of Culture and Politics" [Hebrew], *Teoria u-vikoret* 16 (Spring 2000): 20.

93. Ibid., 24.

94. Ramat Gan may actually be Tel Aviv's new "center," with its considerable group of skyscrapers housing the new money economy. The increasingly intense residential and commercial development within this new cluster of high-rises, nick-

named Ayalon City (after the highway that runs between Tel Aviv and Ramat Gan), coupled with the effective efforts of preservation groups regarding "historic Tel Aviv," may indeed turn Tel Aviv itself into a kind of suburb. At the same time, a former center such as the commercial district surrounding the Old Central Bus Station, is now home to members of Israel's large *gastarbeiter* (foreign workers) population, and consequently viewed as peripheral.

95. Ofrat, "Back Turned to the Sea," 134.

96. Irit Sadan links Zaritzki's abstraction to his personal and professional association with International Style architects. See *Buildings and Vision from a Bird's Eye View: Tel Aviv in the Paintings of Zaritzki, 1930–1945* [Hebrew], exhibition catalog (Tel Aviv: Genia Schreiber University Art Gallery, 2000).

97. Shva, *To Paint the Homeland*, 86–87.

## Chapter 6

The eipgraphs to this chapter are from Brian Ladd, *The Ghosts of Berlin: Confronting German History in The Urban Landscape* (Chicago: University of Chicago Press, 1997), 2; Uzi Weil, "The Man Who Moved the Wailing Wall" [Hebrew], *Happiness* (Jerusalem: Keter, 2001), 158; the poem by Ronny Someck, translated from the Hebrew by Karen Alkalay-Gut, in Karen Alkalay-Gut and Zygmunt Frankel, eds., *Yitzhak Rabin: In Memoriam* (Tel Aviv: Israel Association of Writers in English, Dec. 1995), 4; Amnon Raz-Krakotzkin, "Rabin's Legacy: On Secularism, Nationalism, and Orientalism" [Hebrew], in Lev Grinberg, ed., *Contested Memory: Myth, Nation, and Democracy—Thoughts after Rabin's Assassination* (Beer Sheva: Ben Gurion University Press, 2000), 104; Stephen Barber, *Fragments of the European City* (London: Reaktion, 1995), 51; and Avot Yeshurun, *Kol shirav*, vol. 2 (Tel Aviv: Ha-kibbutz ha-meuchad, 1997), 33.

1. Michel de Certeau, "Walking in the City," in Graham Ward, ed., *The Certeau Reader* (Oxford: Blackwell, 2000), 108.

2. Shmuel Avitsur, "Groves and Agricultural Areas in Tel Aviv before the City's Founding" [Hebrew], *Ariel* 48–49 (1987): 57–62. Members of the Felman family are buried in the Old Cemetery near Bialik's grave.

3. See Ya'akov Shavit and Gideon Birger, *The History of Tel Aviv*, vol. 1, *The Birth of a Town (1909–1936)* [Hebrew] (Tel Aviv: Ramot, 2001), 148–51. Nachman Ben-Yehuda analyzes the Rabin assassination in the context of the scores of political murders carried out by the Zionist movement in Palestine over the past 100 years, whose targets were not only Arabs and the British, but also Jews who were perceived as "strangers" or somehow deviant from the collective. See Nachman Ben-Yehuda, "One More Political Murder by Jews," in Yoram Peri, ed., *The Assassination of Yitzhak Rabin* (Stanford, CA: Stanford University Press, 2000), 63–95.

4. The history of the square has been vividly depicted by filmmakers Moish Greenberg and Yonatan Garfunkel in their 2001 documentary *The Arena* (Ha-zira).

5. See Tali Hatuka, "Moments of Repair: Rabin Square as a Space of Cultural Negotiation" [Hebrew], *Teoria u-vikoret* 24 (Spring 2004): 85–111, a fine study that explores the site's recent evolution.

6. See *Map of Memory: Spectrum of Commemoration in Memory of Yitzhak Rabin* [Hebrew], exhibition catalog (Tel Aviv: Museum of the History of the Land of Israel, 1996).

7. Michael Feige, "Yitzhak Rabin: His Commemoration and the Commemoration of His Commemoration" [Hebrew], in Grinberg, *Contested Memory*, 39–64.

8. See Maoz Azaryahu, "The Spontaneous Formation of Memorial Space: The Case of *Kikar Rabin*, Tel Aviv," *Area* 28, 4 (1996): 501–13; Mira Engler, "A Living Memorial: Commemorating Yitzhak Rabin at the Tel Aviv Square," *Places* 12, 2 (Winter 1999): 4–11; and even the more critical arguments by Ayal Dotan, "The End of Trauma: Sterilization and Blurring in the Representation of Memory" [Hebrew], *Teoria u-vikoret* 17 (Fall 2000): 27–34.

9. Azaryahu, "The Spontaneous Formation of Memorial Space," 502.

10. See the conceptual design competition outlined in *Studio* 131 (Feb.–Mar. 2002): 54–61.

11. See the discussion of Avot Yeshurun's poetry about Tel Aviv in Chapter 1.

12. Michael Karpin and Ina Friedman, *Murder in the Name of God: The Plot to Kill Yitzhak Rabin* (London: Granta, 2000), 54.

13. Doron Rosenblum, "The Arena" [Hebrew], *Israeli Blues* (Tel Aviv: Am Oved, 1998), 94. Originally published in *Ha-aretz*, 10 Nov. 1995.

14. Dan Bar-On, "The Rabin Assassination as the Final Step in the Breaking the Monolithic Construction of Israeli Identity" [Hebrew], in Grinberg, *Contested Memory*, 66.

15. See Vered Vinitzky-Seroussi, "'Jerusalem Assassinated Rabin and Tel Aviv Commemorated Him': Rabin Memorials and the Discourse of National Identity in Israel," *City and Society* 10, 1 (1998): 183–203.

16. Quoted in Tamar Rappaport, "The Many Voices of Israeli Youth: Multiple Interpretations of Rabin's Assassination," in Peri, *The Assassination of Yitzhak Rabin*, 199.

17. Ibid., 201–8.

18. Etgar Keret, "Rabin met," in Asaf Givron, ed., *Ototo* (Tel Aviv: Zmora Bitan, 1999), 7.

19. Ibid., 8.

20. Ibid.

21. Alona Kimchi, *Susannah ha-bokhiya* (Jerusalem: Keter, 1999), 64. Subsequent citations of this work appear in the text.

22. Rosenblum, "Ha-zira," 93.

23. Raz-Krakotzkin, "Rabin's Legacy," 95.

24. Ironically, Amir had intentionally removed his head covering before approaching the square that night, in order to deflect suspicion. The phrase was deleted after some public protest.

25. See Walid Khalidi, ed., *All That Remains: The Palestinian Villages Occupied and Depopulated by Israel in 1948* (Washington, D.C.: Institute for Palestine Studies, 1992).

26. Cited in Shavit and Birger, *History of Tel Aviv*, 198.

27. Alter Druyanov, ed., *Sefer Tel Aviv* (Tel Aviv: Va'adat sefer Tel Aviv, 1936), 298.

28. TAMA (Tel Aviv Municipal Archives) 4-2237, 5 Nov. 1944.

29. TAMA 4-2237. The letter, dated 19 Dec. 1943, is in Hebrew, the signature in Arabic.

30. Khalidi, *All the Remains*, 249.

31. From Yitzhak Bezalel, *Everything Is Writing in the Book: Interviews with Contemporary Israeli Writers* [Hebrew] (Tel Aviv, 1969), 39.

32. Yeshurun, *Kol shirav*, vol. 2, 37.

33. Originally appeared in *Ha-aretz* (2 Feb. 2002). English translation by Peter Cole in Aharon Shabtai, *J'Accuse* (New York: New Directions, 2003), 44–45.

34. See Meron Benvenisti, *Sacred Landscape: The Buried History of the Holy Land since 1948* (Berkeley: University of California Press, 2000).

# Index

Note: Page numbers in italic type refer to illustrations.